READING
PRACTICE BOOK
ACT®

ADVANCED
PRACTICE
SERIES

ies
TEST
PREP

D1361388

Authors
Arianna Astuni, President IES
Khalid Khashoggi, CEO IES

Editorial
Patrick Kennedy, Executive Editor
Rajvi Patel, Editor
Yasmine Gharib, Assistant Editor

Design
Kay Kang, Creative Director

Contributors
Arianna Astuni
Larry Bernstein
Emily Blake
Katie Donovan
Yasmine Gharib
Cynthia Helzner
Chris Holliday
Caitlin Hoynes-O'Connor
Michael Ivkov
Charles Kennedy
Patrick Kennedy
Khalid Khashoggi
Paul King
Rajvi Patel
Jeremy Wheeler

ILEX
Educational Publishers

ies
TEST
PREP

Published by ILEX Publications
24 Wernik Place
Metuchen, NJ 08840
www.ILEXpublications.com
© ILEX Publications, 2014

ON BEHALF OF
Integrated Educational Services, Inc.
355 Main Street
Metuchen, NJ 08840
www.ies2400.com

We would like to thank the ILEX Publications team as well as the teachers and students at IES2400 who have contributed to the creation of this book. We would also like to thank our Chief Marketing Officer, Sonia Choi, for her invaluable input.

The SAT is a registered trademark of the College Board, which was not involved in the production of, and does not endorse, this product.

ISBN: 978-0991388387
QUESTIONS OR COMMENTS? Email us at info@ilexpublications.com

TABLE OF CONTENTS

Dear Student:

   In today's competitive world of test prep and college admissions, students are studying more aggressively than ever before for the ACT. At first, some of the greatest challenges here are posed by the intense Reading section, with its four long passages and forty evidence-based questions. Yet we at IES Test Prep and ILEX Publications are certain that the ACT Reading section can be mastered. To achieve such mastery, you will need a solid overall strategy, memorable tips and tricks, and the best ACT practice material on the market.

   These are exactly the advantages that this practice book provides. All of the methods in our ACT Reading Technique have been tested in live classrooms, and have been proven to increase test-taking comprehension and efficiency. All of our passages and questions have been crafted and edited by seasoned test prep educators. And all of our practice tests are accompanied by potent special features: self-assessments, answer explanations, and 24-hour assistance from the ILEX Publications Team.

   Get ready to learn about the four passage types on the ACT: Literary Narrative, Social Science, Humanities, and Natural Science. But get ready, too, to discover how this book can lead you to a powerful score increase – or perhaps to a coveted perfect-36 score. Read carefully, practice consistently, and control the ACT! I wish you the best of luck in all of your academic endeavors.

Sincerely,

Arianna Astuni
President, IES

ACT
Reading Technique

ACT
Reading Essentials

Each ACT Reading test follows the same format:

- ♦ **35 Minutes** to complete **40 questions**
- ♦ **Four Passage Sections**, each with **10 questions**
- ♦ **Four answer choices** per question, NO wrong answer penalty
- ♦ **Always One Passage** in each of the following topics, and always in the following order:

I.	**Literary Narrative**
II.	**Social Science**
III.	**Humanities**
IV.	**Natural Science**

The passages that occur on the ACT will typically adhere to the following guidelines:

All Passages: Approximately **750-850 words**. The standard passage will have a tangible but not overbearing or distracting tone, and will make use of specific evidence and episodes. However, there will be no field- or discipline-specific jargon unless absolutely necessary (and accompanied by explanations).

Satire and social critique are both appropriate on the ACT, but within tight moderation. Like most standardized tests, the ACT avoids controversy: as a result, topics that involve extensive discussions of violence, sexuality, substance abuse, religious belief, and divisive or partisan political opinions are prohibited.

> ✔ **Quick Tip**
>
> When you are starting out, try to figure out your STRONGEST THREE passage types. If you can't finish all the passages, at least you can make it through these three with confidence.

The Four ACT Passage Types

LITERARY NARRATIVE:

These passages are often taken from fiction from the recent past (post-1950) and address a range of cultural and social contexts. Many Literary Narrative passages focus on a single conflict, incident, issue, or episode. The ACT emphasizes everyday individuals dealing with relatively normal events and dilemmas, but often chooses material that relates to broader themes in art, education, cultural exchange, or economic advancement. The passages often deal with no more than two or three principal characters, since a larger number would lead to confusion; there is also often a very clear sense of structure, since most passages used on the test deal with an evident character contrast or with an important change or revelation.

Although the literary passages can sound simple, they can actually be quite demanding. Many of these passages 1) involve subtlety or complexity of tone and attitude, and address such features in the more difficult questions, and 2) leave some matters involving the repercussions of the characters' actions and the characters' ultimate fates open to doubt or questioning. As a rule of thumb, do NOT attempt to figure out what happens to the characters after the passage concludes: such interpretations can distort your understanding or cause you to be preoccupied with issues unrelated to the questions.

SOCIAL SCIENCE:

These are single-focus passages that address major or important aspects of history, sociology, economics, political philosophy, social psychology, or social approaches to technology. Although the Social Science passages are not long enough to go off-topic, the topics chosen can be fairly broad: "individualism," "suburban sprawl," and "the influence of the Cuban Revolution" would all be appropriate social science topics. Some of these passages will also have apparent biases, yet the authors will still be careful to include highly concrete historical, sociological, and anthropological information.

There is also variation of tone and tactics in the Social Science passages: ACT passages frequently consider qualifications, logical assumptions, counter-arguments, logical repercussions, and important paradoxes and ironies. All of these factors make the passages more complex, and the questions may ask directly about some of these factors.

HUMANITIES:

These are single-focus passages relating to art, culture, or entertainment. Arguably, the humanities passages offer greater flexibility than the other nonfiction passages; this section occasionally includes entries in autobiography, with an emphasis on the author's personal development. The ACT takes a very broad definition of the humanities: television shows, pop music, and audio recordings of Shakespeare have been among past topics. These readings, however, entail the same standards of nuanced language and critical analysis that can be seen in passages treating more traditional topics in the humanities.

NATURAL SCIENCE:

These are single-focus passages relating to developments in biology, chemistry, physics, astronomy, or geology. Technology, psychology, and ecology are also possible topics for the ACT Natural Science passages, but these topics will be discussed from an experimental or empirical standpoint; in other words, the passage cannot be too close to a Social Science passage in approach. Passages will often cluster different news items, experiments, observations, and speculations around a single core topic such as the exploration of Mars, the formation of snowflakes, or the evolution of deep-sea organisms.

Although Natural Science passages do not bring in much autobiography or narrative, they will often consider the consequences, social value, and historical context of particular discovers. Many of these passages contrast older and newer ideas, or present new research on longstanding issues.

> ✓ **Quick Tip**
>
> Recently, the ACT has begun to include two paired passages in one of the four topic areas. Although the Real ACT Book does not include these, we at IES have modeled our book to reflect this change.

Now that you know what to expect, you will need the techniques on the following pages to complete ACT Reading Passages with efficiency, accuracy, and confidence.

Timing

To complete ALL FOUR of the ACT Reading passages, you will need to time each passage in the following way:

8. 5 min read ing
5 min

3.5 MINUTES to read the **PASSAGE**

5 MINUTES to answer the **QUESTIONS**

Answering the Questions

1. Read the Italicized blurb at the beginning of the passage, but do so QUICKLY. Focus on the TITLE and any NOTES that explain special terms or concepts in the passage

2. Read whole passage for STRONG COMPREHENSION. Make sure you have a sense of the main topic, themes, and opinions. Avoid notes; these will only slow you down.

3. Go to the first question. Read carefully to achieve a FULL UNDERSTANDING OF THE QUESTION

4. Underline/bracket any lines from the passage that could serve as evidence for your answer.

5. Now, you are going to develop your own answer. We will refer to these answers as your **MARGIN ANSWERS:**

> ✔ **Remember**
>
> **Margin Answers and POE were created to eliminate the habit of analyzing every answer choice, which is time consuming. If you find that Margin Answers are taking you too long, you may not have broken this habit yet.**

BEFORE looking at multiple choice answers: Answer the question yourself by writing in the margin. Ask yourself these questions:

- ◆ WHO will my answer be about?

- ◆ WHAT action will my answer be about?

- ◆ What will the TONE (+, –) of my answer be?

You may not use all of these tools every time, but using at least one will help with a quick and precise process of elimination (POE)

6. Process of Elimination: As you are doing POE, do NOT consider every answer choice. Instead, cross out answer choices by locating FALSE WORDS that do not match your Margin Answers.

10 DOs and 10 DON'Ts for the ACT Reading Test

10 DOs	10 DON'Ts
Do read the whole passage carefully	Don't highlight anything in the passage as you're reading
Do allow yourself about 3.5 minutes to read the passage	Don't take notes in the margins of the passage while you're reading
Do allow yourself about 5 minutes to answer the questions for each passage	Don't skim the passage and rush to the questions
Do all the questions that are not line reference questions first	Don't read all the questions before you read the passage
Do all the line reference questions last	Don't take longer than 9 minutes per passage (including questions)
Do use your pencil as a pacer to increase reading speed without losing comprehension	Don't do the line reference questions first
Do answer every question	Don't leave any questions blank
Do guess when unsure	Don't attempt to read the whole passage twice
Do work on improving your overall reading speed	Don't "sub-vocalize" (imagine the words being spoken aloud)
Do cross out false words	Don't fall for trap answers

Learn More: To train you to focus on the passages themselves, we have left author and copyright out of our passage blurbs. Discover more about our sources at sources.ilexpublications.com

---

13

The Seven Major Question Types

1) MAIN IDEA

As you are reading each ACT passage, make sure you grasp the author's main topic, and try to figure out the stance or position that the author is taking. You should also think about how (in terms of writing strategies) the author develops particular ideas. The ACT Reading sections will often test you directly on these issues using **Main Idea** questions.

A sample Main Idea question would be the following:

1. The main purpose of the passage is to:

    A. discuss the origins of windmills in ancient Persia.
    B. suggest that the benefits of wind turbine technology vastly outweigh its drawbacks.
    C. list the different problems associated with fossil fuels.
    D. lament the ways that turbines have transformed the natural landscape.

The Main Idea answers will often address topics that seem similar, but that have subtle differences in logic, tone, and presentation. Make sure that you use specific, underlined references to justify your correct answer; however, make sure you are not losing sight of the passage as a **whole composition**.

Although Main Idea questions are common in the Social Science, Humanities, and Natural Science passages, they can also occur in the Literary Narrative passages. An example would be the following:

2. Which of the following statements best describes the plot of the passage?

    F. A young man wants to be a jazz writer but finds the business too challenging.
    G. A young man decides to prioritize his education after an intervention by a figure he respects.
    H. A young man is angry with his mother until a radio personality helps them to negotiate calmly.
    J. A young man and his hero explain a challenging goal to the young man's mother.

main purpose or plot

14

2) EXPLICIT DETAIL

In the Explicit Detail questions, you will be asked directly about the content that occurs in a passage. Here is an example:

3. According to the passage, evidence that the city of Heracleion was a religious site for Greeks has been provided by:

    A. statues of a few Greek gods and goddesses.
    B. the presence of a large sycamore barge.
    C. the abundance of anchors discovered by Godda.
    D. the gravestone of a young Greek soldier.

Note that the question never asks you about how this content functions or what can be concluded from it: you only need to consider **whether or not it appears** in the passage.

The ACT will also frequently ask questions about content that does not appear in the passage. Such Explicit Detail questions use the words NOT and EXCEPT in all caps; here is an example:

4. As stated in the narrator's account, all of the following were features of the narrator's family living space EXCEPT:

    F. candles to provide lighting.
    G. a propane tank.
    H. a worn and dirty rug.
    J. a bamboo ladder.

To address this question, use re-reading and check off, one by one, the explicit details that occur within the passage. Often, the four answers will have similar tones, or will describe similar objects or themes. Because of this, direct evidence and careful process of elimination are essential.

3) VOCABULARY

The ACT will often require you to determine the meanings of particular words from the passages. Here are two examples:

5.   In line 10, *clunky* most nearly means:

    A. unmovable.
    B. stubborn.
    C. huge.
    D. dull.

6.   As it is used in line 73, the word *keeping* most nearly means:

    F. maintaining.
    G. isolating.
    H. preventing.
    J. stockpiling.

These Vocabulary questions can be tricky because all of the answer choices are valid dictionary definitions for the word in the question. However, you need to decide which word **fits the context of the passage**. For this, use the Margin Answer method. Read around for synonyms, antonyms, and context clues, and then answer the following questions:

    ♦ WHAT does the word mean?
    ♦ Which TONE should the word take?

Then, use POE to eliminate all words that do not fit your predictions. And always make sure you **plug your answer choice into the passage** to make sure it makes sense. In fact, if you are pressed for time, quickly plugging in all four choices one by one can help you sense which one might be the right answer.

4) DEVELOPMENT

With Development questions, the ACT will ask you about the functions and purposes of individual parts of the passage, from short phrases to groups of paragraphs.

7. The function of the quotation from Oliver Sacks in lines 13-16 is to:

    A. question whether the reaction was in fact a traditional explosion.
    B. emphasize the popularity of the chemical reaction between sodium metal and water.
    C. underscore the intensity of the chemical reaction between sodium metal and water.
    D. illustrate what most oxidation-reduction reactions look like.

8. The fourth paragraph (lines 25-34) primarily emphasizes:

    F. the growing practice among retailers of staying open on Thanksgiving.
    G. the defining differences between Kmart and its present-day successor Walmart.
    H. the unwillingness of consumers to reflect on the drawbacks of new developments in retail.
    J. the ability of most retailers to quickly adapt to the newest marketing trends.

In order to answer Development questions, you will often be required to place individual sentences and paragraphs in the context of larger arguments—sometimes, in the context of the entire passage. What point does a given sentence or paragraph make? How might it advance the author's overall argument? Considering such factors, while paying close attention to textual evidence, is essential to mastering Development questions.

[Handwritten note in right margin: The function of the lines -or purpose of a particular paragraph on the context of the passage]

17

5) IMPLIED IDEAS

On the ACT, Implied Idea questions will require you to use specific pieces of evidence to arrive at larger points supported by the passage. Often, these questions will require you to arrive at a slightly broader characterization of a person or an item described in the passage, as in the following example:

9. As described in the fourth paragraph, classrooms can be understood as:

    A. disregarded by most psychological studies.
    B. premised on simplistic concepts of organization.
    C. important to developmental learning.
    D. disadvantageous to highly creative children.

Sometimes, however, Implied Idea questions will require you to understand the assumptions that lie behind an author's argument. The following is one example of an assumption question:

10. Throughout the passage, the author makes the assumption that:

    F. the reader of the passage is not a practicing or professional actor.
    G. the reader of the passage falsely believes that acting is a uniformly exciting profession.
    H. most actors would be incapable of pursuing more traditional career paths.
    J. it is impossible to understand the motives of those who choose acting careers.

Note that neither type of Implied Idea question involves interpretation: you must still find specific evidence from the passage that gives you a Margin Answer, and helps you to eliminate false answers.

can be understand as ———
makes the assumption that ————

6) APPLICATION

The Application questions on the ACT will ask you to draw logical conclusions and connections based on the textual evidence that a given passage presents. Think of these as questions that **link** important items. The most basic type involves establishing what a specific word or phrase **refers to** elsewhere in the passage:

11. The "area" mentioned in line 17 most nearly refers to:

    A. the nuns' original territory in Poland.
    B. the outskirts of the city.
    C. the acres of land occupied by the convent.
    D. the businesses that surround the convent.

Application questions may also ask you to determine which evidence supports a particular point, or to notice similarities and differences when revisiting the passage's evidence. The phrasing of these questions can be considerably more complex than that of the linkage questions. Here is an example:

12. It can be reasonably inferred from the passage that one similarity between John Merryman and Lambdin P. Milligan was that both men were:

    F. directly connected to United States legislatures.
    G. ultimately sentenced to death for their actions.
    H. apparently hostile to Lincoln's government.
    J. unwilling to deal directly with the Supreme Court.

Handwritten margin notes: Application Q's / what a word refers to in the passage / it can be inferred

7) TONE/VOICE/ATTITUDE

On the ACT, Tone/Voice/Attitude questions can take the following forms:

13. In this passage, the author describes Winston Churchill in a manner that is:

    A. dramatically mournful.
    B. thoroughly appreciative.
    C. intentionally exaggerated.
    D. subtly pessimistic.

14. At the beginning their conversation, the narrator's mother ad-dresses the narrator in a manner that is:

    F. furious and unpredictable.
    G. composed and intimidating.
    H. unexpected and reassuring.
    J. serious and insensitive.

To address these properly, pay special attention to the designated content (since tone can vary for different content and different paragraphs) and the TONE of your Margin Answer (since basic +/- can quickly eliminate some of the answers).

Now that you know what will be on the ACT Reading, you are ready to begin your practice. As always, if you have any questions, contact us at info@ilexpublications.com.

[handwritten margin note: In / Emotions with which author discusses something]

Test 1

READING TEST
35 Minutes—40 Questions

DIRECTIONS: There are four passages in this test. Each passage is followed by several questions. After reading a passage, choose the best answer to each question and fill in the corresponding oval on your answer document. You may refer to the passages as often as necessary.

Passage I

LITERARY NARRATIVE: This passage is adapted from the short story "Biggest Fan." The primary characters are members of a Chinese-American family living in New York City.

One of my earliest memories is of my father, perched in front of our black-and-white, eight-inch by eight-inch cubical TV, a cigarette between his lips, a sodden New York Yankees baseball cap on his head. It must have been a big game, for
5 he was often on his feet, sometimes pacing, sometimes crouched down and squinting hard at the minuscule screen. He was a practitioner of both meditation and *tai chi*, and I wonder now if he may have believed that his intense concentration could actually *make* the Yankees' hits sail
10 farther, out and over the wall for a home run. Still, despite the fact that the antenna extended all the way up to the ceiling (with a ball of aluminum foil wrapped around the end of it for good measure), the broadcast occasionally cut out, leaving my father staring at fuzz and snow, and yelling in
15 Cantonese.

According to my mother, my father had never watched baseball before they immigrated to America.

"It wasn't a popular sport in China," she told me, when I visited her recently, in the apartment where I had spent my
20 girlhood and where she still lived, down near Canal Street. "But as soon as we arrived in New York City, he found an old Yankees cap at the Salvation Army down the block. He put it on his head, and that was that. He was a fan for the rest of his life."

25 I nodded, listening to the pleasant lilt and sway of my mother's Cantonese, and thinking about my father in that baseball cap. I smiled at the pleasant memory, but also felt a pang of sadness for him. Isolated in his new country, and too old to really start learning English, my father had learned
30 baseball instead. On buses and on subway cars, he would often greet strangers with a shout of "Let's go Yankees!" if he saw that they, too, were wearing a cap or a shirt or a jersey with the iconic blue and white logo on it. Invariably, these strangers would smile at my father, the cheerful Asian man
35 with the thick accent, and yell back to him, "Let's go

Yankees!" Even as a child, I could tell that these encounters always filled my father with pride and happiness. I am sure that in other ways he was lonely, living so far from his home; from what I can recall, he and my mother never had friends
40 over to the apartment. They were a unit of two, their boat adrift on strange and unknown seas, raising me, their only daughter, even though here in America they could have had more children, had they wished. Baseball was my father's mooring; for brief moments, it allowed him to feel that he
45 belonged here, in this sprawling metropolis.

As far back as I can remember, he had worked on the docks, down at the southern tip of Manhattan, loading and unloading the various shipments that came in. His job was something he never talked about with me, which I attributed
50 to the fact that it was hard, grueling work—hardly the best topic to bring home to a delicate young girl. And yet his reticence lent him an air of mystery—he was a man who disappeared at dawn, only to reappear at night, smelling of fish and brine and smoke. That was how it was until the day
55 he died, fifteen years ago, of a heart attack. It was tragic, of course, but neither my mother nor I had been all that surprised: my father had smoked his whole life, and his father before him had succumbed in just the same way, and at an even younger age.

60 Now, every year since his passing, I've visited my mother, to be with her and to support her, and to remember my father. And as the years have gone by, I've come to look forward to this annual rendezvous of ours.

"Are you ready?" I said to my mother, and she nodded.
65 Reaching into my purse, I pulled out two tickets, and placed them down on the small kitchen table.

"Yankees vs. Phillies," my mother said, reading the tickets aloud. "Game starts in two hours."

We walked out, and down to the street. I hailed a cab,
70 and held the door open for my mother, before getting in behind her.

"Yankees Stadium," I told the driver, and he nodded,

GO ON TO THE NEXT PAGE.

perhaps with the same pride my father would have felt, knowing that we were off to one of his favorite destinations.
75 After all, the stadium was our family's proof, in a way, that it's possible for one to find and make a home almost anywhere.

1. As it is used in line 19, the word *spent* is understood to mean:

    A. reduced.
    B. wasted.
    C. invested.
    D. passed.

2. The description of the TV antenna in the first paragraph serves to:

    F. indicate that the narrator's parents are eccentric in their habits.
    G. refute an earlier claim about the luxury of the family apartment.
    H. demonstrate the narrator's awareness of advanced technology.
    J. suggest that the narrator's father tried to find the best possible television reception.

3. The narrator suggests that her father's greeting of "Let's go Yankees!" (line 31) was intended to:

    A. discourage fans of other baseball teams.
    B. socially connect her father to other Yankees fans.
    C. help him remember the Yankees team players.
    D. prove that her father wanted to learn English.

4. The narrator gives all of the following reasons for believing that her father felt lonely in America EXCEPT:

    F. he didn't get along with his coworkers.
    G. his knowledge of the English language was limited.
    H. he didn't have friends who visited him at home.
    J. he lived far from his homeland.

5. The narrator believes that her father didn't talk to her about his job because:

    A. he was aware that she would find the job uninteresting.
    B. his job was not an ideal topic for a girl in her position.
    C. he did not think that she would understand his job duties.
    D. he felt ashamed of his job and his low wages.

6. The passage suggests that all of the following are true of the narrator's father EXCEPT that:

    F. he wanted to feel a connection to other people in Manhattan.
    G. he worked long hours at the dock.
    H. he tried to quit smoking.
    J. he grew up in China.

7. According to the passage, the narrator's grandfather died from:

    A. lung cancer.
    B. an accident at work.
    C. food poisoning.
    D. a heart attack.

8. The question "Are you ready?" in line 64 refers to:

    F. going to a baseball game.
    G. getting dressed in Yankees attire.
    H. visiting the grave of the narrator's father.
    J. watching a baseball game on television.

9. The main purpose of the third paragraph (lines 18-24) is to:

    A. tell how the narrator's mother and father first met.
    B. describe a struggle from the narrator's childhood.
    C. explain how the narrator's father became a Yankees fan.
    D. compare life in China to life in the United States.

10. The tone of the last paragraph is:

    F. arrogant and insistent.
    G. nostalgic and content.
    H. backward-looking and mournful.
    J. giddy and patriotic.

GO ON TO THE NEXT PAGE.

Passage II

SOCIAL SCIENCE: This passage is adapted from the essay "Egypt's Remains: Recent Events in the History of Archaeology."

If you don underwater exploration gear and set out to recover the remains of one or two warships that sank off the coast of Egypt in the time of Napoleon, you probably won't expect to come across the remains of a 2,300 year-old city.
5 Yet this is what happened to French archaeologist Franck Godda in the year 2000. When he was about 6.5 kilometers off the coast of Alexandria, Godda discovered, among other items, 64 ships, about 700 anchors, a treasure trove of gold coins, and a series of giant granite statues. Also scattered
10 around on the sandy bottom were small and delicately decorated sarcophagi. It quickly became clear that many of these items had once been offerings to the Temple of Amun Gereb, a structure that also lay there, on the floor of the Mediterranean Sea, in almost pristine condition. Godda did
15 not know it at the time, but he had discovered what had once been the most important port of Ancient Egypt. This trading center was known to the Egyptians as Thonis; the Greeks called it Heracleion.

There was little surviving record of Thonis-Heracleion
20 or its importance to the ancient Egyptians before the port was discovered by Godda. However, archaeologists and expert historians are beginning to discern not only the city's significance during its commercial heyday but also the particulars of its fate—how it came to be where it is now.

25 As can be seen from the position of the city, the Egyptian coastline once extended farther out into the sea; it is hard to say exactly how and why the coastline contracted. Initially, some thought that the changes in the coastline might have been the result of a tsunami—not something that most of us
30 would associate with the Mediterranean, despite theories that a volcanic explosion on the island of Santorini caused such an event around 3000 B.C. Such theories, however, seem flimsy when subjected to scrutiny. Indeed, the artifacts that Godda unveiled are so lightly damaged that the tsunami
35 hypothesis seems implausible. In addition, Alexandria is just a short distance along the coast from where Heracleion once stood. There is no evidence that the better-known city was touched by anything so devastating as a tsunami.

But one thing has not been disputed: the city's crucial
40 place in Egyptian commerce. Heracleion is located right at the mouth of the Nile, which has always been one of the most important rivers in the world. In Egypt at the time of the Pharaohs, this waterway fed the people both bodily and spiritually. Annually, with its floods, it deposited silt that
45 gave renewed life to the soil; from the Nile's Pyrus reeds came the papyrus scrolls on which the Egyptians could write in hieroglyphics. It provided fish and fresh water. It was a barrier against invading armies. Among the boats discovered in Heracleion are sturdy cargo vessels and a long, sleek vessel

50 crafted in sycamore. It is a barge, most likely one of the sacred barges so often depicted on Egyptian tomb paintings. It is clear that this vessel was made downriver in Memphis and then brought to the city. Perhaps it carried the statuette of a Pharaoh—a possible offering to the god Osiris—that has
55 also been found in Heracleion. Thus, the city was also a sacred center, and not simply for Egyptians: the tombstone of a young Greek soldier has been identified among the city's ruins.

Although Heracleion served as a gateway to Egyptian
60 cities farther south, its site was eventually compromised by geologic forces. The Nile becomes sluggish and meanders as it approaches the Mediterranean, losing its singular directness, dividing and breaking into six or seven branches that weave their way through low-lying islands. These islands were
65 originally created by silt, which, due to the weakening of the river's force, eventually sank to the river's bed. It is on one of these islands that Thonis-Heracleion was built. After a time, built-up silt began to block the waterway that led to Memphis. Perhaps that is why Alexander the Great created a new port
70 farther along the coast: Alexandria is on higher and more solid land.

Yet this still does not explain why the city disappeared from sight and history. However, a new suggestion is being seriously considered: liquefaction.

75 We often associate sand with the dryness of deserts. However, sand can be both porous and unstable, as we all know from our childhood days on the beach. The definition of liquefaction is "a process by which water-saturated sediment loses strength and acts as a fluid, an effect that can
80 be caused by an earthquake or other upheaval." While there is no evidence that an earthquake affected Thonis-Heracleion, the rest of that definition is viable. Could it be that, over time, the city simply sank gently beneath the waters of the Nile? It would explain the preservation of those artifacts. What it
85 cannot explain is why, so far, no written reference to a "disappearing city" appeared before our own century.

GO ON TO THE NEXT PAGE.

11. The main purpose of the passage can best be described as an effort to:

A. praise archaeologist Franck Godda for adapting to an unusual set of circumstances.
B. describe in detail an archaeological discovery that involves an unresolved issue.
C. outline and encourage documentary research that would find written records of Heracleion.
D. explain how the founders of Heracleion planned a city that would surpass Memphis in importance.

12. When the author declares that "one thing has not been disputed" (line 39), he most likely means that:

F. the disappearance of Heracleion has often been explained by the natural movement of the Nile.
G. the tsunami hypothesis has not always been popular, but has always appeared in discussions of the fate of Heracleion.
H. Heracleion is regarded as an important economic center, though other topics related to the city remain open to debate.
J. Heracleion's religious importance is evident, though the city's role in commerce has less often been appreciated.

13. The passage states that the city of Heracleion was discovered by an architectural expedition that set out with the original intention of:

A. understanding Napoleon's role in Egyptian history.
B. locating a few warships that had sunk near Egypt.
C. recovering gold and statues from ancient Alexandria.
D. explaining how underwater sand deposits can help to preserve artifacts.

14. It can be reasonably inferred that the author regards the "tsunami" theory described in the third paragraph (lines 25-38) as:

F. an idea incompatible with the liquefaction theory.
G. a suggestion that seems dishonest at first.
H. a source of ongoing scholarly controversy.
J. a speculation that can be confidently rejected.

15. As it is used in line 60, the word *compromised* most nearly means:

A. undermined.
B. rejected.
C. discredited.
D. balanced.

16. According to the passage, all of the following were benefits that the Nile gave to the people of ancient Egypt EXCEPT:

F. writing materials.
G. sources of nourishment.
H. protection from enemies.
J. power for grain mills.

17. Which of the following does the author of the passage NOT do in the final paragraph?

A. Define a term
B. Reject a possibility
C. Refer to an expert
D. Present an assumption

18. According to the passage, evidence that Heracleion was a religious site for Greeks has been provided by:

F. statues of a few Greek gods and goddesses.
G. the presence of a large sycamore barge.
H. the abundance of anchors discovered by Godda.
J. the gravestone of a young Greek soldier.

19. Which of the following questions is it NOT possible to answer based on the passage?

A. How did Heracleion sink beneath the sea without being destroyed?
B. Why was the city of Heracleion important to Egyptian commerce?
C. Why did Alexander the Great build a second city comparable to Heracleion?
D. What uses did the Egyptians find for the natural resources of the Nile?

20. It can be reasonably inferred that both the "sarcophagi" (line 11) and the "Temple of Amun Gereb" (lines 12-13) are significant because they were:

F. signs that Napoleon had never been present in the region Godda had chosen.
G. important to individuals from both ancient Greece and ancient Egypt.
H. relatively well preserved when they were discovered by Godda.
J. extracted from the floor of the ocean by Godda's expedition.

GO ON TO THE NEXT PAGE.

Passage III

HUMANITIES: This passage is adapted from the short art critical profile "Garaicoa and His Rugs, 2005-Present."

The first time you glimpse one of Carlos Garaicoa's works at a museum exhibition, you will probably assume that you are looking at a piece of pavement, extracted straight from a city street. But that assumption will be wrong. What
5 you are actually looking at is a rug made out of wool, cotton, and a few other materials—including filaments of aluminum and infusions of mercury. All of this allows the Cuban-born Garaicoa to create rugs that look just like stretches of the street and sidewalk surfaces of his native Havana. It's a
10 clever (though apparently costly) sleight of hand, but Garaicoa's camouflaged rugs are much more than artistic parlor tricks.

Offbeat though his art can seem, Garaicoa is working within an artistic tradition that flourished in the early
15 twentieth century and that continues strong to this day. Artists, in modern times, have become masters of objects that aren't what they seem to be. Perhaps it all started when Belgian artist René Magritte painted a straightforward, realistic image of a tobacco pipe, then added in a teasing
20 caption: "This is not a pipe." The tradition continued with American artists Robert Gober (who created replicas of ceramic sinks using plaster and enamel) and Jeff Koons (who created replicas of inflatable pool toys using polychromed aluminum). Even photographers have gotten in the habit of
25 making objects that aren't quite true to material: German photographer Thomas Demand, for instance, has used cardboard and layered paper to create replicas of everything from subterranean caves to the Oval Office. Then he photographs his replicas, and nobody—except the most
30 attentive viewers—will ever know the difference.

This is an international tradition, and Garaicoa is an unabashedly international artist. As he declared in a 2003 interview, he wants his art to trace "broad global paths." But he is interested in something far more urgent than playing
35 mind games with objects and materials. Beyond the rugs, Garaicoa is an architect and a photographer. It is best to place the rugs within a larger body of work that aspires to be both fanciful and useful—to express Garaicoa's personality and to address problems such as sustainability, overpopulation, and
40 resource allocation, in Cuba and beyond.

According to art and design critic Lowery Stokes Simms, the street for Garaicoa "becomes a vehicle for social commentary simply by naming it for a person, date, or event. Such tributes encourage civic pride and memorial sentiment."
45 Return here to Garaicoa in exhibition. Often, Garaicoa's rugs are accompanied by video projections of life on actual human streets. At this point, his art ceases to be little more than clever mimicry, and becomes a spectacle that encourages visitors to see life in lower- to middle-class Havana up

50 close—or as up close as a museum in New York or Los Angeles will allow.

Already passports to modern Cuba, the rugs are also guides to meditation. Even a quick glance will show that something of this sort is Garaicoa's intention: as installed at a
55 recent showcase at Manhattan's Museum of Arts and Design, the rugs and their video projections were presented in an airy room with dusky, comforting lighting. Move past this general aura, and you will see that the rugs are adorned with words and slogans that translate to "Change," "The General
60 Sadness," and "The Fight Is Everywhere and Everyone Is Fighting." We are thus invited to contemplate these themes, both how they play out within modern cities and how they resonate through the course of civilization at large. Perhaps this invitation is most evident in Garaicoa's rug *El*
65 *Piensamento* (a title that translates to "a thought"), which precisely recreates a two-tone stone surface. To *El Piensamento*, Garaicoa adds yet another layer of simulation: shadow. The darkened outline of a pedestrian can be seen on this rug, and this "shadow" takes a passing presence and
70 gives it permanence. With this play of permanence and impermanence, Garaicoa questions humanity's role within the cities it creates. Do we each leave a mark, or are we all just passing through?

All of this is in sharp contrast, so it seems, to the spirit
75 of Garaicoa's architectural designs. Here, the artist can seem much more whimsical: he has devised everything from glowing yellow plans for entire future cities to individual structures inspired by the mind-bending fictions of Jorge Luis Borges. Of course, such projects continue Garaicoa's
80 emphasis on how we make use of our living spaces, and aspire to forms that are at once visually pleasing and socially responsible. They also, and unexpectedly, continue the conversation that the rugs initiate. The rugs ask us how we respond to the urban spaces we already have; the architecture
85 asks us what we want our cities to become.

21. The author's purpose in writing this passage is most likely to:

A. point out the specific political events that Carlos Garaicoa commemorates with his rugs.
B. explain why Garaicoa has become more popular in the United States than in Cuba.
C. profile Garaicoa and show how his works respond to major issues in urban society.
D. present a series of contrasts between Carlos Garaicoa and earlier replica-making artists.

GO ON TO THE NEXT PAGE.

22. As described in the passage, Garaicoa's art involves all of the following EXCEPT:

    F. video projections.
    G. architectural models.
    H. metal sculptures.
    J. rugs made from a variety of materials.

23. The passage directly indicates that Garaicoa's rugs can be characterized as all of the following EXCEPT:

    A. expensive.
    B. humorous.
    C. socially suggestive.
    D. initially deceptive.

24. The question that the author of the passage poses in lines 72-73 serves to call attention to:

    F. a point of ideological similarity between Garaicoa and Jorge Luis Borges.
    G. a broad issue that Garaicoa's *El Piensamento* encourages its viewers to confront.
    H. a reason why Garaicoa's rugs are now featured prominently in museums.
    J. an idea that is much less prominent in the works of other artists who create elaborate replicas.

25. As it is used in line 63, the word *course* most nearly means:

    A. defined schedule.
    B. formal study.
    C. historical progress.
    D. specific territory.

26. According to Lowery Stokes Simms, Garaicoa's rugs are significant because they allude to:

    F. historical reminders.
    G. multimedia experiments.
    H. rebellious gestures.
    J. indicators of the future.

27. The second and third paragraphs (lines 13-40) function to:

    A. argue that Garaicoa's art is concerned with issues that are not unique to Cuba.
    B. show why art that involves mimicry of everyday objects has rarely been practical or useful.
    C. highlight the reasons why museum visitors continue to enjoy detailed replicas of objects.
    D. explain that even the artists who admire Garaicoa have little interest in imitating his methods.

28. In lines 29-30, the author mentions the "most attentive viewers" of Thomas Demand's photographs in order to indicate that:

    F. today's advanced modeling technologies are used more often by photographers than by sculptors.
    G. Demand's innovations shock and puzzle even those viewers who are accustomed to Magritte.
    H. inattentive museum viewers have allowed Demand to achieve a positive reputation that he does not deserve.
    J. Demand's photographed items are mistakenly regarded as real, not as replicated, on a regular basis.

29. As described in the passage, the rug entitled *El Piensamento* is notable because it presents its viewers with:

    A. the shadow of a human figure.
    B. a series of political slogans.
    C. colors and textures that mimic high-quality marble.
    D. philosophical meanings that Garaicoa never intended.

30. The author refers to Jorge Luis Borges (lines 78-79) in order to emphasize:

    F. the presence of mimicry as a theme in literature.
    G. a precedent for Garaicoa's beliefs about society.
    H. the fanciful nature of Garaicoa's architecture.
    J. the ways Garaicoa uses narrative in his rugs.

GO ON TO THE NEXT PAGE.

Passage IV

NATURAL SCIENCE: Adapted from Philipp Henschel, "Where Are All the Leopards?" and Jan Kamler, "Cambodia's Last Leopards." Both articles are © Panthera.org, 2016.

Passage A by Philipp Henschel

When I started my research on leopards in Gabon in 1999, every single researcher or conservationist I came across was studying great apes or forest elephants. At international conferences, the researchers I met who were also working on
5 large carnivores pretty much all focused on tigers, lions, or cheetahs. When I asked why nobody seemed to be studying leopards, I would hear things like: "they are not really threatened," "they are a dime a dozen," "they are too elusive, too hard to study," and so on.

10 The general consensus seemed to be that the leopard wasn't worth any specific research or conservation effort–that there were bigger and seemingly more threatened species to study. (Conveniently, some of those species were also considerably easier to observe and count; studying leopards
15 involves hacking your way through dense forest or bush, packed like a mule with remote camera traps while one can research lions and cheetahs from the driver's seat of a Land Rover.) Very few people seemed to consider the possibility that the lack of concern about leopard numbers wasn't because they
20 weren't threatened, but rather because nobody had ever bothered to rigorously count them at a meaningful scale.

My colleagues at Panthera and I are changing that. Between 2009 and 2012, I led big cat surveys in West Africa's 21 largest protected areas. We found leopard presence in 7 of
25 them, and only one of the remaining West African populations numbered over 100 individuals. Today, in all of West Africa, as few as 500 breeding adults may remain. While we knew that wildlife had declined in these areas due to poor funding and protection, those findings were much more sobering than we
30 had feared. Even worse, our survey results from other geographic regions in Africa and Asia showed very similar patterns.

At Panthera, we are initiating and supporting conservation projects that protect leopards in 30 countries across Africa, the
35 Middle East, and tropical Asia. In addition to identifying where sustainable leopard populations exist or can be rebuilt, we work with local and national governments and NGO partners to stop the illicit trade of leopard fur, protect leopard habitat, reduce conflict between leopards and people, stabilize and
40 increase prey populations, and scale down unsustainable legal trophy hunting.

If the international conservation community can double down in support of initiatives like these, there is real hope for the leopard. Our next steps in this very moment will determine
45 the fate of this incredible species.

Passage B by Jan Kamler

The Indochinese leopard—a genetically unique subspecies of leopard—has only three remaining strongholds in the world: Peninsular Malaysia, the Northern Tenasserim Forest Complex along the Myanmar-Thailand border, and Cambodia's Eastern
50 Plains Landscape (EPL), where Panthera recently initiated camera trap surveys to monitor the population.

What's immediately noticeable about Indochinese leopards is that they don't look like other leopards; most individuals are black, or melanistic, enabling them to
55 camouflage into the dark, shadowy forest floor of Southeast Asia's evergreen forests. In order to monitor the species, a special camera trap equipped with infrared light is necessary, because only in infrared light do the "hidden" spots of black leopards become visible, thereby allowing for individual
60 recognition. The population we are monitoring in EPL, however, is different from the rest of the subspecies – likely because the landscape is characterized by dry, open, savanna-like forests. All the Indochinese leopards here are spotted, making them Southeast Asia's last population of spotted-only
65 leopards – and all the more important to monitor and protect.

A typical day in the field in Cambodia starts at sunrise, when the birds wake us at our campsite. After cooking rice, eating breakfast, and packing a lunch, we set off in teams of two to place camera traps. On flat terrain, we use motorbikes,
70 while more hilly and inaccessible areas require hiking. When not setting or checking camera traps, we carefully survey the dirt roads and trails looking for signs of leopards (prints or droppings) to get a better idea of leopard numbers in areas without camera traps. We typically return after dark because
75 the protected areas in which we work are between 3,000 to 4,000 km^2 – a lot of ground to cover.

Previous studies show that this population has been in decline, largely because of poaching for the illegal wildlife trade. Leopard parts are used as substitutes for tiger parts in
80 traditional Asian medicines, so as tigers decline throughout the region, there is increasing demand for leopard parts. No matter what our data yields about the population in EPL, one thing is certain: it's vital we protect this fascinating and unique animal.

GO ON TO THE NEXT PAGE.

Questions 31-34 ask about Passage A.

31. It can reasonably be inferred that the "consensus" described in line 10 of Passage A involved agreement among:

A. experts who were not actively studying leopards.
B. activists interested in performing fieldwork with Panthera.
C. scientists who feared leopard population declines.
D. students who learned of Henschel's leopard research.

32. One of the important functions of the second paragraph (lines 10-21) is to:

F. sarcastically criticize the researchers mentioned in the first paragraph.
G. summarize a memorable episode from the author's research on lions and cheetahs.
H. propose a new method for counting and studying leopards.
J. explain why leopards have not received the same level of attention from conservationists that other species have.

33. As it is used in line 32, the word *patterns* most nearly means:

A. shapes.
B. obsessions.
C. tendencies.
D. gestures.

34. The leopard conservation efforts which the author of Passage A advocates can most accurately be described as:

F. groundbreaking and controversial.
G. improvised and desperate.
H. multi-national and collaborative.
J. experimental and inconclusive.

Questions 35-37 ask about Passage B.

35. Which of the following statements about the type of Indochinese leopard that the author is studying is best supported by Passage B?

A. Its geographical range once extended to Africa.
B. Its spots can only be detected using special equipment.
C. It closely resembles the tiger in size and temperament.
D. It is most active at night.

36. Which of the three areas described in the first paragraph is the site of the fieldwork that the author is performing?

F. Peninsular Malaysia
G. The Norther Tenasserim Forest Complex
H. Cambodia's Eastern Plains Landscape
J. The author is active in all three areas.

37. The author of Passage B indicates that "signs of leopards" (line 72) are important because:

A. the area inhabited by the Indochinese leopard has not been fully mapped.
B. the Indochinese leopard cannot be observed directly.
C. these signs can signal poaching activity.
D. these signs can allow for more accurate population estimates.

Questions 38-40 ask about both passages.

38. Which of the following is present in Passage B but not in Passage A?

F. A description of a full day of fieldwork
G. A reference to one of Panthera's initiatives
H. A quotation from one of the author's colleagues
J. An estimate of the size of a leopard population

39. Both Passage A and Passage B describe leopard fieldwork that involves:

A. government funding.
B. camouflage gear.
C. tranquilizer darts.
D. camera traps.

40. The primary purpose of each passage is to discuss:

F. a large animal researcher's attempts to change the opinions of his colleagues.
G. the different forms of poaching and habitat loss that threaten leopards.
H. a species of leopard that was recently discovered by Panthera researchers.
J. a leopard population that the author believes should be aggressively protected.

END OF TEST 1.
STOP! DO NOT TURN THE PAGE UNTIL TOLD TO DO SO.

Answer Key: TEST 1

Test 1

LITERARY NARRATIVE

1. D
2. J
3. B
4. F
5. B
6. H
7. D
8. F
9. C
10. G

HUMANITIES

21. C
22. H
23. B
24. G
25. C
26. F
27. A
28. J
29. A
30. H

SOCIAL SCIENCE

11. B
12. H
13. B
14. J
15. A
16. J
17. C
18. J
19. A
20. H

NATURAL SCIENCE

31. A
32. J
33. C
34. H
35. B
36. H
37. D
38. F
39. D
40. J

To see your scaled ACT Reading Score (1-36), determine how many questions you answered correctly and consult the Scoring Chart on Page 186 of this book.

Post-Test Analysis

This post-test analysis is essential if you want to see an improvement on your next test. Possible reasons for errors, both for the test overall and for each of the four reading passages, are listed here. Place check marks next to the types of errors that pertain to you, or write your own types of errors in the blank spaces provided.

GENERAL

◇ Spent too much time reading the passages
◇ Spent too much time answering the questions
◇ Did not attempt to finish all of the passages
◇ Did not create effective margin answers
◇ Did not use process of elimination
◇ Could not find evidence to answer the questions
◇ Could not comprehend the topics and ideas in the passages
◇ Could not understand what the questions were asking
◇ Interpreted the passages rather than using evidence
Other: _____

LITERARY NARRATIVE

◇ Spent too long reading the passage
◇ Spent too long answering the questions
◇ Could not identify the setting and characters
◇ Could not understand the plot or action
◇ Could not work effectively with tone and clues to tone
Other: _____

> **Use this form** to better analyze your performance. If you don't understand why you made errors, there is no way that you can correct them!

SOCIAL SCIENCE

◇ Spent too long reading the passage
◇ Spent too long answering the questions
◇ Could not understand the author's position or arguments
◇ Used outside knowledge rather than using evidence
Other: _____

HUMANITIES

◇ Spent too long reading the passage
◇ Spent too long answering the questions
◇ Could understand the themes and organization of the passage
◇ Could not understand the author's ideas and uses of evidence
Other: _____

NATURAL SCIENCE

◇ Spent too long reading the passage
◇ Spent too long answering the questions
◇ Found the concepts and ideas in the passage confusing
◇ Found the questions confusing
◇ Could not effectively work with the inference and logic questions
Other: _____

TEST 1 Answer Explanations

1. Correct Answer: D

In lines 19-20 of the passage, the narrator refers to "the apartment where I had spent my girlhood." Thus, *spent* in this context has to do with the passage of time. Choice **D**, *passed* (as in "passed the time"), is the best match. *Reduced* (**A**) and *wasted* (**B**) both take negative tones that the passage does not support. *Invested* (**C**) refers to a financial transaction or a use of assets, and would not accurately describe time spent.

2. Correct Answer: J

Lines 10-13 state that "despite the fact that the antenna extended all the way up to the ceiling (with a ball of aluminum foil wrapped around the end of it for good measure), the broadcast occasionally cut out." Thus, it can be inferred that the antenna must have been extended and covered with foil to prevent the broadcast from cutting out, or to produce fairly good reception. So, choice **J** is the best answer. At this point, only the father has been mentioned and only one of his "habits" has been described, so that choice **F** is too broad in scope. Both **G** and **H** rely on inaccurate descriptions of the parents' living space: with its "minuscule screen" (line 6) and faulty reception, the television set indicates an absence of *luxury* (**G**) and *advanced technology* (**H**) in the narrator's family apartment.

3. Correct Answer: B

The narrator notes that her father felt "pride and happiness" (line 37) upon having his "Let's go Yankees!" greeting returned by strangers. The narrator also posits that "in other ways he was lonely," (line 38) and so baseball "allowed him to feel that he belonged here" (lines 44-45). Choice **B** is the only choice about social connection. The other answers can be eliminated for various reasons: **A** is too negative in tone, **C** would require references to specific Yankees players, and **D** cannot be justified because the father makes no effort to learn English and "learned baseball instead" (lines 29-30).

4. Correct Answer: F

The narrator says that her father was "too old to really start learning English" (lines 28-29), which eliminates choice **G**. She also states that he "never had friends over to the apartment" (lines 39-40), which eliminates choice **H**, and that he was "living so far from his home" (line 38), which eliminates choice **J**, leaving only choice **F**. In fact, it is impossible to know how the father interacted with his coworkers because he "never talked about" his job with his daughter (line 49).

5. Correct Answer: B

In explaining why her father's "job was something he never talked about with me" (lines 48-49), the narrator states that it was "hardly the best topic to bring home to a delicate young girl" (lines 50-51). A "girl in her position" in choice **B** matches "delicate young girl" (line 51). Choices **A** and **C** would require further information about the father's thoughts on his job, yet the father exhibited a "reticence" that ruled out such further disclosures (lines 52). Choice **D** is based on a misinterpretation of the passage: the father's wages may not be high (as is clear from the family's lonely and spare lifestyle), but this situation is never explicitly identified as a source of shame for him.

6. Correct Answer: H

Choice **F** can be eliminated because baseball "allowed him [the narrator's father] to feel that he belonged here" (lines 44-45). The narrator's father "worked on the docks" (lines 46-47) and "disappeared at dawn, only to reappear at night" (line 53), eliminating choice **G**. His interest in baseball developed only after the family "immigrated to America" (line 17), not *in China* (line 18) eliminating choice **J** and leaving choice **H**. The father in fact "smoked his whole life" (line 57) and his death is linked to this persisting habit.

7. Correct Answer: D

The narrator's father "died, fifteen years ago, of a heart attack" (line 55), and "his father before him had succumbed in just the same way" (lines 57-58). Thus, choice **D** is correct. Although the father's lifestyle is difficult, do not falsely assume that he died as a result of something in his environment, such as an accident at work (**B**) or food poisoning (**C**). Choice **A** is a trap answer: though a habitual smoker and indeed open to the threat of lung cancer, the father is actually killed by a heart attack.

8. Correct Answer: F

After posing the question in the line reference, the narrator "pulled out two tickets" (line 65). Her mother replies, "Yankees vs. Phillies . . . Game starts in two hours" (lines 67-68). Thus, choice **F** is correct. Be careful not to falsely relate this reference to ideas elsewhere in the passage: the father's death is described in lines 57-59 (**H**) and the process of watching a baseball game is described in the first paragraph (**J**). Neither, however, relates directly to the narrator's dialogue and subsequent actions. Although trap answer **G** can seem closer to the topic of a Yankees game, it is ultimately inaccurate. The only pieces of *Yankees attire* mentioned in the passage are the clothes of the father and the random people he meets: whether the mother and daughter are dressed similarly is never specified.

9. Correct Answer: C

The second paragraph states that the narrator's father didn't watch baseball in China. The third paragraph explains the change: he "found an old Yankees cap" (lines 21-22) and became "a fan for the rest of his life" (lines 23-24). Thus, choice **C** is correct. Although the mother narrates much of this paragraph, she does not describe her relationship with the narrator's father (**A**) or adopt a negative tone and describe a struggle (**B**). Choice **D** is too broad: the mother presents a contrast involving the narrator's father, not a larger contrast involving lifestyles in two countries.

10. Correct Answer: G

Going to a Yankees game, the narrator witnesses "the same pride my father would have felt" (line 73), which supports choice **G**. The tone is strongly positive (*pride*) and the narrator is looking nostalgically backward (*my father*). Choices **F** and **H** include strong and inappropriate negatives (*arrogant* and *mournful*, respectively). Choice **J** distorts the ideas in this final paragraph: the

TEST 1 Answer Explanations

narrator is pleased but not giddy (or happy yet unsettled) and is performing actions that commemorate her father (not that exhibit patriotism).

SOCIAL SCIENCE

11. Correct Answer: B

The passage is about how *Godda discovered* (line 7) Heracleion and how current theories *cannot explain* (line 85) the city's fate, thus supporting *archaeological discovery* and *unresolved issue* in choice **B**. Do not mistake the author's interest in Heracleion for strong supportive emotions: though an important figure in the passage, Godda is never explicitly praised, eliminating choice **A**. And the author's tone is not *encouraging* but rather informative, eliminating choice **C**. Much remains unknown about Heracleion, and the exact "founders of Heracleion" and their intentions are not mentioned at all in the passage: thus, eliminate choice **D**.

12. Correct Answer: H

Lines 39-40 state that "one thing has not been disputed: the city's crucial place in Egyptian commerce." This supports *economic center* in choice **H** and implies that other aspects of Heracleion are disputed, thus supporting the idea that *other topics related to the city remain open to debate* in choice **H**. Lines 39-40 do not mention anything about the *disappearance of Heracleion*, thus eliminating choice **F**. Lines 39-40 do not reference a *tsunami*, thus eliminating answer choice **G**. (Although line 38 does mention a *tsunami*, be sure to look for what the questions specifically asks.) Lines 39-40 also make no mention of *Heracleion's religious importance*, even though this issue is central to other portions of the passage, thus eliminating choice **J**.

13. Correct Answer: B

Lines 1-3 reveal that Godda "set out to recover the remains of one or two warships that sank off the coast of Egypt," making choice **B** correct. Lines 1-3 designate *Napoleon* only as a time reference for the original artifacts Godda was seeking (not as a person linked to the artifacts in any other way), thus eliminating choice **A**. Lines 6-7 explicitly state Godda's findings to be "6.5 kilometers off the coast of Alexandria," not "from ancient Alexandria," thus making choice **C** faulty and incorrect. The author makes no mention of the precise processes involved in *preserving artifacts* until the final paragraph of the passage, thus making it possible to eliminate choice **D**.

14. Correct Answer: J

The author rejects the tsunami theory as *flimsy* (line 33) and *implausible* (line 38). In addition, the author finds "no evidence that the better-known city [Alexandria, near Heracleion] was touched by anything so devastating as a tsunami" (lines 37-38). Thus, choice **J** is correct. The author never directly compares the tsunami idea to the *liquefaction theory* (described only in lines 75-86) in the third paragraph, although the author seems to favor liquefaction as a more likely explanation for the fate of Heracleion. Thus, choice **F** does not relate to the author's immediate

discussion. Line 35 clearly states that a *tsunami* is highly unlikely due to the lack of damage to the artifacts. This idea is supported throughout the passage, which makes answer choice **G** faulty in that it uses *at first* to indicate that the tsunami idea could actually be acceptable. (Moreover, theorists could put forward a flawed idea without necessarily having *dishonest* motives: be careful of how the negative tone operates here.) Lines 25-38 do not mention anything about *scholarly controversy*: the author does disagree with the "some" who have set forward the tsunami theory (lines 28-29), yet it is not evident that these "some" are scholars or that there is disagreement or controversy on a broader scale.

15. Correct Answer: A

Compromised in line 60 should describe a negative effect because the relevant paragraph describes the downfall of Heracleion, which "sank to the river's bed" (line 66). Choice **A** (*undermined*) is the best match. For **B**, *rejected* is an illogical choice since the sentence refers to *geological forces*; to describe these as *rejecting* would be to give *geological forces* decision-making properties. Choice **C**, *discredited*, can be eliminated for the same reason: *to discredit* should refer to the action of a person, not of a geological force. Choice **D** is clearly wrong; the word *balanced* does not match the writer's discussion of the forces that negatively impacted Heracleion and that could explain the city's disappearance.

16. Correct Answer: J

The Nile provided reeds that the Egyptians used as *papyrus scrolls* (line 46), so that choice **F** should be eliminated. The Nile also "provided fish and fresh water. It was a barrier against invading armies" (lines 47-48). This evidence eliminates choices **G** and **H**, leaving choice **J**. *Grain mills* are mentioned nowhere in the passage, and it cannot be assumed that the Egyptians (despite their commerce and manufacturing) used the Nile to power these structures.

17. Correct Answer: C

Line 75 puts forward the assumption that sand is found primarily in *deserts*, thus eliminating choice **D**. The author then defines the term *liquefaction* in lines 78-80, thus eliminating choice **A**. However, because a source is not specified, it cannot be concluded that the quoted definition is a quotation from an expert (so keep choice **C**). Choice **B** can be eliminated because the author rejects the possibility that "an earthquake affected Thonis-Heracleion" (line 81).

18. Correct Answer: J

The author states in lines 55-56 that "the city [Heracleion] was also a sacred center," as shown by the fact that "the tombstone of a young Greek soldier has been identified among the city's ruins" (lines 56-58). Thus, choice **J** is correct. In lines 39-58, the author never mentions finding "statues of a few Greek gods and goddesses" thus easily eliminating choice **F**. (Do not conclude wrongly, based on the evidence of the Greek soldier's tombstone, that such Greek statues were necessarily present.) Likewise, an *abundance of anchors* is mentioned in the beginning of the passage (line 8) and is not brought back as evidence that *Heracleion* was a Greek religious site, thus eliminating choice **H**. Choice **G** should also be disqualified, because the sycamore *barge* (lines 50-51) only indicates that Heracleion was a religious site for Egyptians. This artifact is in no way related to the Greeks.

19. Correct Answer: A

Lines 39-40 introduce "the city's crucial place in Egyptian commerce," and the following sentences give reasons for Heracleion's important status: the Nile provided "papyrus scrolls, . . . fish and fresh water" (lines 46-47), thus eliminating choices **B** and **D**. Lines 69-71 demonstrate "why Alexander the Great created a new port," thereby answering the question posed in choice **C**. Thus, choice **A** remains. Be careful of misinterpreting the final paragraph as a justification for A: here, the author provides an idea that *would explain* why Heracleion sank beneath the water (lines 82-84), not a definitive or indisputable reason why the city sank.

20. Correct Answer: H

Lines 10-11 state that the sarcophagi were *delicately* decorated (and thus not harmed), and line 14 states that the temple was found "in almost pristine condition." These descriptions support the idea that these artifacts were *well preserved*, as stated in choice **H**. Line 3 clearly states that Godda was initially seeking "two warships that sank off he coast of Egypt in the time of Napoleon." Though Napoleon's time period is referenced, the author never indicates whether Napoleon was present in Godda's chosen region or not, thus eliminating choice **F**. Lines 16-18 do indicate that Thonis-Heracleion in general was known to both Egyptians and Greeks; however, it is never specified whether Greeks took any interest in the structures mentioned in the question. Thus, eliminate choice **G**. Nor is it specified whether Godda *extracted* any structures or artifacts from the floor of the sea: the author only states that Godda discovered the buildings of Heracleion, without describing the later stages of Godda's expedition. Thus, eliminate choice **J**.

HUMANITIES

21. Correct Answer: C

This passage outlines the career of Garaicoa and describes how he uses his artwork to "address problems such as sustainability, overpopulation, and resource allocation" (lines 39-40). Thus, choice **C** is correct. Although Garaicoa's rugs generally "encourage civic pride and memorial sentiment," the author never points to specific events that the rugs commemorate, thus making choice **A** incorrect. The author also indicates that Garaicoa is popular in American museums, but never contrasts Garaicoa's status in the United States with his status in Cuba, thus making choice **B** incorrect. For choice **D**, line 34 states that Garaicoa "is interested in something far more urgent than playing mind games with objects and materials," aligning Garaicoa with other replica-making artists. However, such other artists are only mentioned in the second paragraph, and as artists who are working the same "artistic tradition" (line 14) as Garaicoa. Thus, choice **D** misstates the relationship between Garaicoa and these artists; this answer also refers to an issue that is only secondary in the passage.

22. Correct Answer: H

The reference to *video projections* in line 56 eliminates choice **F**. Later references to Garaicoa's *architectural designs* (line 75) and *plans* (line 77) eliminate choice **G**. The multi-material "rug made out of wool, cotton, and a few other materials" (line 5-6) eliminates choice **J**, leaving choice **H**. Garaicoa uses "filaments of aluminum and infusions of mercury" in his rugs (lines 6-7), but this information does not indicate that he makes *metal sculptures* as well.

23. Correct Answer: B

The rugs are describes as *costly* (line 10) and *camouflaged* (line 11) because they "look just like stretches of the street and sidewalk surfaces" (lines 8-9), thus eliminating choices **A** and **D**. Garaicoa uses his artwork to "address problems such as sustainability, overpopulation, and resource allocation" (lines 39-40). Thus, choice **C** is out, leaving choice **B**. Do not assume that, because some of the other artists described in the second paragraph might be humorous, Garaicoa must be described as humorous himself.

24. Correct Answer: G

The author asks, "Do we each leave a mark, or are we all just passing through?" (lines 72-73) to show how *El Piensamento* "questions humanity's role within the cities it creates" (lines 71-72). Thus, choice **G** is correct. The lines above present no clear that indicates that they serve "to point to ideological similarities between Garaicoa and Jorge Luis Borges," who is only mentioned later on and only in reference to Garaicoa's architecture. Thus, choice **F** is incorrect. Nor do the referenced lines provide "a reason why Garaicoa's rugs are now featured prominently in museums," since museums are not mentioned at all at this point. Thus, choice **H** is incorrect. **J** can be eliminated because it refers to the wrong element of the passage: other artists who create replicas are mentioned in the second paragraph, but have disappeared from the discussion by the time the relevant line reference appears.

25. Correct Answer: C

The author discusses how Garaicoa's themes "resonate through the course of civilization" (line 63). Thus, *course* in this context has to do with history or past time. Choice **C** is the best match. The phrases *defined schedule and formal study* both refer to the activities of individual people, not to the nature of civilization as a whole, thus making answer choices **A** and **B** incorrect. The final words of line 63, *civilization at large*, contradict the idea of *specificity* in answer choice **D**; the answer itself also refers to physical *territory*, not to the nature of civilization.

26. Correct Answer: F

Lowery Stokes Simms states that, in Garaicoa's rug artwork, the street "becomes a vehicle for social commentary simply by naming it for a person, date, or event" (lines 42-43), which induces *memorial sentiment* (line 44) in the viewer. This evidence matches choice **F**. Lowery Stokes Simms does not make a linkage between the significance of Garaicoa's rugs and *multimedia experiments* (which are mentioned only by the author of the passage in line 46). Thus, eliminate choice **G**. Choice **H**, *rebellious gestures*, contradicts the tone and meaning of the passage, since the rugs involve social pride and commemoration rather than social re-

TEST 1 Answer Explanations

bellion. Furthermore, Lowery Stokes Simms links the rugs to the past (commemoration) and the present (civic pride) but never to the future, so that answer choice **J** is incorrect.

27. Correct Answer: A

The third paragraph explains that the *artistic tradition* (line 14) in the second paragraph "is an international tradition, and Garaicoa is an unabashedly international artist" (lines 31-32). Lines 32-40 further explain the word-wide nature of Garaicoa's art. Thus, choice **A** is correct. To eliminate **B**, keep in mind that lines 41-42 present the idea that "the street for Garaicoa 'becomes a vehicle for social commentary.'" Art that functions in this manner could be socially *useful* and *practical*; moreover, the author never explains whether the other artists mentioned have succeeded in creating useful art. We are simply told what the other artists have created, now how these creations function. *Museum visitors* are not mentioned in lines (13-40), thus eliminating answer choice **C**, while *artists who admire Garaicoa* are not mentioned at all in lines (13-40), thus eliminating answer choice **D**. Do not falsely assume that the other artists mentioned admire, or even know of, Garaicoa.

28. Correct Answer: J

Describing the process of observing Demand's replicas, the author notes that "nobody—except the most attentive viewers—will ever know the difference" (lines 29-30) between replica and original. Thus, the replicas are perceived as real by most people, so that choice **J** is correct. Despite the precision of some of the replicas described by the author, specific *modeling technologies* were not mentioned at all in the passage, thus eliminating answer choice **F**. The author does not directly oppose *Demand* and *Magritte*, and in fact groups them as part of the same *artistic tradition* (line 14), thus eliminating answer choice **G**. In addition, choice **H** is too negative in tone and discusses Demand's reputation, an issue that the author never addresses. Thus, this choice is incorrect.

29. Correct Answer: A

In *El Piensamento*, "the darkened outline of a pedestrian can be seen " (lines 68-69) and is described as a *shadow* (line 69). Thus, choice **A** is correct. In the passage, *El Piensamento* was not described as transmitting a *series of political slogans*, even though other Garaicoa rugs bear political sayings; thus, answer choice **B** is incorrect. *Marble* is not referenced at all in the passage; thus, answer choice **C** is incorrect. In the passage *El Piensamento* was never described to bring about unintended *philosophical mean-ings*; thus, eliminate answer choice **D**.

30. Correct Answer: H

The reference to "the mind-bending fictions of Jorge Luis Borges" (lines 78-79) serves to support the author's claim that Garaicoa's architectural work is *whimsical* (line 76). Thus, choice **H** is the most accurate answer. **F** is incorrect since it references Borges's relation-ship to *literature*, while the purpose of the comparison is to explain Garaicoa and his art. **G** is incorrect since the passage does not mention any social beliefs that link Jorge Luis Borges and Garaicoa (or define Borges's social beliefs at all); rather, the two men are linked by artistic style. Although the rugs described in lines 52-73 involve narrative elements, the lines referenced for this question do not make any mention of Garaicoa's rugs; thus, choice **J** is incorrect.

NATURAL SCIENCE

31. Correct Answer: A

In the first paragraph, the author discusses conservationists and explains that "nobody seemed to be studying leopards (lines 6-7); then, the author explains that there is a "consensus" among these individuals that "the leopard wasn't worth any specific research or conservation effort (lines 10-11). This information directly supports choice **A**. Choice **B** refers to the wrong individual: Henschel is working with Panthera, but we are not told of the experts' relationship to the organization. Choice **C** distorts the stance of the experts (who are in fact not concerned about the leopards), while **D** wrongly identifies the experts as students, even though it offers some of the right context.

32. Correct Answer: J

In this paragraph, the author explains that other species are "considerably easier to observe and count" (line 14) than leopards are: while leopards involve difficult fieldwork in forest and brush, "lions and cheetahs" (line 17) can be observed with relative ease. These factors explain why conservationists have not attempted to "rigorously count" (line 21) leopards, thus justifying choice **J**. The author is simply explaining facts (not using sarcasm, eliminating choice **F**) and only describes his direct work with leopards (not with lions and cheetahs, eliminating choice **G**). Choice **H** is inaccurate because, even though the author supports attempts to study leopards, a new "method" is not defined here: the lack of study is the author's main focus.

33. Correct Answer: C

The word *patterns* is presented in the context of "survey results" (line 30) which show wildlife population declines: such declines are a tendency that the authors have observed, justifying choice **C**. Choices **A** and **D** wrongly assume that the author is referring to FORMS or MOVEMENTS, not to a group of related EVENTS, while choice **B** is out of context. The author is indeed interested in wildlife decline, but cannot be negatively described as "obsessed" with the issue.

TEST 1 Answer Explanations

34. Correct Answer: H

In outlining proactive efforts to protect leopards, the author of Passage A promotes the idea of working "with local and national governments and NGO partners" (line 37) and points to the "international community" (line 42) as a playing a potentially important role. Choice **H** rightly indicates that international forces will work together. Choices **F**, **G**, and **J** are all problematic because they involve negatives. The researchers and conservationists mentioned in the first paragraph might disapprove of the author's focus on leopards, but there is no logical reason why the author would "advocate" plans that are "controversial" (when in fact his plans involve consensus), "desperate," or "inconclusive" (when in fact he has very firm ideas in mind).

35. Correct Answer: B

In the second paragraph of Passage B, the author explains that a "special camera trap equipped with infrared light" (line 57) is needed to detect the hidden black spots of the Indochinese leopard. This information supports choice **B**, but should not be confused as evidence for choice **D**. (The forests inhabited by the leopards are shadowy, but the leopard's own sleep and waking schedule is never explained). Choices **A** and **C** distort details from the passage: the leopard has a limited range (not a range that once involved "Africa", which is in fact never mentioned) and is used as a replacement for the tiger in "traditional Asian medicines" (line 80, but is never COMPARED to the tiger in any other way).

36. Correct Answer: H

The author defines three Indochinese leopard sites in the first paragraph of Passage B, then goes on to describe a "typical day in the field in Cambodia" (line 66), where he works on an open landscape. It can be inferred from this information that the author is active in Cambodia's Eastern Plains Landscape, or choice **H**. Choices **F** and **G** refer to other sites in the first paragraph of Passage B, and choice **J** wrongly assumes that the author is active in all three when only the Cambodian site is explicitly mentioned for fieldwork.

37. Correct Answer: D

The author of Passage B explains that the "signs" are important because they enable researchers to "get a better idea of leopard numbers in areas without camera traps" (lines 73-74). This information directly supports choice **D**, since leopards in these areas must be taken into account for accurate estimates. Choice **A** is contradicted by the first paragraph (which defines the Indochinese leopard's range), choice **B** wrongly assumes that the leopard cannot be seen by researchers (when in fact only its SPOTS cannot be observed directly), and **C** refers to a topic from the final paragraph ("poaching"), NOT to a topic that the author ties directly to the leopard traces.

38. Correct Answer: F

In lines 66-76, the author of Passage B describes "A typical day in the field" and explains how a team tracks Indochinese leopards: the account concludes with an explanation of why the researchers typically "return after dark". This information supports choice **F**: the author of Passage A is well aware of how leopard fieldwork operates, but never describes a "full day" in this manner. Both passages refer to one of Panthera's initiatives (eliminating **G**). Only Passage A includes quotations (lines 7-9, eliminating **H**) and a direct measurement of a population size (lines 24-27, eliminating **J**). The author of Passage B does mention that the Indochinese leopard populations are declining, but does NOT provide a number for the approximate size of the population.

39. Correct Answer: D

The author of Passage A references the "camera traps" used in leopard fieldwork in line 16; the author of Passage B mentions "camera traps" in line 69. This information supports Choice **D**. Only Passage A discusses government activity (lines 35-41, eliminating **A**), while neither passage mentions camouflage gear (eliminating **B**) or tranquilizer darts (eliminating **C**). Do not wrongly assume that the difficulty of tracking leopards makes these tools, which are not specifically mentioned, in any way necessary.

40. Correct Answer: J

While Passage A focuses on the author's conservation work with "West African populations" (line 25) of leopards, Passage B focuses on the author's conservation-oriented fieldwork involving "The Indochinese leopard" (line 46). This information directly supports **J**. Choice **F** brings up an issue that is only addressed in the first paragraph of Passage A, choice **G** mistakes a secondary issue (forms of poaching, only discussed near the end of each passage) for the main focus, and choice **H** makes a faulty assumption. The leopards in both passages INTEREST Panthera researchers, but are never designated as DISCOVERED by Panthera itself.

Test 2

READING TEST

35 Minutes—40 Questions

DIRECTIONS: There are four passages in this test. Each passage is followed by several questions. After reading a passage, choose the best answer to each question and fill in the corresponding oval on your answer document. You may refer to the passages as often as necessary.

Passage I

PROSE NARRATIVE: The following two passages are adapted from memoirs written by career educators: Holliday's appeared in 2013 while Jervaise's appeared in 1976.

Passage A by Chris Holliday

It was 1960. I was a young man of twenty-one, just out of college and ready to try my hand at teaching at a vocational school. At the North Monmouthshire College of Commercial Training in Wales, Mr. Walby was the Head of the English
5 Department and my very first boss.

Mr. Walby was a man of great girth. In fact, he was the fattest man I had ever seen in my life. He had jowly cheeks and his small eyes were hidden behind thick-rimmed spectacles. His sparse hair was spread flat and thin against the top of his
10 head, and his dark moustache drooped a little at each end. When he walked, he lumbered at a sedate yet stately pace, although he rarely moved from his office when he was actually present in the college. Looking rather like a walrus at ease, he leaned back in his straining leather chair, clasped his vast
15 pudgy hands at the nape of his neck, and stared, in supreme content, at the opposite wall. On this wall was framed his one great achievement of each year: the timetable for his department.

The timetable was his pride and joy. Once it was completed, it was absolutely inviolable. In fact, in the five years that I was
20 at the college, the timetable never changed. A lesson in any of the subjects that came under Mr. Walby's loving care lasted one hour. Each subject was allotted ten hours a week. Thus, each class received a double lesson, in each subject, at the same time, every day for five school days. In Mr. Walby's eyes, this
25 was the perfect timetable. Teachers were less impressed, and the college inspectors, when they made their biennial visit, critically demanded that Mr. Walby revise his system. Mr. Walby nodded his head in grave agreement with the inspectors' commands and, once the uncomprehending outsiders had left,
30 continued to pass his day, gazing at what he had wrought. A slight twitch of his moustache, and the memory of the invaders became no more.

Passage B by Geoffrey Jervaise

The boarding house for me and the other first-year students was a very small section of the school, and there were
35 two male teachers in charge of it, Mr. Jones and Mr. Charlton— but we called them "Moe" and "Dez" behind their backs, affectionately, in the same way in which people refer to familiar and famous comedy double acts. Like all good duos, they complemented each other like a well-worn pair of
40 mismatched shoes. Individually, they contrasted with each other so sharply in appearance and wit that it was hard to predict how well they worked as a team. Moe was slim, always sharply dressed, holding a pose at the front of the class, apparently imperturbable and (though taciturn at most times)
45 in possession of an astringent wit, which never allowed an adversary in conversation a chance to deliver the punch line. Dez, on the other hand, was a sprawling figure, always comfortably rather than smartly dressed. He was most at ease in the worn, coffee-stained leather armchair of his study from
50 which he conversed with rather than lectured to his pupils, always willing to embark on long—and always hilarious— series of reminiscences to illustrate a point. This odd couple also shared the task of teaching my group in English; both had an immense knowledge of their subject, and they balanced out
55 each other's opinions with subtle digs that produced a simultaneous belly laugh from Dez and wry smile of acknowledgment from Moe. They clearly shared the ease and respect that accompany a true friendship.

They saved me. I wanted so much to be like them, and to
60 impress them. So I worked (at least in their lessons), and, as I read the books they discussed, I began to grow up and accept myself in a way I had never done before. They never sat me down and droned on to me about my situation, as child psychiatrists and education specialists would do today; rather,
65 they just made me feel, gradually, more secure about myself. Once, in the middle of a long story retold to me on the school's main staircase, Dez threw in, a propos of nothing, the following remark: "You know, of course, that a lot of people here are quite easily influenced by you, don't you? You should
70 use that." He never expanded on that remark. Before I had the chance to recover, Dez had moved on to some piece of reminiscence that I have long forgotten.

GO ON TO THE NEXT PAGE.

Questions 1-3 ask about Passage A.

1. On the basis of the information in Passage A, approximately how old was the narrator when he departed from Mr. Walby's college?

    A. 21
    B. 22
    C. 26
    D. 31

2. It can be reasonably inferred that the author of Passage A refers to the "college inspectors" (line 26) for what reason?

    F. To foreshadow Mr. Walby's dismissal from his post.
    G. To show that Mr. Walby's opinions were not shared.
    H. To make Mr. Walby seem oblivious and incompetent.
    J. To praise Mr. Walby for his spirit of defiance.

3. As it is used in line 16, the word *framed* most nearly means:

    A. accused.
    B. highlighted.
    C. contextualized.
    D. mounted.

Questions 4-7 ask about Passage B.

4. The narrator refers to famous comedy double acts primarily to:

    F. explain the oddly harmonious relationship between Moe and Dez.
    G. imply that Moe and Dez were much more competitive than their students intuited at the time.
    H. introduce the strange and unflattering descriptions of Moe and Dez.
    J. specify one of the forms of entertainment that Moe and Dez discussed at length in their courses.

5. In addition to teaching, Moe and Dez were assigned the responsibility of:

    A. telling amusing stories to help their students learn.
    B. mentoring students from difficult backgrounds.
    C. supervising the narrator's boarding house.
    D. publishing research on topics in English.

6. Which of the following does the narrator NOT describe in an approving manner?

    F. "Moe" (line 42)
    G. "Dez" (line 47)
    H. "their subject" (line 54)
    J. "education specialists" (line 64)

---

7. In what way does the second paragraph of Passage B differ from the first paragraph of Passage B?

    A. The first paragraph describes general tendencies; the second describes a specific scene.
    B. The first paragraph includes quoted dialogue; the second only includes paraphrased dialogue.
    C. The first paragraph presents Moe and Dez in a positive light; the second suggests their personal failings.
    D. The first paragraph focuses on the narrator's classmates; the second explains why the narrator had trouble relating to those classmates.

Questions 8-10 ask about both passages.

8. The descriptions of Mr. Walby in Passage A differ from the descriptions of Moe and Dez in Passage B in that the author of Passage A never considers:

    F. how Mr. Walby interacts with students.
    G. what other teachers think of Mr. Walby.
    H. the physical appearance of Mr. Walby.
    J. a few of the emotions felt by Mr. Walby.

9. Of the following characters, which one is described as the most talkative?

    A. Mr. Walby in Passage A.
    B. The narrator of Passage A.
    C. Moe in Passage B.
    D. Dez in Passage B.

10. Another author has written the following about the role of the ideal teacher:

    It is such a teacher's role not to impart his style to you, but to elevate you to a style of your own.

    Which passage most closely echoes the view presented in the quotation?

    F. Passage A, because the narrator admires Mr. Walby's diligence.
    G. Passage A, because the narrator is inspired to rebel against Mr. Walby.
    H. Passage B, because Moe and Dez inspired the narrator to become confident in his own personality.
    J. Passage B, because Moe and Dez encouraged the narrator to find his own way to a career in education.

GO ON TO THE NEXT PAGE.

Passage II

SOCIAL SCIENCE: This passage is adapted from the essay "Welcome to China, President Nixon." The Vietnam War lasted from 1959-1975, with the level of U.S. involvement varying over time.

"The week that changed the world," is how President Richard Nixon characterized his February 1972 visit to China. The first United States President to enter China in twenty-five years, Nixon made his visit in the midst of the
5 Cold War, with conflict in Vietnam raging and tensions with Communist China running deep.

Even though President Nixon had decided to prioritize relations with China upon entering office in January 1969, the reasons for his trip were anything but simple. Had they
10 been widely known at the time, his motivations would have surprised many.

President Nixon had made his name as a conservative politician, and had made his anti-communist feelings evident years before assuming the Presidency. During a
15 1964 trip to Asia, he had announced that "it would be disastrous to the cause of freedom" for the U.S. to formally recognize Red China. Yet this is exactly what he did in 1972, and this move shocked America's allies, altered the global balance of power, and shook the status quo of world
20 politics. Although President Nixon may have been ready to reach out to China, members of the State Department were concerned that Nixon's plan would only irritate America's allies. Ultimately, President Nixon disregarded State Department skeptics and proceeded with his initiative.

25 China had its own reasons for agreeing to the meeting. The Chinese sovereign, Mao Tse-tung, viewed the Soviet Union as a threat and felt that a relationship with the United States would be strategically wise. This was not the only regional consideration, either: Mao felt that cooperation
30 with the United States could help him reclaim Taiwan as a Chinese territory, and was concerned about Japan's rapidly growing, export-based economy. A favorably-inclined Washington would be in a position to check any Japanese tendencies toward militarism and political expansionism.
35 Yet hardliners in the Chinese government—remembering American military activity against North Korea, one of China's allies—did not want to normalize relations.

President Nixon had his own reasons for improving
40 relations. Both he and National Security Advisor Kissinger believed that ties to China would give the United States more flexibility on the world scene. When it came to the communist countries, the United States had been dealing primarily with the ideologically hostile Soviet Union. By
45 reaching out to China, Nixon could break up the Communist Bloc by leveraging China's interests against those of the Soviets.

More basically, opening relations with China would catch the Soviet Union's attention. A relationship with
50 China would cause the Soviet Union to become paranoid, concerned that its Communist partner was breaking away. Ultimately, President Nixon hoped that the Soviet Union would see an impending danger and become increasingly compliant with the diplomatic demands of the United
55 States.

But Nixon also wanted help in resolving the Vietnam War. He aimed to decrease the amount of aid provided to North Vietnam by China, and also hoped to persuade the Soviet Union and China to take diplomatic action in the
60 conflict. A successful effort here would create a sense of isolation on North Vietnam's part; its two big supporters would be dealing with the United States, its enemy.

In setting up such a delicate meeting, Mao and Nixon were aided by officials from Pakistan, a country friendly
65 with both China and the United States. On his own, Kissinger took two trips to China: one to secretly lay the groundwork for President Nixon's trip, one to plan out the exact itinerary.

The trip itself was akin to a television mini-series.
70 American audiences tuned in for eight days and nights of images broadcast directly from China—the first such images to reach America in twenty years. The visit was also big news in China itself. Mao's citizenry listened to the official radio broadcasts and newspapers featured
75 Nixon's visit on the front page.

In his own metaphor, President Nixon remembered the trip as "a voyage of philosophical discovery as uncertain, and in some ways as perilous, as the voyages of geographical discovery of an earlier time." Such rhetoric
80 aside, the trip was only a qualified success in geopolitical terms. Shortly after his time with Chairman Mao, President Nixon negotiated the first step in a Strategic Arms Limitation Treaty with the Soviet Union, ushering in a new era of diplomacy and easing worldwide fears concerning
85 nuclear war. Unfortunately for Nixon, the China trip did not accomplish everything that he and Kissinger had wanted: the United States did not receive much diplomatic help when it came to the Vietnam War. Instead, the United States gradually withdrew its forces and Saigon, the
90 country's capital, became the property of Vietnamese communists.

GO ON TO THE NEXT PAGE.

11. The passage states that Nixon's 1972 trip to China was met with direct opposition from:

    A. diplomatic officials from Pakistan.
    B. large portions of the American public.
    C. members of the U.S. State Department.
    D. Vietnamese communists.

12. According to the passage, what major accomplishment resulted from Nixon's visit to China?

    F. Reduction of Chinese aid to North Vietnam
    G. Improved relations with the Soviet Union
    H. Renewed interest in Chinese culture throughout the United States
    J. An international ban on nuclear weapons

13. It can be reasonably inferred from the passage that one similarity between "State Department skeptics" (lines 23-24) and "hardliners in the Chinese government" (line 35) was:

    A. strong support for military measures that gave rise to worldwide fears of nuclear war.
    B. dissatisfaction with the outcome of the American military activity against North Korea.
    C. unwillingness to publicize diplomatic efforts that would reconcile China and the United States.
    D. opposition to the 1972 meeting between Richard Nixon and Mao Tse-tung.

14. The passage states that Nixon first made relations with China one of his priorities in:

    F. 1947.
    G. 1964.
    H. 1969.
    J. 1972.

15. As it is used in line 33, the word *check* most nearly means:

    A. completely erase.
    B. critically analyze.
    C. attentively watch.
    D. act against.

16. The author uses the term *impending danger* (line 53) to describe:

    F. the threat of escalating hostilities in Vietnam.
    G. a stronger relationship between China and the United States.
    H. the potential alliance of China and Vietnam.
    J. the unlikelihood of breaking up the Communist Bloc.

17. It can be reasonably inferred from the passage that all of the following were similarities between China and the Soviet Union EXCEPT:

    A. active support of North Vietnam.
    B. paranoia resulting from Nixon's 1972 trip.
    C. ideological differences with the United States.
    D. willingness to negotiate with the United States.

18. The quotations included in the passage indicate that President Nixon regarded his trip to China as:

    F. enlightening yet old-fashioned.
    G. remarkable and wholly successful.
    H. dangerous and disorienting.
    J. risky yet transformative.

19. It can be reasonably inferred from the passage that, before 1972, the United States government was unwilling to:

    A. formally recognize Red China.
    B. send diplomatic officials into Chinese territory.
    C. intervene in regional conflicts involving China and the Soviet Union.
    D. offer military protection to Taiwan.

20. The author of the passage mentions Pakistan as an example of a country that was:

    F. unlikely to play a large role in international diplomacy, but ultimately crucial to improving relations between China and the United States.
    G. visited by Henry Kissinger, but that ultimately took on only a very small role in planning President Nixon's trip to China.
    H. on positive terms with both China and the United States, and capable of aiding these countries in their diplomatic efforts.
    J. friendly with several other military and economic powers in Asia, and determined to limit the influence of the Soviet Union.

GO ON TO THE NEXT PAGE.

Passage III

HUMANITIES: This passage is adapted from the essay "Film This Life: The New Biopic." The initial release dates for some of the films discussed are provided in parentheses.

One of the great ironies of film is that the lives of great men and women often make mediocre movies—or worse. Stocked with big-name actors, executed with top-quality cinematography, and released right in the midst of awards
5 season, these movies don't set out to be mediocre. Yet somehow, mediocrity is where these films wind up, award caliber actors and all. A trend this consistent can't be accidental, can it? How do dynamo subjects—generals, statesmen, scientists, artists—inspire (if that is the word)
10 such clunky films?

Those who view studio film-making and media marketing generally as exercises in cynicism have a few ideas about how this trend established itself. "Moviegoers buy on impulse, and the people who hand out movie awards
15 are no different," notes Paula Welton, a popular film blogger and the author of the recently-published *Silver Screen Economics: Supply, Demand, and the Film Industry*. "Create a movie with a 'great' subject and 'great' actors, put it out in November, watch the awards roll in by January. By the time
20 the awards voters realize that they have voted for a great big piece of hokum, it will be too late." This, according to Welton, is what happened with the film *A Beautiful Mind*, which was based on the life of celebrated mathematician John Nash and swept the 2002 Academy Awards. By the time
25 anyone realized that *A Beautiful Mind* was (in Welton's words) "triumph-of-the-will drivel parading as art," the ballots had already been cast.

As persuasive and entertainingly combative as Welton's approach is, there is more to the story of why the lives of
30 renowned men and women suffer on the silver screen. (Nor am I wholly in agreement with her verdict on *A Beautiful Mind*: not a flawless film, but really that dreadful?) There have, after all, been great movies that tell the stories of great historical figures: *Patton, Lawrence of Arabia, Malcolm X,*
35 and *The Coal Miner's Daughter* are peak accomplishments from past decades, and "biopics" (or biographical motion pictures) such as *American Splendor* and *Capote* are easily among the best films of the past ten years. The question then changes: Why are films like these such exceptions to the
40 rule?

Of course, films that rise above mediocrity will always be the exception to the rule. But the exceptions here are so noticeable because the conventions of the "great individual" biopic have become so rigid in the past fifteen years: find a
45 troubled historical figure, add "colorful" supporting characters, a "life-changing" love interest, and "impossible" odds, trudge along from set piece to set piece, then wind up with a big "victory over impossible odds" finale. The setup

worked well enough in *My Left Foot* (1989), which balanced
50 out its workmanlike plotting with edgy camera work and impeccable acting. Still, there is an expectations game that must be played. It is not enough for a film to tell General George Patton's story: the film needs to feel as large and as great and as unconventional as Patton himself, or risk seeming
55 like an insult.

Greatness of this sort is precisely what can be seen in *Patton*, a film that barely hangs together for its first hour and coheres brilliantly at the end, the kind of maverick maneuver that Patton would have loved. It also happens, almost
60 miraculously, in director Steven Spielberg's *Lincoln* (2012)— and imagine the nerve it took to tackle *that* subject. The movie is as canny and rousing as Abraham Lincoln himself. But both *Lincoln* and *Patton* feature something that more "reverent" biopics never successfully summon, but that just
65 about any aliens-and-explosions blockbuster does: an element of crisis and surprise.

As a medium, film is not designed for civics class portraits of largeness and greatness in the first place. In truth, great movies are so often premised on visions of failure,
70 weirdness, loneliness, catastrophe—have been since funny-disturbing silent films such as *The Cabinet of Doctor Caligari*, and always will be. Showing the world as a fragmentary and unpredictable place is what film is good at: after all, what place in the world will bring you more fragmentary and
75 unpredictable visions than a movie theater? Perhaps this is why good biopics (*Patton, Lincoln, Capote*) are often high tension fragments of larger biographies, or are sagas that thunder past (*Lawrence of Arabia, Malcolm X*) in their violent, often confusing grandeur.

80 Human greatness is not easy to understand: it may be impossible to understand, even for the people who achieve it. Sudden, swift, dreamlike, movies are a medium that can capture the blunt energy of personal drama and historical change, or that can be used to perpetuate the most tired
85 conventions. It is up to the filmmakers to find remarkable ways to tell remarkable life stories.

21. The passage as a whole can best be described as:

A. a discussion of why films such as *Lincoln* and *Patton* have not been fully understood.
B. an explanation of the qualities necessary to create a great film that is biographical in content.
C. an overview of the biographical films that movie award voters have over-valued.
D. an argument against film criticism that is not based on historical research.

GO ON TO THE NEXT PAGE.

22. In line 10, *clunky* most nearly means:

F. unmovable.
G. stubborn.
H. huge.
J. dull.

23. Paula Welton's comments in lines 17-21 are most notable for their:

A. unconcern.
B. cynicism.
C. enthusiasm.
D. fury.

24. It can reasonably be inferred from the passage that films depicting high-profile historical figures are often produced with the expectation that they will:

F. win a number of awards.
G. break box office records.
H. shock audiences with previously unrevealed information.
J. sway public opinion on a variety of social issues.

25. The author's comments within the parentheses in lines 30-32 primarily serve to:

A. show annoyance with Welton's harsh criticism methods.
B. indicate unqualified agreement with Welton.
C. distance himself from Welton's opinion of a particular film.
D. clarify the high standards that should be applied to biographical films.

26. It can reasonably be inferred from the last sentence of the second paragraph that:

F. film award voters are often swayed more by a film's promotional tactics than by its actual quality.
G. the procedure for determining film awards is often mysterious.
H. different types of films have used different formulas to earn positive press.
J. Welton is annoyed that she cannot nominate films for awards.

27. The author considers all of the following to be among the most praiseworthy biopics produced by Hollywood EXCEPT:

A. *A Beautiful Mind.*
B. *Patton.*
C. *Malcolm X.*
D. *American Splendor.*

28. The author takes a strong stance against mediocre biopics because these films:

F. have confusing and experimental plots.
G. play down the greatest accomplishments of their subjects.
H. do not promote the work of talented but unknown actors.
J. depict remarkable individuals but are themselves unimpressive.

29. The author mentions the film *The Cabinet of Doctor Caligari* primarily in order to:

A. give an example of a biographical film that was once immensely popular.
B. claim that films have been portraying the same universal themes throughout history.
C. criticize the film for its use of conventions that are becoming outdated.
D. modify the earlier claim that "reverent" biopics cannot make good films.

30. It can reasonably be inferred from the passage that the films *Patton*, *Lincoln*, and *Capote* are notable in that they:

F. focus on single periods in the lives of their protagonists.
G. depict characters who are both high-achieving and controversial.
H. include flashbacks to the early lives of their subjects.
J. combine historical facts with invented characters.

GO ON TO THE NEXT PAGE.

Passage IV

NATURAL SCIENCE: This passage is adapted from the essay "A Windmill in My Mind."

Since the earliest times, builders and engineers have recognized that gales of wind contain a kinetic energy that can be converted into mechanical power. Of course, in Persia in 200 B.C., the phrase "kinetic energy" was not commonly
5 used: nonetheless, it was in Persian civilization that the positive force of wind power was first explored. The result was the windmill. Today, such a device might be regarded as a primitive form of energy production, but the earliest windmills did make it so that the grinding of corn and the
10 irrigation of fields were no longer quite so labor intensive. It was not until the Middle Ages that windmills appeared in Europe.

Human civilization has evolved well beyond those first Persian contraptions, building ever larger networks of energy
15 and utility. We now live in a Technicolor world, where the flick of a switch creates instant communication, entertainment, warmth, food, and, above all, light throughout every day and night. It is the production of electricity that has achieved this level of ease and comfort for most of us. Until now, solid
20 fuels have been fundamental to the production of electricity. However, we have become aware that such power sources are damaging both to ourselves and to our environment. Increasingly, fossil fuel dependency is becoming economically non-viable for developing nations in Africa
25 and South America, since coal and petroleum can be expensive to import and difficult to distribute.

Rather than return to an age of darkness in any capacity, scientists have reconsidered the possibilities inherent in the wind. The result has been the creation of the wind turbine. At
30 first glance, the slim towers and whirling blades may seem extremely sophisticated, but in reality the collective wind farms that are springing up near coastlines and along hillsides are merely the offspring of those primitive original windmills—and are just as revolutionary. How these
35 machines work is quite easy to explain. A modern fan uses electricity to create wind: a wind turbine uses wind to make electricity. The wind turns the huge steel blades, which in turn spin a shaft, which is itself connected to a generator. The kinetic energy in the wind has been transformed into electrical
40 power—just like that.

While the physics and economics involved are not especially taxing to understand, other elements of wind power give rise to substantial problems. The first wind turbines have been a source of contention ever since they
45 were built, both because their usefulness seems questionable and because their presence can appear invasive. Of course, it is a universal social tradition that anything strikingly innovative is necessarily suspect, particularly if it is as immediately visible as a thirty foot-tall wind turbine. Wind
50 farms have sprung up and changed the cherished seaside and countryside landscapes. To stand on the high cliffs and gaze across the vast emptiness of the ocean is no longer possible in many places: the poetical vastness of the sea has been interrupted by these steel giants. Look up at the forested
55 mountains: there will be spaces where trees, which had been there for centuries, have been felled and replaced by ranks of turbines. As a result, those who live in areas where there is the potential to erect wind turbines are suspicious and hostile. They do not believe that their quality of life will be improved
60 tangibly by these machines.

In vain do the proponents of wind turbines argue that wind power has the lowest potential to contribute to global warming. Never mind that wind power produces none of the damaging toxic agents produced by fossil fuels, and never
65 mind that turbines pose no danger of radioactive fallout. The public is unconvinced. Communities dislike turbines for reasons that are aesthetic: despite their stately and streamlined appearance, turbines are by no means silent and in fact produce a constant, irritating hum. Communities also fear the
70 environmental impact of the turbines' presence. Birds and bats may find their traditional flight patterns interrupted by the turbine towers; the choice between preserving native songbirds and saving a few cents on energy costs is, for many people, no choice at all. Other people fear that the underwater
75 vibrations produced by ocean turbines will disturb traditional breeding and feeding grounds for fish. Perhaps most irrational—yet most persistent, among communities that do not fully understand turbine technology—is the fear that local weather will be affected by the presence of these
80 monolithic pylons.

One wonders if the Persians met with the same hostility in 200 B.C. Possibly. Until humanity either gets used to the turbines or rejects these machines altogether, the scientists can only agree with Shakespeare: "Blow, blow, thou winter
85 wind, thou art not so unkind as man's ingratitude."

31. The primary purpose of the passage is to:

   A. discuss the origins of windmills in ancient Persia.
   B. suggest that the benefits of wind turbine technology vastly outweigh its drawbacks.
   C. list the different problems associated with fossil fuels.
   D. lament the ways that turbines have transformed the natural landscape.

GO ON TO THE NEXT PAGE.

32. The author indicates that the use of windmills in ancient Persia was a measure that:

F. met with local resistance.
G. had widespread and beneficial consequences.
H. helped to resurrect other old technologies.
J. led to an initial waste of resources.

33. The passage mentions "the grinding of corn" and "the irrigation of fields" in the first paragraph as two activities that were:

A. made easier by the invention of the windmill.
B. important to the economy of ancient Persia.
C. mostly undertaken by slaves.
D. completed with relative ease.

34. The author uses the word *contraptions* in line 14 to emphasize the idea that:

F. current windmills closely resemble Persian windmills in appearance.
G. the Persian windmills were primitive and unsophisticated.
H. the ancient Persians would have been surprised by present-day uses of wind energy.
J. people today are not impressed by ancient technologies such as windmills.

35. As it is used in line 42, the word *taxing* means:

A. hardworking.
B. difficult.
C. precise.
D. expensive.

36. According to the passage, the most significant obstacle in the construction of new wind turbines is:

F. misunderstanding of the physics involved in producing wind energy.
G. mistrust of the new technology by local residents.
H. the physical difficulty of clearing rocks and trees.
J. the remoteness of the sea and mountain sites often chosen for turbines.

37. According to the passage, all of the following are problems associated with typical fossil fuels EXCEPT:

A. expenses related to importation.
B. relative difficulty of transportation.
C. damage to the environment.
D. public resistance to new power plants.

38. According to the passage, wind turbines generate electricity by:

F. using the kinetic energy of wind to power a generator, which then spins the shafts of a series of windmills.
G. using electricity produced by a generator to set the turbine blades in motion, so that the wind increases and multiplies the energy produced.
H. using wind energy to create underwater vibrations, which then produce electricity.
J. using the kinetic energy of wind to spin a shaft, which is connected to a generator.

39. According to the passage, all of the following are current objections to wind turbines EXCEPT that:

A. they create an irritating noise.
B. they pose a threat to birds and bats.
C. they disturb the breeding grounds of fish.
D. they are associated with radioactive fallout.

40. In the passage, the author uses a quotation from Shakespeare in lines 84-85 to call attention to what idea?

F. Wind has been a source of power for centuries.
G. Humanity is ungrateful for inventions that are immensely beneficial.
H. Shakespeare's civilization made use of wind turbine technology.
J. People should be criticized for lacking scientific knowledge.

END OF TEST 2
STOP! DO NOT TURN THE PAGE UNTIL TOLD TO DO SO.
DO NOT RETURN TO A PREVIOUS TEST.

Answer Key: TEST 2

Test 2

LITERARY NARRATIVE

1. C
2. G
3. D
4. F
5. C
6. J
7. A
8. F
9. D
10. H

HUMANITIES

21. B
22. J
23. B
24. F
25. C
26. F
27. A
28. J
29. B
30. F

SOCIAL SCIENCE

11. C
12. G
13. D
14. H
15. D
16. G
17. B
18. J
19. A
20. H

NATURAL SCIENCE

31. B
32. G
33. A
34. G
35. B
36. G
37. D
38. J
39. D
40. G

To see your scaled ACT Reading Score (1-36), determine how many questions you answered correctly and consult the Scoring Chart on Page 186 of this book.

Post-Test Analysis

This post-test analysis is essential if you want to see an improvement on your next test. Possible reasons for errors, both for the test overall and for each of the four reading passages, are listed here. Place check marks next to the types of errors that pertain to you, or write your own types of errors in the blank spaces provided.

GENERAL

◇ Spent too much time reading the passages
◇ Spent too much time answering the questions
◇ Did not attempt to finish all of the passages
◇ Did not create effective margin answers
◇ Did not use process of elimination
◇ Could not find evidence to answer the questions
◇ Could not comprehend the topics and ideas in the passages
◇ Could not understand what the questions were asking
◇ Interpreted the passages rather than using evidence
Other: _____

LITERARY NARRATIVE

◇ Spent too long reading the passage
◇ Spent too long answering the questions
◇ Could not identify the setting and characters
◇ Could not understand the plot or action
◇ Could not work effectively with tone and clues to tone
Other: _____

Use this form to better analyze your performance. If you don't understand why you made errors, there is no way that you can correct them!

SOCIAL SCIENCE

◇ Spent too long reading the passage
◇ Spent too long answering the questions
◇ Could not understand the author's position or arguments
◇ Used outside knowledge rather than using evidence
Other: _____

HUMANITIES

◇ Spent too long reading the passage
◇ Spent too long answering the questions
◇ Could understand the themes and organization of the passage
◇ Could not understand the author's ideas and uses of evidence
Other: _____

NATURAL SCIENCE

◇ Spent too long reading the passage
◇ Spent too long answering the questions
◇ Found the concepts and ideas in the passage confusing
◇ Found the questions confusing
◇ Could not effectively work with the inference and logic questions
Other: _____

TEST 2 Answer Explanations

LITERARY NARRATIVE

1. Correct Answer: C

In the first paragraph of Passage A, the narrator notes that he was "a young man of twenty-one" (line 1) when he decided to try teaching at Mr. Walby' vocational school. Later, the narrator refers to the "five years that I was at the college" (lines 19-20): because the narrator stayed for five years, he was roughly twenty-six when he left. Thus, **C** is the best answer. **A** wrongly takes the narrator's initial age as the age at which he left, **B** wrongly assumes that he only stayed for one year, and **D** wrongly assumes that he stayed for ten.

2. Correct Answer: G

The narrator explains that the college inspectors would visit Mr. Walby and "critically" demand "that Mr. Walby revise his system (line 27): however, the system in question is the timetable that was Mr. Walby's "pride and joy" (line 18). Thus, the inspectors and Mr. Walby are in disagreement about the value of the timetable, making **G** the best answer. Although the narrator's discussion of Mr. Walby is mostly comical and ironic (eliminating the too positive **J**) the narrator does not actually criticize Mr. Walby as a generally ineffective or incompetent instructor. **F** wrongly assumes that the instructors will take action against Mr. Walby (when in fact he is allowed to stay in his post), while **H** presents a stance that is much too harshly negative.

3. Correct Answer: D

In using the word *framed*, the narrator is describing Mr. Walby's "timetable for his department" (line 17), which is *positioned* or *mounted* on Mr. Walby's wall. **D** is thus the best choice. **A** wrongly assumes that a negative tone is being introduced at this point (when the timetable is only described negatively in the next paragraph), and **B** and **C** would both refer to acts of observation or interpretation, not to the simple physical act of mounting a picture on a wall.

4. Correct Answer: F

After the narrator compares Moe and Dez to "famous and familiar double comedy acts" in line 38, the narrator goes on to explain that these two teachers "complemented each other" (line 39). Because the two men were quite different, "it was hard to predict how well they worked as a team" (lines 41-42). Thus, **F** effectively describes the harmonious relationship between Moe and Dez. **G** ("competitive") attributes the wrong dynamic to these cooperative teachers, while **H** wrongly assumes that the narrator's descriptions are negative ("unflattering") overall, when in fact the narrator respects Moe and Dez. **J** is out of scope: Moe and Dez are only described as "English" teachers (line 52), so that there is no way to tell if they did in fact introduce the narrator to "comedy double acts".

5. Correct Answer: C

In the first paragraph, the narrator mentions the "boarding house for me and the other first-year students" (lines 33-34) and introduces the "two male teachers in charge of it" (line 35), Moe

and Dez. Thus, choice **C** is the best answer. **A** and **B** are actions that Moe and Dez may perform in assisting their students, but are not designated as "duties". Although they two teachers also specialize in English, they are never mentioned as researchers: do not wrongly assume that **D** describes a duty of theirs.

6. Correct Answer: J

In the final paragraph of Passage B, the narrator explains that child psychologists do not take the best approach to handling problems: instead of reaching out in the (approved) manner of Moe or Dez, a child psychologist would have "droned on" (line 63) about the young narrator's situation. Thus, **J** is the best choice. Although the narrator does offer comical observations about Moe and Dez, he praises their "immense knowledge of their subject" (line 54), English. Eliminate **F, G,** and **H** on account of the narrator's positive tone in each case.

7. Correct Answer: A

In the first paragraph, the narrator introduces Moe and Dez, explaining how well they generally "worked as a team" (line 42). In the second paragraph, the narrator focuses on a more specific scene, which took place "on the school's main staircase" (lines 66-67). This information supports choice **A** and can also be used to eliminate choice **B**, since the only quoted dialogue occurs in the "scene" in the second paragraph. **C** is problematic because the second paragraph presents the positive influence of Moe and Dez, while **D** wrongly shifts the emphasis of the passage as a whole to the narrator's classmates.

8. Correct Answer: F

In the second passage, the author describes how Moe appeared "at the front of the class" (line 43) and how Dez "lectured" (line 50). In contrast, Mr. Walby only interacts with "Teachers" (line 25) and "college inspectors" (line 26). This information can be used to justify **F** and to eliminate **G**, since the teachers are not impressed by Mr. Walby's timetable. Both **H** and **J** describe important elements of Passage A: Mr. Walby's physical appearance is described in detail in lines 6-17, and it is explained that he takes "pride and joy" (line 18) in his yearly timetable.

9. Correct Answer: D

In Passage A, the narrator never explains either Mr. Walby's conversation habits or his own: the focus is on Mr. Walby's position, appearance, and fixation on the timetable. In Passage B, Moe is described as "taciturn [or reserved] at most times" (line 44) while Dez is described as "always willing to embark on long —and always hilarious—series of reminiscences" (line 51-52). This information supports **D**: no relevant information is given to justify **A** or **B**, while the description of Moe directly disqualifies **C**.

10. Correct Answer: H

This quote describes a teacher who plays an indirect, highly positive role. Moe and Dez in Passage B never force the narrator into a particular style or career, but instead, in the narrator's words, "just made me feel, gradually, more secure about myself" (line 65). Thus, **H** is a highly effective answer. Eliminate **F** and **G** because the narrator of Passage A sees Mr. Walby only as a pleasantly comical figure, while **J** is incorrect because Passage

TEST 2 Answer Explanations

B (though written by a teacher) does not actually show HOW the narrator decided to enter education.

SOCIAL SCIENCE

11. Correct Answer: C

Lines 21-22 state that "members of the State Department were concerned" about Nixon's 1972 trip. Thus, choice **C** is correct. Pakistani officials assisted with the meeting (**A**); thus, they were not opposed to Nixon's trip. The opinions of Vietnamese Communists (**D**) and the American public (**B**) are not given in the passage.

12. Correct Answer: G

The author writes that, "ultimately, President Nixon hoped that the Soviet Union would see an impending danger and become increasingly compliant with the diplomatic demands of the United States" (lines 52-55). Thus, Nixon's ultimate goal was to make the Soviet Union respect the demands of the United States, which matches choice **G**. Nixon "aimed to decrease the amount of aid provided to North Vietnam by China" (lines 57-58) but he did not accomplish that goal (**F**). American interest in Chinese culture (**H**) is not discussed in the passage, although Americans did take an interest in Nixon's trip (lines 69-75). Nixon negotiated the first part of a nuclear weapons treaty with the Soviet Union but did not create an international ban on nuclear weapons (**J**).

13. Correct Answer: D

Lines 21-22 state that "members of the State Department were concerned" about Nixon's 1972 trip. Similarly, lines 35-37 state that "hardliners in the Chinese government . . . did not want to normalize relations" between China and the United States, which was the goal of Nixon's 1972 meeting. Thus, choice **D** is correct. "Worldwide fears of nuclear war" (**A**) were eased by a nuclear weapons treaty with the Soviet Union, not with China. "Hardliners in the Chinese government" (line 35) were displeased with "American military activity against North Korea" (line 36), but there is nothing to indicate that that U.S. State Department was similarly displeased (**B**). According to lines 70-71, Nixon's trip was in fact publicized on American television (**C**).

14. Correct Answer: H

Lines 7-8 state that "President Nixon had decided to prioritize relations with China upon entering office in January 1969," and so choice **H** is correct. The year 1947 (**F**) is not mentioned in the passage. 1964 (**G**) was the year of Nixon's somewhat antagonistic Asia trip and 1972 (**J**) was the year of Nixon's China trip.

15. Correct Answer: D

Mao "was concerned about Japan's rapidly-growing, export-based economy" (lines 31-32), and hoped that the United States "would be in a position to check any Japanese tendencies toward militarism and political expansionism" (lines 33-34). Because Mao didn't want Japan to expand, *check* must mean limit or hinder. Choice **D** is the best match. Choices **B** and **C** do not mean hinder; although appropriately negative, choice **A** is too extreme and, in context, would involve completely debilitating an entire country.

16. Correct Answer: G

"President Nixon hoped that the Soviet Union would see an impending danger" (lines 52-53) if he were to succeed in "opening relations with China" (line 48). Thus, the *impending danger* was improved diplomacy between the United States and China, and so choice **G** is correct. Choices **F**, **H**, and **J** do not involve diplomacy between the United States and China, but can be tricky because they refer to terms and ideas from elsewhere in the passage.

17. Correct Answer: B

The "Soviet Union and China" (line 59) are listed as "North Vietnam's . . . two big supporters" (line 61), which eliminates choice **A**. References to "the ideologically hostile Soviet Union" (line 44) and "tensions with Communist China running deep" (lines 5-6) eliminate choice **C**. Lines 43-44 ("the United States had been dealing primarily with the ideologically hostile Soviet Union") and line 25 ("China had its own reasons for agreeing to the meeting") eliminate choice **D**, leaving choice **B**. Only in line 50 is paranoia (as related to the Soviet Union alone) described.

18. Correct Answer: J

Nixon's trip was "the week that changed the world" (line 1) but it was also *uncertain* and *perilous* (lines 77-78). Thus, choice **J** is correct. Choice **F** is wrong because Nixon's trip was groundbreaking, not old-fashioned. "Unfortunately for Nixon, the China trip did not accomplish everything that he and Kissinger had wanted" (lines 85-87), and so it was not a complete success (**G**). Finally, the trip was *dangerous* but was not *disorienting* (**H**): Nixon had set goals in mind and was able to explain the results of his trip without confusion.

19. Correct Answer: A

In 1964, Nixon stated that "'it would be disastrous to the cause of freedom' for the U.S. to formally recognize Red China" (lines 15-17). Thus, choice **A** is correct. Other answers either contradict the passage or rely on information that is nowhere provided. Henry Kissinger, a U.S. official, took two trips to China before Nixon went (**B**). Prior to Nixon's trip, the U.S. had already been involved with the Soviet Union; there is nothing to indicate that the U.S. refused to "intervene in regional conflicts involving China and the Soviet Union" (**C**). Mao felt that "the United States could help him reclaim Taiwan" (line 30) but no mention is made of offering military protection *to* Taiwan (**D**).

20. Correct Answer: H

"In setting up such a delicate meeting, Mao and Nixon were aided by officials from Pakistan, a country friendly with both China and the United States" (lines 63-65). Thus, Pakistan was a mutual ally and was willing to help (choice **H**). The passage makes note of Henry Kissinger's visits to China, not Pakistan (**G**). And the passage does not state that Pakistan was "unlikely to play a large role in international diplomacy" (**F**) or that it was "determined to limit the influence of the Soviet Union" (**J**); the most that is known is that Pakistan assisted China and the United States in their diplomatic efforts.

TEST 2 Answer Explanations

HUMANITIES

21. Correct Answer: B

The passage discusses the traits that make films about "the lives of great men and women" (lines 1-2) *mediocre* (line 5) versus *great* (line 33). Thus, choice **B** is correct. The passage is about film quality, not ability to be understood (**A**). It discusses overrated films (**C**) and misguided film critics (**D**) but does not focus on either topic. (In addition, the film critics are not misguided by a lack of historical knowledge; rather, manipulative advertising is the dilemma that the passage cites here.)

22. Correct Answer: J

The author discusses mediocre (line 5) films and then refers to them as *clunky* (line 10) despite having *dynamo subjects* (line 8). Thus, clunky means the opposite of dynamo (high-energy, exciting). Choice **J** is thus the best answer. Choices **F** and **H** are physical attributes of actual objects, and so they would not be used to describe a film and the ideas behind it. Choice **G** would be used to describe a personality, not a film.

23. Correct Answer: B

Paula Welton is presented as an example of "those who view studio filmmaking and media marketing generally as exercises in cynicism" (lines 11-12). Thus, choice **B** is correct. Of the other choices, **A** neglects her strong bias, **C** is too positive, and **D** is too strongly negative for a sarcastic dismissal of poor filmmaking.

24. Correct Answer: F

Welton states that biographical films rely on their high-profile subjects to win *movie awards* (line 14); the creators of the films in question "watch the awards roll in by January" (line 19). Thus, choice **F** is correct. Box office records (**G**) and public opinion regarding social issues (**J**) are not mentioned. The passage does not suggest that biopics are made to be shocking or to expose audiences to new facts (**H**); in fact, the author often seems to be judging these films based on style and artistry, not on the facts that they use.

25. Correct Answer: C

In the author's parenthetical comment "Nor am I wholly in agreement with her verdict on *A Beautiful Mind*" (lines 30-32), *her* refers to Welton. Thus, the author is showing disagreement with Welton's opinion of *A Beautiful Mind*, and so choice **C** is correct. Choice **B** is the opposite of the author's intention and choice **A** is too extreme. Choice **D** is off-topic, since it does not refer to Welton's judgment.

26. Correct Answer: F

A Beautiful Mind "swept the 2002 Academy Awards" (line 24). Thus, *the ballots* in line 27 are Academy Award votes. The film followed the "'great' subject and 'great' actors" formula in line 18 but ended up as a "piece of hokum" (line 21), and so choice **F** is correct. The sentence does not mention award procedures (**G**). The passage is about biopics, not various types of films (**H**). And despite her apparent dissatisfaction with recent film awards, Welton does not openly state a desire to nominate films for awards (**J**).

27. Correct Answer: A

Patton and *Malcolm X* "are peak accomplishments from past decades" (lines 35-36) and *American Splendor* is "easily among best films of the past ten years" (lines 37-38). These lines eliminate choices **B**, **C** and **D**, leaving choice **A**. Furthermore, the author uses *A Beautiful Mind* as an example of a deficient film (line 32).

28. Correct Answer: J

In film, "the lives of great men and women often make mediocre movies" (lines 1-2). Choice **J** is thus the best answer. Choice **G** misdirects the author's criticisms: the author objects to films that are not pleasing, but says little about how well these films line up with the historical record. Choice **H** misdirects the author's discussion, since the author never discusses the kinds of actors used in great biopics. Choice **F** contradicts the author's ideas, since "violent, often confusing" biopics (line 79) are among those praised by the author.

29. Correct Answer: B

The author lists the themes of great movies as "failure, weirdness, loneliness, catastrophe" (lines 69-70). The author then goes on to say that those themes have been used "since funny-disturbing silent films such as *The Cabinet of Doctor Caligari*" (lines 70-71). So, choice **B** is correct because it involves consistency of film themes over time. Choices **A**, **C** and **D** are not about the consistency of film themes over time. In addition, **A** and **D** falsely assume that *The Cabinet of Doctor Caligari* is a biopic (though this is never specified) and **C** takes a negative tone toward this film (which the author sees as an important and meaningful film precedent).

30. Correct Answer: F

The author believes that "good biopics (*Patton, Lincoln, Capote*) are often high-tension fragments of larger biographies" (lines 76-77), and so choice **F** is correct. In contrast, choices **G** and **J** are not about focusing on a small time-frame. **H** mentions the fragmentary technique of flashbacks, but flashbacks are earlier time periods presented in addition to, not instead of, present time in a given film. Thus, they would expand rather than limit the timframe of the film.

NATURAL SCIENCE

31. Correct Answer: B

The passage discusses the benefits (e.g. "wind power has the lowest potential to contribute to global warming" in lines 62-63) and lesser drawbacks (e.g. "reasons that are aesthetic" in line 67 and *irritating hum* in line 69) of wind power. So, choice **B** is correct. The history of Persian windmills (**A**) is only discussed as an introduction to these other considerations, the problems associated with fossil fuels (**C**) are listed to contrast with the cleanliness of wind energy technology, and the visual effects of turbines (**D**) are listed late in the passage as examples of why some people oppose turbines. Thus, none of those three answer choices is the focus of the passage.

TEST 2 Answer Explanations

32. Correct Answer: G

Persian windmills benefited society: they made "it so that the grinding of corn and the irrigation of fields were no longer quite so labor intensive" (lines 9-10). Thus, choice **G** is correct. Local resistance (**F**) is discussed in contemporary society, not in ancient Persia. Choices **H** and **J** are not mentioned in the passage: the author is concerned only with the windmill (**H**) and does not describe possible drawbacks for the Persians (**J**).

33. Correct Answer: A

The author states that "the earliest windmills did make it so that the grinding of corn and the irrigation of fields were no longer quite so labor intensive" (lines 8-10) as support for the idea that windmills harnessed the "positive force of wind power" (line 6) to do work. Thus, choice **A** is correct. The economic importance (**B**) of grinding corn and irrigating fields is not discussed at any length, nor is slave labor (**C**) mentioned at all. These labor-intensive tasks were themselves made *easier* by wind technology, but the passage does not actually say that they were *easy* compared to other tasks (**D**).

34. Correct Answer: G

In stating that "human civilization has evolved well beyond those frst Persian contraptions" (lines 13-14), the author contrasts our current *evolved* technology with earlier *contraptions*, and so *contraptions* implies the opposite of highly evolved. Thus, choice **G** is correct. Choice **F** gives the opposite relationship (similarity). The hypothetical reactions of ancient Persians to present day technology (**H**) are not discussed. Modern people have indeed improved upon ancient technology, but whether or not ancient technology impresses people today is an issue that the author never addresses (**J**). If anything, the author himself seems impressed by the usefulness of ancient windmills.

35. Correct Answer: B

Because the context is "taxing to understand" (line 42), *taxing* must mean either *hard* or *easy*. "Not especially taxing to understand" (lines 41-42) is contrasted with *substantial problems* in line 43, and so *taxing* must be negative. Thus, "taxing to understand" means *hard* to understand, and so choice **B** makes sense. Choices **A, C** and **D** do not describe the state of being hard to understand: though both appropriately negative, **A** refers to people and **D** refers to goods.

36. Correct Answer: G

The author laments the fact that "those who live in areas where there is the potential to erect wind turbines are suspicious and hostile" (lines 57-58). This matches choice **G**. The passage states that the physics involved is not hard to understand (**F**). The diffculty of clearing rocks and trees (**H**) is not mentioned at all, though such work may be involved in some real-life cases. The remoteness of turbine sites (**J**) is mentioned, but is not defined as an obstacle to turbine construction.

37. Correct Answer: D

Choices **A** and **B** can be eliminated by lines 25-26: "coal and petroleum can be expensive to import and difficult to distribute." Choice **C** can be eliminated by line 64: "damaging toxic agents produced by fossil fuels." Thus, choice **D** remains. Remember, the passage is concerned with public resistance to windmills, not with public resistance to other forms of energy.

38. Correct Answer: J

In a wind turbine, "the wind turns the huge steel blades, which in turn spin a shaft, which is itself connected to a generator" (lines 37-38). This directly supports choice **J**. Choices **F** and **G** put the same steps in incorrect orders. Underwater vibrations (**H**) are a fear of some opponents of turbines (lines 74-75), not a step in electrical generation.

39. Correct Answer: D

Turbines "produce a constant, irritating hum" (line 69), which eliminates choice **A**. "Birds and bats may find their traditional flight patterns interrupted by the turbine towers" (lines 70-72), which eliminates choice **B**. "Ocean turbines will disturb traditional breeding and feeding grounds for fish" (lines 75-76), which eliminates choice **C**. Thus, choice **D** remains. Do not use outside knowledge: some communities may fear radioactive fallout from energy sources, but there is no proof from the passage that wind turbines are associated with such fallout.

40. Correct Answer: G

The Shakespeare quotation states that wind is "not so unkind as man's ingratitude" (line 85). The author extends that sentiment to wind technology, and thereby makes the point than mankind is ungrateful for wind technology. This matches choice **G**. The first sentence of the last paragraph mentions time (**F**), but the Shakespeare quotation does not itself describe the history of wind energy. The wind in the quotation is merely wind, not wind used to power turbines (**H**). And the quotation is about being ungrateful, not about lacking scientific knowledge, and is not being used as an argument for criticizing people (**J**). Instead, the quotation indicates in context that humanity's criticisms of wind energy are unfair.

Test 3

READING TEST
35 Minutes—40 Questions

DIRECTIONS: There are four passages in this test. Each passage is followed by several questions. After reading a passage, choose the best answer to each question and fill in the corresponding oval on your answer document. You may refer to the passages as often as necessary.

Passage I

LITERARY NARRATIVE: This passage is adapted from the short story "To Build a Home." "*Pour manger?*" translates roughly as "To eat?" in French.

Sudan was yesterday: hot, sticky, noisy, infuriating, and alive, the streets were packed with erratic cars and buses, changing lanes at will and racing through stoplights and, at the last moment, narrowly avoiding pedestrians and the
5 occasional camel. The market stalls had been full of shouts and laughter. Cafés spilled out onto the pavements, where the men seated themselves around small tables bearing exotic hookah pipes, each group chatting late into the night beneath the velvety, star-spattered sky.

10 Today was the northern coast of France. No cars, no buses, not even a bicycle broke the stillness. No people walked the streets. Simon shivered as the icy wind scraped and swirled dead leaves into the corners of the low walls of the square. It was only six o'clock, yet already the silent
15 darkness was gathering. He looked up. There were no stars, just a creeping, deepening gloom over the bare straight streets.

Last night he had flown from Khartoum to Paris. This morning he had mounted the train to Rennes, then had taken
20 an empty bus here, to Pontivy. Through it all, Simon's intention had been to look at houses to buy in preparation for his intended retirement. Under the desert sun of Sudan, he had dreamed of efficient, sophisticated Europe. He had been a little surprised to find that there were no cabs about; he
25 walked nearly a mile to the nearest hotel and the hotel itself seemed nearly deserted. Grudgingly, the concierge had pointed Simon to a small, cold room on the second floor, payment required in advance. Simon dumped his bag in the little room and set out to explore the town.

30 The town itself was shut tight against the cold drizzle. The central square was empty, and most of the streets looked no different.

Simon crossed a small side road. He glanced along it, and saw that it seemed to rise steeply. A few doors up from
35 where he stood was the dimly lit sign of a small café. The café itself was open but empty, apart from a woman polishing water glasses behind the counter. Well, Simon thought, better than nothing. He entered. The woman looked up. She nodded. Simon gestured with his hand and said, "Pour manger?" She
40 pointed to a table by the widow. He sat. She brought a menu. It was in French. He pointed at an item. She nodded and retreated through a small door behind the counter. He looked around. On the wall was a colored print of a bluish seascape. On the table was a small vase with a red flower.

45 The door to the kitchen area opened. The woman brought Simon's order to the table, muttered "bon appétit," and retired behind the counter. The kitchen door opened again; a second woman entered—the cook, Simon assumed— and the two women stood together, positioned side-by-side
50 but expressing no particular familiarity. They chatted offhandedly. Now and again, one or the other of them glanced at a clock set amidst the café's shelves of aperitifs and wines. It crossed Simon's mind that perhaps they were waiting for him to finish eating so that they could close up and go home.

55 The bell above the entrance to the café jangled, the door opened, and it was as though a wave of energy swept into the room in the guise of a lithe young man laughing and calling out to the two women—sweeping past in his jeans, sweater, and stylish jacket, a scarf carelessly thrown around his neck.
60 A student, perhaps, but in reality a magician, for his entrance changed the entire room. The lights gleamed more brightly, the seascape on the wall came to life.

It seemed to Simon that the curtain of a stage had risen and a play had begun. The two women were now transformed,
65 crying out in eagerness and delight. They kissed the young man on both cheeks. He hugged them both, grinning. Maternally, they ruffled his hair and patted his back. There were exclamations among the three of them as the young man launched into an excited account of something that was
70 far beyond the limits of Simon's French.

The woman who had served Simon saw Simon signal and brought him the bill. She was laughing as she reached the table. He put down exact change and said his thanks and left

GO ON TO THE NEXT PAGE.

the café to a chorus of farewells, before the three gathered
75 back into their conversation.

In the street outside, Simon could hear their excited laughter. He looked up at the sky. The rain had stopped. A thin moon was visible. Simon thought he could see a few stars sparkling.

1. At the time of the events of the story, Simon is:

   A. in search of pleasing companions during a brief stay in France.
   B. attempting to adjust to a culture that is completely unfamiliar.
   C. trying to find a new house in preparation for his retirement.
   D. determined to forget his earlier home and lifestyle.

2. The passage contains recurring references to which of the following?

   F. Stars
   G. Animals
   H. Airplanes
   J. Mountains

3. The primary setting for the events that take place in this passage is:

   A. Sudan.
   B. Paris.
   C. Rennes.
   D. Pontivy.

4. Details in the passage most strongly suggest that, in relation to the two women and the young man, Simon is:

   F. an aspiring collaborator.
   G. a complete stranger.
   H. a forgotten acquaintance.
   J. an intimidating intruder.

5. As presented in the first two paragraphs (lines 1-17), the contrast between Sudan and France, respectively, can best be understood as a contrast between:

   A. harmony and silence.
   B. liveliness and stillness.
   C. chaos and hopefulness.
   D. luxury and wisdom.

6. It can reasonably be inferred that the author of the passage notes that Simon "had dreamed of efficient, sophisticated Europe" (line 23) in order to indicate that:

   F. Simon was somewhat surprised by the actual conditions he encountered in France.
   G. Simon's unrealistic expectations are inappropriate for a man of his age.
   H. Simon's desire to enjoy the sophistication of Europe will remain unfulfilled.
   J. Simon is beginning to favor a change of plans and might return to Sudan.

7. In the passage, the young man's entrance can best be described as changing the mood of two women from:

   A. reserve to excitement.
   B. timidity to aggression.
   C. sadness to celebration.
   D. caution to courage.

8. It can be reasonably inferred from the passage that Simon's ability to understand the French language is:

   F. frequently disputed.
   G. immensely embarrassing.
   H. apparently imperfect.
   J. personally inspiring.

9. In lines 37-38, the phrase "better than nothing" refers to:

   A. the possibility of eating at the café.
   B. Simon's desire to return to Sudan.
   C. the casual conversation of the two women.
   D. the depressing appearance of the town as a whole.

10. The point of view from which the passage is told can best be described as that of:

   F. an inhabitant of a small French town who is trying to find explanations for the activities of a visitor from abroad.
   G. an elderly man who is determined to find new companions in order to settle into a radically new culture more easily.
   H. a knowledgeable observer who uses scholarly research to explain puzzling aspects of contrasting Sudanese and French lifestyles.
   J. a detached narrator explaining a traveler's expectations and describing the traveler's experiences of new settings.

GO ON TO THE NEXT PAGE.

Passage II

SOCIAL SCIENCE: This passage is adapted from "Insane for the Holidays."

The day after Thanksgiving is known as Black Friday, a title that was bestowed upon it in 1966 by a disgruntled Philadelphia policeman. As retail scholar Michael Lisicky has noted, looking back at Black Friday's origins, "The
5 stores were just too crowded; the streets were crowded; the buses and the police were just on overcall and extra duty." Sometimes, violence ensued as well. Due to these troubles, Black Friday scared shoppers away.

Yet in the 1980s, Peter Strawbridge, former owner of
10 the now-defunct Strawbridge & Clothier's department store in Philadelphia, invented a new explanation for the term. He said Black Friday was the day when business profits went into the black.

Regardless of why it is called Black Friday, the day
15 after Thanksgiving has always been a dramatic start to the holiday shopping season. For decades, it was an unwritten rule that Christmas advertising did not start till after Thanksgiving. This unwritten rule caused retailers great distress in 1939, when Thanksgiving arrived relatively late,
20 on November 30. Retailers petitioned President Franklin D. Roosevelt to change the date of Thanksgiving in order to guarantee a longer shopping season. In December of 1941, Congress officially set aside the fourth Thursday in November as Thanksgiving.

25 Kmart, which once ranked among America's most prominent superstores, has been opening its doors on Thanksgiving since 1991. In so doing, it became the first such retailer to break the threshold and turn Thanksgiving into something other than a day of leisure. By 2009, Walmart, the
30 present-day successor to Kmart's huge share of the market, was also keeping its outlets open on Thanksgiving. *If you can't beat them, join them* seems to be the attitude of retailers, since the number of retailers open on the holiday has only continued to grow.

35 And what has been the attitude of consumers? More or less, *let the games begin!* After all, who wants to wait in line on Black Friday when you can expect good deals and tiny crowds just one day earlier? Apparently, everybody wins.

Not so fast. As noted in one recently-posted editorial,
40 "Retailers that open their doors on Thanksgiving Day in hopes of boosting holiday sales are shifting purchases away from Black Friday, rather than increasing the number of overall transactions." But even if stores, technically, are not doing more business, consumers are encouraged to pace their
45 purchases: some on Thanksgiving, some on Black Friday, no more one-day stampede.

However, there are also arguments that the traditional chaos of Black Friday has simply been redistributed, so that consumers and store employees face new dilemmas.
50 According to *Time* Magazine, "hundreds of thousands of consumers have resorted to online petitions and even worker strikes to voice their anger at retailers that decided to open their doors—thereby requiring employees to work—on Thanksgiving." In New Jersey, State Senator Richard Cody
55 has expressed sympathy for store employees and is trying to get legislation passed that would prohibit stores from opening before 9:00 p.m. on Thanksgiving. He said of store workers, "They are put in a position to either work on Thanksgiving or risk losing their jobs. This [the proposed legislation] would
60 allow them to be with their families and to give thanks, as other families do." Currently, three states—Maine, Massachusetts, and Rhode Island—have blue laws that restrict stores from opening on Thanksgiving.

Such controversies aside, a commercialized
65 Thanksgiving is firmly embraced by at least one group: millennials. A 2013 survey undertaken by LoyaltyOne showed that 50% of consumers in the 18-24 age bracket say that all-day shopping on Thanksgiving is a great idea. This is significantly higher than the figure for the general population,
70 only 33% of whom endorse all-day Thanksgiving shopping. Conversely, the survey noted that 50% of respondents, of all ages, believe that all-day shopping hours on Thanksgiving Day is a bad idea because it distracts from celebrating Thanksgiving.

75 The economic benefits to retailers of opening on Thanksgiving Day seem mixed at best, and the psychological benefits appear to be even more uncertain. Are we as a society becoming so commercialized that we can't even take one day off from our beloved malls? Is nothing sacred? Many
80 consumers and retail employees want the Thanksgiving tradition of a family-and-friends day upheld; however, the number of those who want Thanksgiving to be another day of buying and selling is significant. And therefore, commerce on Thanksgiving seems to be here to stay. We just need to figure
85 out how to keep the turkey moist until after the shopping is done.

11. One of the functions of the first two paragraphs (lines 1-13) is to

    A. offer testimonies from individuals present at the earliest and most violent Black Friday events.

    B. undermine the widely-held idea that Black Friday is a day when businesses experience losses.

    C. take a position in an ongoing controversy about the benefits and drawbacks of Black Friday.

    D. provide two alternative explanations of the origins of the name "Black Friday."

GO ON TO THE NEXT PAGE.

12. According to the passage, all of the following are possible drawbacks of a commercialized Thanksgiving EXCEPT:

   F. plummeting retail profits.
   G. the risk of job loss.
   H. decreased family time.
   J. strikes among workers.

13. The author mentions Maine, Massachusetts, and Rhode Island in order to emphasize the point made in the passage that:

   A. the emotions associated with Black Friday can vary significantly depending on time and location.
   B. the idea of Thanksgiving as a day of shopping has been met with active opposition.
   C. the controversy associated with a commercialized Black Friday has been most intense in these states.
   D. the legislation proposed by Richard Cody is likely to be successful because of these precedents.

14. In the passage, the author presents clear oppositions between all of the following EXCEPT:

   F. consumers and store owners.
   G. superstores and smaller businesses.
   H. retailers and legislators.
   J. millennials and older Americans.

15. The fourth paragraph (lines 25-34) primarily emphasizes:

   A. the growing practice among retailers of staying open on Thanksgiving.
   B. the defining differences between Kmart and its present-day successor Walmart.
   C. the unwillingness of consumers to reflect on the drawbacks of new developments in retail.
   D. the ability of most retailers to quickly adapt to the newest marketing trends.

16. The author cites the survey undertaken by LoyaltyOne as support for the idea that:

   F. only a few states have blue laws that are related to Thanksgiving.
   G. shopping on Thanksgiving is not the only economic issue that divides millennials from older Americans.
   H. millennials are an age group that supports all-day shopping on Thanksgiving.
   J. the commercialization of Thanksgiving has ceased to be a source of dispute.

17. According to the passage, the enactment of State Senator Richard Cody's legislation would result in:

   A. the widespread disappearance of the chaos associated with Black Friday.
   B. greater publicity for Thanksgiving-related petitions and worker strikes.
   C. retailers in New Jersey opening no earlier than 9:00 p.m. on Thanksgiving.
   D. the adoption of a policy that would prevent all New Jersey stores from opening on Thanksgiving.

18. The author of the passage most strongly indicates that stores that stay open on Thanksgiving do not increase their profits because:

   F. sales are shifted from Black Friday to Thanksgiving, yet the number of transactions does not increase overall.
   G. the need for family celebration keeps the vast majority of customers from buying new items on Thanksgiving.
   H. awareness of legislation that could limit shopping on Thanksgiving has caused consumers to do most of their shopping on Black Friday.
   J. only superstores such as Kmart and Walmart have found ways to profit from Thanksgiving shopping.

19. It can reasonably be inferred that the author uses the questions in the final paragraph to call attention to:

   A. topics that the author avoided earlier.
   B. possible drawbacks of Thanksgiving-day shopping.
   C. the likelihood of a compromise involving consumers and retailers.
   D. the skepticism of marketing experts.

20. In the final two paragraphs (lines 64-86) the author most strongly suggests that public acceptance of a commercialized Thanksgiving is:

   F. an idea that millennials will be unlikely to support once they are more mature.
   G. a position with psychological consequences that remain misunderstood.
   H. a policy that even its harshest critics will soon endorse.
   J. a growing trend that may become even more firmly established.

GO ON TO THE NEXT PAGE.

Passage III

HUMANITIES: Passage A is from the book *Or So It Goes: A Survey of 20th Century Art.* Passage B is from Peter Kristoff, "The Heath Is the Universe: Meaningful Art in a 'Meaningless' World" (1983).

Passage A from *Or So It Goes*

By the middle of the 20th century, visual art had abandoned many of the philosophical ambitions that once defined it. Man's place in the universe. Gone. Man's understanding of his own essence. Gone. The shift began when Marcel Duchamp in
5 the 1910s selected shovels and coatracks and bicycle tires from the run of everyday life and called them "art"; the transformation was complete when Andy Warhol, at midcentury, shunted Brillo boxes and big, campy prints of Elvis into American museums. What could such art do but suggest a world without
10 hierarchy—without art vs non-art, without order vs. disorder— and thus without meaning? Art had become a mirror not of the soul or the universe, but of the tackiness, hilariousness, and pointlessness of so much human action.

Literature, however, took longer to abandon the quest for
15 meaning, perhaps because so many of the greatest 20th-century playwrights and poets also moonlighted as moral and existential philosophers. Perhaps also, it was because literature was never mere "decoration" as so many of the visual arts once were: it was always a way to instruct and delve, for the Greeks, for
20 Shakespeare, for 20th century masters as different as T.S. Eliot, Virginia Woolf, and Ernest Hemingway.

Instead of renouncing its age-old search for meaning, literature reduced that search to an absurdity, a grotesque. This is exactly what happens in *Cosmos* (1965), a dementedly
25 ingenious satire of man's place in the universe written by Polish modernist Witold Gombrowicz. The plot is simple: the narrator of the story is walking through the countryside when he sees a dead bird hanging from a twig. Determined to get to the bottom of this "mystery", the narrator notices patterns
30 involving cracks in walls and the shapes of his acquaintances' noses, and struggles mightily to make sense of it all. The narrator kills a cat; later, one of the narrator's acquaintances kills himself. Just as the narrator is working himself into a hopeless welter of over-interpretation, the novel ends abruptly
35 with the sentence "Tonight we will be having chicken fricassee for dinner." Humor, banality, and absurdity conquered literature after all.

Passage B by Peter Kristoff

In their tragedies, the Greeks implied that if a man defies the gods by searching for his own answers, he is on his own.
40 Later, in Christopher Marlowe's play *Doctor Faustus*, the demon Mephistopheles delivers his judgment of the world: "Why, this is hell, nor am I out of it." The isolation, the terrifying disorientation of the solitary individual has been the very basis not only of theatre, but of all literature. Indeed, the
45 novelist Thomas Hardy clearly expresses the insignificance of the individual in *The Return of the Native.* This masterful Victorian novel focuses on the character of Mrs. Yeobright and evokes her life on the bleak and isolated Egdon Heath. At one point, Mrs. Yeobright glimpses an unknown man on the distant
50 horizon:

"The silent being who thus occupied himself seemed to be of no more account of life than an insect. He appeared as a mere parasite of the heath, fretting its surface in his daily labour as a moth frets a garment, entirely engrossed with its
55 products, having no knowledge of anything but the fern, furze, heath, lichens, and moss."

Egdon Heath, in Hardy's novel, represents the universe; "the great inviolate place (that has) an ancient permanence that the sea cannot claim. Who can say of a particular sea that it is
60 old? Distilled by the sun, kneaded by the moon, it is renewed in a year, in a day, or in an hour. The sea changed, the fields changed, the rivers, the villages, and the people changed, yet Egdon remained." There the universe, in all its intimidating permanence, is defined for you.

65 Now, the basic tenets that lie behind twentieth-century writing that embraces the absurd are not new ideas. What is new, perhaps, is that we are no longer provided with characters who struggle and strive to formulate ideas about themselves, their place, their purpose; we encounter only people who have
70 given up and simply accept that nothing can be done about anything. Not that the authors of the absurd who emerged in the 1940s and 1950s really care one way or the other: they do not defend their ideas, they just blankly present their beliefs.

But is acceptance an appropriate answer to the human
75 condition? Or is it just an evasion ? Surely, literature is meant to motivate us to demand a meaning to life. Look up at the stars at night. There is a meaning somewhere out there. We have to find it.

Questions 21-23 ask about Passage A.

---

21. As it is used in line 2, the phrase *defined it* most nearly means

   A. been its primary characteristics.
   B. been its major limitations.
   C. caused it to become indisputable.
   D. led to stereotypes about it.

22. One of the themes of the novel *Cosmos*, as it is described in Passage A, is:

F. romance.
G. pollution.
H. materialism.
J. death.

23. The primary purpose of Passage A is to:

A. contrast artists such as Duchamp and Warhol with their predecessors.
B. show how different types of art and literature embraced the idea of meaninglessness.
C. compare writers such as Eliot and Woolf to their contemporaries.
D. urge authors to return to a type of writing that is philosophically meaningful.

Questions 24-27 ask about Passage B.

---

24. In the first paragraph of Passage B, the author mentions the Greek "tragedies" (line 38) and *Doctor Faustus* (line 40) as examples of works that:

F. are in continuity with *The Return of the Native* in their understanding of the individual.
G. had a great influence on Hardy when he was composing *The Return of the Native*.
H. are similar to the writings about absurdity that appeared in the 1940s and 1950s.
J. have been criticized on account of their strong religious content.

25. The author of Passage B explains that the setting of Egdon Heath in *The Return of the Native* is:

A. unpopulated.
B. symbolic.
C. infamous.
D. fantasy-like.

26. As described in the excerpt from *The Return of the Native*, the "unknown man" (line 49) in Passage B appears to be:

F. heroic and persevering.
G. insignificant and self-absorbed.
H. confused and melancholy.
J. secretive and distrustful.

27. Does the author of Passage B see acceptance as "an appropriate answer to the human condition" (lines 74-75) or as "an evasion" (line 75)?

A. An appropriate answer, because the author speaks positively of authors who embrace the absurd
B. An appropriate answer, because the author notes that indifference to philosophical questions is an increasingly popular attitude
C. An evasion, because the author speaks positively of authors who investigate man's place in the universe
D. An evasion, because the author explains that Hardy's writing is still enormously popular despite new ideas about absurdity

---

Questions 28-30 ask about both passages.

---

28. One difference between Passage A and Passage B is that, unlike Passage B, Passage A explicitly discusses:

F. politics.
G. Greek writing.
H. visual art.
J. works of drama.

29. Both Passage A and Passage B consider:

A. broad shifts in perspective as they relate to literature.
B. the social problems that have been depicted in literature.
C. philosophers who also wrote popular literature.
D. the humorous techniques used in modern literature.

30. As described in Passage A, how does the narrator of *Cosmos* differ from the "characters" (line 67) described near the end of Passage B?

F. The narrator of *Cosmos* believes that life is meaningless.
G. The narrator of *Cosmos* is unconcerned about death.
H. The narrator of *Cosmos* realizes that he is ridiculous.
J. The narrator of *Cosmos* endeavors to interpret the world around him.

GO ON TO THE NEXT PAGE.

Passage IV

NATURAL SCIENCE: This passage is adapted from the article "The Prototyping Revolution." All acronyms and abbreviations are defined within the passage: RP stands for "rapid prototyping."

Three-dimensional printing (3DP) is a flexible and cost-effective digital modeling technology that is stimulating economies all over the world. And this technology is revolutionizing medicine in the process. While 3DP is still in
5 its early stages, innovations in manufacturing provide compelling evidence that 3DP will significantly impact how healthcare professionals help their patients. Pharmaceutical companies are finding this new technology useful in customizing dosage measurements and in increasing the
10 general reliability of time-release medications. Prosthetics researchers are also enthusiastic, since 3DP can be particularly useful in reducing human error and cutting materials' costs when manufacturing artificial limbs.

Yet perhaps the most compelling medical use for 3DP is
15 generating and printing precise images of organs, which has the potential to solve the problem of organ donor shortages. Although there are limits to how much 3DP can accomplish, there is also evidence that this technology is helping us refine our ways of thinking through age-old problems.

20 Prototyping, the construction of a physical or tactile model of a concept or design, is an essential step in developing a wide range of products; these products can be as simple as plastic consumer toys, or as crucial as medical necessities such as synthetic heart valves. Historically, prototyping has
25 been performed by hand; artisans used various and sometimes incompatible methods, including casting, molding, material removal (for example, cutting and chiseling), and combining material with adhesives such as glue. Before the late twentieth century, prototyping had always involved extensive time and
30 labor, even when the designs in question were relatively simple. But the advent of the computer rapidly changed prototyping methods.

As computers became more affordable, rising industries and small companies began to harness the capabilities of
35 these devices. New software in computer-aided design (CAD) and computer-aided manufacturing (CAM) made virtual or "soft" prototyping possible. The engineering side of design became more cost effective, now that digital models could accurately predict minute structural properties. This
40 method also allowed more intricate product designs and facilitated testing a design's resistance to stress and strain. However, the necessary tactile models were still handmade and, as product design grew increasingly complex, physical prototyping took longer than ever before.

45 Rapid prototyping (RP), the immediate precursor of 3DP, was the first prototyping method to supersede manual prototyping. At last, machines could build prototypes directly from digital information, without the need for a model made

by human hands. This bypassing saved time and avoided
50 human error. The allure of this method is unmistakable; since the invention of RP in 1988, over thirty varieties of RP methods have emerged, and most of these varieties have become commercially viable.

An interesting difference between RP technologies and
55 more traditional prototyping methods is that RP technologies are "additive" processes, while the traditional methods are "subtractive." In other words, RP builds models by combining layer upon layer without ever factoring in unnecessary material. In contrast, traditional models begin with a larger
60 substance and often sculpt a primary form from a solid block.

Despite their variations, all RP methods share a general step-by-step process. The first step to all RP techniques is to create a computerized model of the prototype, generally with CAD or CAM. The most important requirement for this
65 model is that its specified interior, exterior, and boundaries clearly define an enclosed volume. The next step is to transfer this file to a format which expresses the model in geometric shapes that will be easily read by a software program. The last step before physical prototyping is to open this file in
70 software capable of "slicing" the design into stacked levels, or cross-sections. These can subsequently be produced with materials in solid, liquid or powder form. Some RP techniques, including 3DP, use a combination of materials to create the tactile prototype.

75 The Massachusetts Institute of Technology pioneered the first commercially viable 3D printer in 1993. Created by Michael Cima and Emanuel Sachs, this printer was far superior to earlier 3DPs. One feature that set this machine apart from its precursors was its capacity to print with a
80 variety of materials, such as plastics, ceramics, and metals; moreover, this exemplary printer could use both powder and liquid substances to create prototypes. These attributes permitted greater flexibility than ever, and invited even more industries to take advantage of the efficiency of 3DP.

31. The author's purpose in writing this passage is most likely to:

   A. discuss the origins and benefits of three-dimensional printing technology.
   B. give examples of various industrial uses of three-dimensional printing.
   C. outline the drawbacks of creating models through computer prototyping.
   D. hail a breakthrough by researchers at the Massachusetts Institute of Technology.

GO ON TO THE NEXT PAGE.

32. Which of the following methods does the passage identify as the immediate precursor of 3DP?

    F. Manual or hand-made prototyping
    G. Rapid prototyping (RP)
    H. Computer-aided design (CAD)
    J. Computer-aided manufacturing (CAM)

33. According to the passage, all of the following are examples of real-world applications of 3DP EXCEPT:

    A. the construction of new toys for mass production.
    B. the creation of prosthetic limbs.
    C. the development of more precise time-release medications.
    D. the accurate modeling of donor organs.

34. The main purpose of the third paragraph (lines 20-32) is to:

    F. provide an overview of the various problems associated with manual prototyping.
    G. illustrate how prototyping is essential to the medical industry.
    H. give examples of the different methods artisans use to prototype.
    J. argue that prototyping is more efficient than 3DP.

35. The main purpose of the sixth paragraph (lines 54-60) is to explain:

    A. a source of conflict among researchers.
    B. a harmful consequence of new medical technologies.
    C. the high reputation of manual prototyping.
    D. an important distinction in prototyping methods.

36. According to the passage, it can be inferred that rapid prototyping (RP) replaced manual prototyping primarily as a result of the fact that:

    F. RP models could be built without human craftsmanship, which saved time and reduced error.
    G. the manufacturers of RP technology were given generous subsidies from technology institutes.
    H. only a few companies held patents on RP technology, which allowed them to dominate the market.
    J. it became far cheaper to rely on RP technology than to pay for human labor.

37. The author states that all of the following are steps in a typical rapid prototyping (RP) process EXCEPT:

    A. creating a model with the aid of a computer.
    B. transmitting the model to a file that will be readable by a software program.
    C. constructing an initial manual prototype using a mold.
    D. using a software program to split the prototype image into various cross-sections.

38. As described in the passage, the 3D printer developed by the Massachusetts Institute of Technology was notable because this machine made possible the:

    F. use of effective 3D printing in a way that is efficient for businesses.
    G. movement away from RP and toward new forms of 3DP within the medical field.
    H. creation of prototypes both from multiple layers and from a single block of material.
    J. first use of RP technologies in manufacturing prosthetic limbs.

39. It can be inferred from the passage that one of the limitations of the "precursors" (line 79) of the computer created by Cima and Sachs was their:

    A. inefficient use of electricity.
    B. dependency on rare and different power sources.
    C. overly complex operation instructions.
    D. inability to print with a wide variety of materials.

40. The author's attitude towards 3DP technology can best be described as:

    F. objective.
    G. skeptical.
    H. enthusiastic.
    J. defensive.

END OF TEST 3
STOP! DO NOT TURN THE PAGE UNTIL TOLD TO DO SO.
DO NOT RETURN TO A PREVIOUS TEST.

Answer Key: TEST 3

Test 3

LITERARY NARRATIVE

1. C
2. F
3. D
4. G
5. B
6. F
7. A
8. H
9. A
10. J

HUMANITIES

21. A
22. J
23. B
24. F
25. B
26. G
27. C
28. H
29. A
30. J

SOCIAL SCIENCE

11. D
12. F
13. B
14. G
15. A
16. H
17. C
18. F
19. B
20. J

NATURAL SCIENCE

31. A
32. G
33. A
34. F
35. D
36. F
37. C
38. F
39. D
40. H

To see your scaled ACT Reading Score (1-36), determine how many questions you answered correctly and consult the Scoring Chart on Page 186 of this book.

Post-Test Analysis

This post-test analysis is essential if you want to see an improvement on your next test. Possible reasons for errors, both for the test overall and for each of the four reading passages, are listed here. Place check marks next to the types of errors that pertain to you, or write your own types of errors in the blank spaces provided.

GENERAL

◇ Spent too much time reading the passages
◇ Spent too much time answering the questions
◇ Did not attempt to finish all of the passages
◇ Did not create effective margin answers
◇ Did not use process of elimination
◇ Could not find evidence to answer the questions
◇ Could not comprehend the topics and ideas in the passages
◇ Could not understand what the questions were asking
◇ Interpreted the passages rather than using evidence
Other: _____

LITERARY NARRATIVE

◇ Spent too long reading the passage
◇ Spent too long answering the questions
◇ Could not identify the setting and characters
◇ Could not understand the plot or action
◇ Could not work effectively with tone and clues to tone
Other: _____

> **Use this form** to better analyze your performance. If you don't understand why you made errors, there is no way that you can correct them!

SOCIAL SCIENCE

◇ Spent too long reading the passage
◇ Spent too long answering the questions
◇ Could not understand the author's position or arguments
◇ Used outside knowledge rather than using evidence
Other: _____

HUMANITIES

◇ Spent too long reading the passage
◇ Spent too long answering the questions
◇ Could understand the themes and organization of the passage
◇ Could not understand the author's ideas and uses of evidence
Other: _____

NATURAL SCIENCE

◇ Spent too long reading the passage
◇ Spent too long answering the questions
◇ Found the concepts and ideas in the passage confusing
◇ Found the questions confusing
◇ Could not effectively work with the inference and logic questions
Other: _____

TEST 3 Answer Explanations

1. Correct Answer: C

The author directly states that "Simon's intention had been to look at houses to buy in preparation for his intended retirement" (lines 20-22), thus supporting **C**. Choices **A** and **D** list incorrect intentions: Simon does not find any companions in the passage (even though he observes a scene of companionship in the café) and does not dislike his earlier home (which is described somewhat positively as "alive" in the first paragraph). Choice **B** is wrong because Simon is not completely unfamiliar with France: he dreams of "sophisticated Europe" in line 23 and is revealed to have limited French language skills in line 70 and elsewhere.

2. Correct Answer: F

In the passage, the author describes a "star-spattered sky" (line 9), a "sky with "no stars" (line 15), and "a few stars sparkling" (lines 78-79). Together, these pieces of evidence justify **F**. A plane ride (**H**) is only mentioned once ("he had flown" in line 18). *Animals* (**G**) and *mountains* (**J**) are not referenced at all: do not falsely assume that they are present in Simon's settings.

3. Correct Answer: D

The passage establishes that *here* is Pontivy (line 20), so that **D** is the correct choice. The locations listed in choices **A**, **B** and **C** are places that Simon previously visited or passed through: Sudan is his former home, while Paris and Rennes, as described in lines 18-19, are cities along Simon's route to Pontivy.

4. Correct Answer: G

The passage explains that Simon has set out to "explore the town" of Pontivy (line 29), indicating that he is not entirely familiar with this location. Other clues indicate that Simon is a stranger to the three individuals in the café: the do not call him by name or interact with him, beyond serving his food. Moreover, the passage (which is from Simon's perspective) never assigns names to these three characters. Thus, **G** is the most reasonable answer. The second woman was "the cook, Simon assumed" (line 48); thus, he does not know that woman, which eliminates choices **F** and **H**. Choice **J** is wrong because Simon is a customer there for the purpose of *eating* (line 54); he is not an intruder.

5. Correct Answer: B

Sudan is *noisy* (line 1), *alive* (line 2) and *packed* (line 2), while France is *silent* (line 14) and marked by *stillness* (line 11). Thus, **B** is the best choice. Choices **A** and **D** can be eliminated based on their respective descriptions (*harmony*, *luxury*) of Sudan: for **D**, do not confuse a lively location with *exotic* features (line 8) for a place that is *luxurious* or materially rich. Choice **C** can be eliminated based on its description (*hopefulness*) of France, a country that seems quite empty and even takes a negative tone in the first two paragraphs.

6. Correct Answer: F

Because Simon *dreamed* of sophisticated Europe, he may have in mind an image that does not line up with reality. In fact, the statement quoted in the question is followed by the observation that Simon was *surprised* (line 24) by the lack of cabs in Europe itself. Thus, Simon's expectations were wrong. Choice **J** is fundamentally flawed, because Simon's attitude toward Europe and France becomes increasingly positive as the passage progresses. While Simon's expectations were incorrect, they were not inappropriate (**G**) and could have been based on reasonable conclusions. The passage does not state that his expectations would not be fulfilled anywhere in Europe (**H**); we do not learn of his travels beyond Pontivy and thus cannot make this conclusion.

7. Correct Answer: A

The young man's entrance *transformed* (line 64) the women from using only a few words and waiting for Simon to go home (lines 41-54) to "crying out in eagerness and delight" (line 65). Thus, expect a general negative to positive transition, such as *reserve* to *excitement* in choice **A**, but do not neglect the meanings of individual words. The second adjectives in choices **B** and **D** do not directly line up with ideas of *eagerness and delight* (line 69). Although negative, *sadness* in choice **C** is wrong: because the two women say little, we do not know enough about exactly what they are thinking to conclude that they are sad.

8. Correct Answer: H

The young man told a story that was "far beyond the limits of Simon's French" (line 70), a quote which indicates that Simon's French is limited or *imperfect*. Choices **F** and **J** do not work: they are too extreme (**F** too negative, **J** too positive), and assume strong emotional reactions to Simon's French that are not depicted in the passage. Choice **G** implies that Simon's French is limited, but also incorrectly states that he is embarrassed by his language skills: we do not actually learn how he feels about his command of French, so be careful not to misinterpret his general reserve as embarrassment.

9. Correct Answer: A

Simon has just approached (but has not yet entered) a café when he states that it looks "better than nothing" (lines 37-38), which supports **A** and eliminates choice **C**. Choices **B** and **D** refer to topics in the passage but are not directly about the café. Thus, they should be eliminated.

10. Correct Answer: J

Throughout, the narration of the passage registers exactly what Simon thinks and how Simon feels after traveling from Sudan to the *new* town location of Pontivy. The narrator third-person, however, never assumes a defined identity or voices independent opinions, and thus remains *detached*. This evidence supports **J**; other answers distort the content of the passage. Since the identity of the narrator is never defined, **F** (which assumes that the narrator is an *inhabitant* of a French town) is incorrect. In the third paragraph, the author explains that "Simon's intention had been to look at houses to buy in preparation for his intended retirement" (lines 20-22). Thus, choice **G** attributes incorrect intentions to Simon. Choice **H** is wrong because the passage uses sensory impressions (not scholarly research) to establish the contrast between Sudan and France.

TEST 3 Answer Explanations

11. Correct Answer: D

As described in the first paragraph, *Black Friday* was at one point a negative term coined "by a disgruntled Philadelphia policeman" (lines 2-3) due to the day's crowding and violence; however, Peter Strawbridge described Black Friday as "the day when business profits went into the black" (lines 12-13). These two alternative explanations point to choice **D**. Choice **B** goes against the positive tone that Strawbridge gives Black Friday, while choice **A** incorrectly assumes that the policeman and Strawbridge are describing the *earliest* and *most violent* Black Fridays. (They could, instead, be describing typical Black Friday events.) The author does not give an opinion this early in the passage as to the benefits and drawbacks of Black Friday (**C**), even though the later stages of the passage do weigh Black Friday pros and cons.

12. Correct Answer: F

Among the commercialized Thanksgiving drawbacks listed in the passage are the following: workers being "put in a position to either work on Thanksgiving or risk losing their jobs" (lines 58-59), losing "the Thanksgiving tradition of a family-and-friends day" (lines 80-81), and "worker strikes" as a means of voicing anger (lines 51-52). This information eliminates **G**, **H**, and **J**, respectively. The author nowhere discusses falling retail profits: at most, the passage suggests that stores, "technically, are not doing more business" but are not watching their profits *plummet* either (lines 43-44), so that **F** is the best answer.

13. Correct Answer: B

The author mentions that "three states—Maine, Massachusetts, and Rhode Island—have blue laws that restrict stores from opening on Thanksgiving" (lines 61-63) in order to support the point that many people have opposed "retailers that decided to open their doors—thereby requiring employees to work—on Thanksgiving" (lines 52-54). The tone applied to Thanksgiving and Black Friday is purely negative here, not varied according to location (**A**). Other states are not compared to Maine, Massachusetts, and Rhode Island. Thus, choices **C** (which would rely on such comparisons) and **D** (which relates to the legislative situation in New Jersey) can be eliminated.

14. Correct Answer: G

The author mentions consumers who have voiced "their anger at retailers" in lines 51-52, refers to legislation "that would prohibit stores from opening before 9:00 p.m." in lines 56-57, and notes that the opinions of "millennials" contrast with the opinions of the larger (and older) American population in lines 65-74. This information eliminates **F**, **H**, and **J**. For **G**, the only *superstores* directly mentioned in the passage are Kmart and Walmart, and these superstores are significant because they stay open on Thanksgiving, NOT because they are contrasted with smaller businesses.

15. Correct Answer: A

This paragraph mentions the open-on-Thanksgiving policy followed by Kmart and Walmart, and concludes by asserting that that "the number of retailers open on the holiday has only continued to grow" (lines 33-34). Thus, **A** is the best answer. Choice **C** is about consumers, not retailers, and adopts a negative tone (drawbacks) that this paragraph does not openly support. Choice **B** misconstrues the passage (since the author cites a similarity between Kmart and Walmart, not multiple differences), while choice **D** is off-topic (since store policies, not marketing trends, are emphasized by this paragraph).

16. Correct Answer: H

The survey is cited to support the paragraph's thesis that "a commercialized Thanksgiving is firmly embraced by at least one group: millennials (lines 64-66), making **H** correct. Choices **F** and **J** are not about millennials at all, while choice **G** is unsupported, since the author does not refer to any "economic issues" beyond a commercialized Thanksgiving in reference to the survey.

17. Correct Answer: C

Cody's legislation "would prohibit stores from opening before 9:00 p.m. on Thanksgiving" (lines 56-57). This information lines up directly with choice **C**. Choice **D** is too extreme, since Cody's policy would only limit store hours on Thanksgiving. Choice **A** is unsupported by the text, since Cody's legislation relates only to Thanksgiving policies (NOT to events on the next day, Black Friday), and choice **B** is illogical, since the workers on strike would be in favor of Cody's legislation. Cody's measures are a possible response to petitions and strikes, but would not necessarily impact future strikes and petitions.

18. Correct Answer: F

In the passage, the author puts forward the idea that "retailers that open their doors on Thanksgiving Day in hopes of boosting holiday sales are shifting purchases away from Black Friday, rather than increasing the number of overall transactions" (lines 40-43). Family celebrations (**G**), legislation (**H**), and superstores (**J**) are not mentioned here: they are mentioned elsewhere in the passage (lines 76-85, 54-64, and 75-85, respectively) and never in connection to the issue of store profits.

19. Correct Answer: B

The questions presented imply that modern American society does not know how to "take one day off" (lines 78-79) from shopping or hold holiday dinners *sacred* (line 79); these are the possible effects of "retailers of opening on Thanksgiving Day" (lines 75-76). Thus, expect a negative answer: **B**, which describes *drawbacks*, is an appropriate choice. The sentiments in the paragraph do not involve compromise (**C**) or marketing experts (**D**). The author did not avoid this issue before (**A**); in fact, family Thanksgiving dinners are discussed in lines 58-63.

TEST 3 Answer Explanations

20. Correct Answer: J

The last two paragraphs cite evidence that many people, particularly the young Americans known as *millennials* (line 66), favor "commerce on Thanksgiving" (lines 83-84); thus, this practice "seems to be here to stay" (line 84). The author does not state that either millennials (**F**) or critics of Thanksgiving retail (**H**) will change their minds. And while the author does state that the *psychological benefits* (lines 76-77) of Thanksgiving retail are *uncertain* (line 77), this does not mean that such benefits are *misunderstood* (**G**). It is possible to know what benefits are possible (or *understand* them) without being certain that these benefits can be found in reality.

HUMANITIES

21. Correct Answer: A

The phrase *defined it* refers to the "philosophical ambitions" (line 2) of visual art: these ambitions would be characteristics of the art that expressed or investigated them. Thus, **A** is the best answer, while other choices apply faulty tones to the phrase *defined it*. Because the phrase involves "ambitions" that artists would see as desirable, **B** ("limitations") and **D** ("stereotypes") involve faulty negatives. **C** is incorrect in context: later artists DID dispute the "philosophical ambitions" of the art described, as explained in the rest of the first paragraph.

22. Correct Answer: J

As described in Passage A, the plot of *Cosmos* involves "a dead bird" (line 28). Elsewhere in the novel the "narrator kills a cat; later, one of the narrator's acquaintances kills himself" (lines 32-33). Together, these pieces of information indicate that death is a theme of the novel. Thus, **J** is an effective answer. Romance (**F**) might be a theme associated with older art than *Cosmos*, pollution (**G**) is never mentioned, and materialism (**H**) is only a theme of the art mentioned in the first paragraph of Passage A.

23. Correct Answer: B

The author explains in the first paragraph that artists in the middle of the twentieth century abandoned philosophical issues such as "Man's place in the universe" (line 3) to embrace the theme of "the tackiness, hilariousness, and pointlessness of so much human action" (lines 12-13). The author develops this discussion by drawing on themes from both art and literature, so that **B** is the best answer. **A** (which only addresses visual artists) and **C** (which only addresses writers) are both too narrow. **D** is problematic because it mistakes the objective tone of the passage for a persuasive tone of defense.

24. Correct Answer: F

In the first paragraph, the author explains that both Greek tragedies and *Doctor Faustus* explore the "terrifying disorientation of the individual" (line 43). This theme is linked to the "insignificance of the individual" (lines 45-46) that is explored in Thomas Hardy's novel *The Return of the Native*; thus, **F** is the best answer. **G** misstates the author's case: while these works all share a theme, there is no argument that Hardy read the other

works. **H** (absurdity, which the author criticizes) and **J** both wrongly assume that the author dislikes the works from the first paragraph, which are in fact presented as meaningful.

25. Correct Answer: B

The author of Passage B explains in line 57 that "Egdon Heath, in Hardy's novel, represents the universe," thus providing direct justification for choice **B**. Choice **A** is incorrect because Mrs. Yeobright does in fact inhabit the Heath, while **C** and **D** may be related to faulty readings of the author's descriptions. The Heath can be very loosely interpreted as disturbing or disorienting as presented, yet the author of Passage B never uses vocabulary that explicitly portrays the Heath as *infamous* or *fantasy-like*.

26. Correct Answer: G

The "unknown man" is described as "of no more account of life than an insect" (line 52) and as "entirely engrossed . . . having no knowledge of anything but the fern, furze, heath, lichens, and moss" (lines 54-56). These line references justify the adjectives "insignificant" and "self-absorbed", respectively, making **G** the best answer. **F** wrongly introduces a positive, while **H** (confused) and **J** (secretive) introduce negatives that do not correspond directly to any element of the description in lines 51-56.

27. Correct Answer: C

In lines 45-46, the author follows his approving discussion of the Greeks and of *Doctor Faustus* by stating that "Thomas Hardy clearly expresses the insignificance of the individual". This information indicates that addressing questions about the universe is a better approach than "acceptance": **C** rightly focuses on the author's praise for writers who avoid the "acceptance" criticized in the passage. **A** and **B** both take the wrong general attitude (and, especially in the case of **B**, are closer to the stance of Passage A), while **D** introduces the issue of Hardy's reputation, which is never considered.

28. Correct Answer: H

Passage A begins with a discussion of "visual art" (line 1) that draws on specific artists such as Marcel Duchamp and Andy Warhol: although some of the broad philosophical ideas in Passage B may be relevant to visual art, visual art and visual artists are never directly mentioned. **H** is the correct answer. Neither passage explicitly discusses politics (eliminating **F**), while Passage B discusses both Greek writing (eliminating **G**) and works of drama (eliminating **J**) in its first paragraph.

29. Correct Answer: A

In Passage A, the author explains how, "Instead of renouncing the age-old search for meaning, literature reduced that search to an absurdity, a grotesque" (lines 22-23) in the 20th century. The author of Passage B also describes broad shift related to 20th-century literature, which lacks" characters who struggle and strive to formulate ideas about themselves" (lines 67-69). Together, these quotations indicate that **A** is the best choice. Though Passage A does discuss consumer objects in visual art, neither passage emphasizes social problems in literature (eliminating **B**) and neither discusses philosophers who wrote literature (eliminating **C**), though both do discuss literature that raises philosophical questions). Choice **D** is only relevant to Passage A, which discusses the "Humor" (line 36) in literature.

30. Correct Answer: J

While the characters in Passage B do not "struggle and strive to formulate ideas" (line 68), the narrator of *Cosmos* observes his surroundings and "struggles mightily to make sense of it all" (line 31). This information justifies **J**, but also indicates the faulty logic in **F**, **G**, and **H**. The narrator appears to believe that what he is observing is meaningful or important: only the author or reader of *Cosmos* would see the narrator's observations as meaningless, insignificant, or ridiculous.

NATURAL SCIENCE

31. Correct Answer: A

Early in the passage, the author establishes that "three-dimensional printing (3DP) is a flexible and cost-effective digital modeling technology that is stimulating economies all over the world" (lines 1-3). The author then describes the development of 3DP, paying special attention to how 3DP represents an improvement over earlier prototyping methods. Thus, the passage describes and lauds 3DP, which eliminates the negative choice **C**. Choice **D** is too narrow: the passage is about 3DP in general, not just the Massachusetts Institute of Technology version (which is only introduced in the final paragraph. In addition, the author focuses mainly on the medical uses of 3DP (lines 7-19) rather than industrial uses (**B**).

32. Correct Answer: G

Lines 45-46 state that "rapid prototyping (RP)" was "the immediate precursor of 3DP." Thus, choices **F**, **H**, and **J** are factually incorrect, leaving **G** as the correct answer. Keep in mind that you must identify the technology that came *immediately before* 3DP: manual prototyping is the earliest form mentioned in the passage, while both CAD and CAM (line 36) are mentioned as leading to RP.

33. Correct Answer: A

In the first two paragraphs, the author mentions that 3DP can assist in "manufacturing artificial limbs" (line 13), "increasing the general reliability of time-release medications" (lines 9-10), and "printing precise images of organs" in order to address organ donor shortages (lines 15-16). These pieces of evidence allow you to eliminate **B**, **C**, and **D**, respectively. The creation of "plastic consumer toys" (line 23) is mentioned only as a typical prototyping task; there is no evidence that 3DP, which is discussed mostly in terms of its medical uses, is itself used to create toys. Thus, **A** is the best answer.

34. Correct Answer: F

The point of this paragraph is that manual prototyping was inefficient; it "had always involved extensive time and labor" (lines 29-30). Thus, all answers other than **F** must be eliminated because they do not list negative traits of manual prototyping. **G**

could accurately describe lines 1-19, but not the line reference for this question; **H** seems roughly on topic, yet the author takes a much more negative tone than **H** entails. **J** reverses the author's logic, since the passage as a whole argues that 3DP is more efficient than earlier methods.

35. Correct Answer: D

The sixth paragraph describes "an interesting difference between RP technologies and more traditional prototyping methods" (lines 54-55). Thus, choices **A** (*researchers*) and **B** (*medical technologies*, not prototyping technologies) do not relate to the main topic as directly as possible, and involve inappropriately negative tones. The high reputation of manual prototyping (**C**) is not discussed in this paragraph either: in fact, the author uses much of the passage to call attention to processes that are more efficient (and thus may have higher reputations) than manual prototyping.

36. Correct Answer: F

The author describes the main benefits of rapid prototyping (RP) in the following manner: "machines could build prototypes directly from digital information, without the need for a model made by human hands. This bypassing saved time and avoided human error" (lines 47-50). This evidence makes **F** the best choice. The idea that RP was financially effective is a reasonable inference, yet the passage does not support the specific logic of **G** and **J**. Subsidies (**G**) and the exact costs of human labor and RP (**J**) not discussed at all. Similarly, choice **H** is wrong because patents are not discussed in relation to the benefits of RP.

37. Correct Answer: C

Outlining the typical steps of RP modeling, the author notes that models are created using "digital information without the need for a model made by human hands" (lines 48-49). It is then necessary to express the model in geometric shapes "that will be easily ready by a software program" (lines 67-68). The author also explains that "RP builds models by combining layer upon layer without ever factoring in unnecessary material" (lines 57-59). Together, this material can be used to eliminate **A**, **B**, and **D**, since *digital information* would naturally be used by software programs. Because RP does not at any point require "a model made by human hands," **C** is not a step in RP modeling.

38. Correct Answer: F

As described in the final paragraph of the passage, "the Massachusetts Institute of Technology pioneered the first commercially viable 3D printer" (lines 75-76). Thus, the Massachusetts Institute of Technology printer was unique in its ability to be used commercially or was *efficient for businesses*, so that **F** is the best choice. The other answer choices refer to issues from elsewhere in the passage: the movement from RP to 3DP is referenced in lines 45-47 (**G**), the use of layering to create prototypes is described in lines 68-71 (**H**), and the importance of RP technologies in creating prosthetic limbs is discussed in lines 11-13 (**J**). These are most likely features that the Massachusetts Institute Technology printer shares with other 3D printers, not features that make it special or *notable*.

39. Correct Answer: D

The author provides the following description of the advantages of the Cima and Sachs printer: "One feature that set this machine apart from its precursors was its capacity to print with a variety of materials" (lines 78-80). Thus, it can be inferred that the precursors could not print with a variety of materials, so that **D** is the best answer. Use this information to eliminate choices **A**, **B** and **C**, since electricity usage, power sources, and operation instructions are never mentioned with reference to earlier printers. The other unique advantage of the Cima and Sachs printer (its status as the "first commercially viable 3D printer, as described in line 76) is not mentioned in the context of the question.

40. Correct Answer: H

Throughout the passage, the author's tone is very positive, and the author is *enthusiastic* about the possibilities presented by 3D printing. For example, 3DP technology is described as "flexible and cost-effective" (lines 1-2) as well as *compelling* (line 14). The author also spends much of the passage showing how 3D printing and related methods were improvements over manual prototyping (lines 45-53) and how 3D printing continues to evolve and improve (lines 75-84). Thus, choices **G** and **J** are wrong because they are negative and indicate resistance to 3DP. Choice **F** is wrong because it is neutral, thus understating the extent of the author's support for the new technologies.

Test 4

READING TEST

35 Minutes—40 Questions

DIRECTIONS: There are four passages in this test. Each passage is followed by several questions. After reading a passage, choose the best answer to each question and fill in the corresponding oval on your answer document. You may refer to the passages as often as necessary.

Passage I

PROSE NARRATIVE: Taken from "El Refugio," a memoir by Michael Ivkov, and the "Ornithologist's Guide to New Jersey," a novella by Patrick Kennedy. Both works describe birdwatching experiences.

Passage A by Michael Ivkov

Over the course of an hour, we took down several "key species," yet my interest didn't grow much. But as we turned back down the path, I turned a quick right, immediately catching sight of a larger bird flapping in circles around our
5 bush. It squawked over the bush repeatedly and then erratically began dive-bombing the bush, its talons exposed. No warning. I gawked at the scene. It captured my attention completely. Forget the boring rep I assigned to birds, or the mild enjoyment I got out of looking at a cute little thing—this was something
10 new. This was exciting.

The bird was called a Cooper's Hawk, I later discovered, and it had a dramatic look—maybe a foot and a half long, with bright orange eyes, a short wingspan, a long tail streaked with black and brown, and a white and copper colored breast. It was
15 probably hunting a rat or a shrew or a smaller bird—perhaps the one we spotted earlier, in the bush.

After this, nothing was truly the same. My interest in birding didn't manifest itself immediately, but over the course of several weeks it emerged. I went out to the North Woods
20 twice a week during the winter months to look for Cooper's Hawks hunting in the late afternoon. Quiet and elusive, these elegant hawks dwell exclusively in heavily wooded areas, where they can quickly dive down from heights and pick up easy prey. The more I watched them waltz in the air as they
25 dived down on the hunt, the more I grew impatient to see additional Cooper's Hawks. I wanted to be part of the cast (hawks' version of a "flock"). When winter came to a gradual close and the hawks migrated out, I was debilitated, like a smoker who had just burned out his last cigarette.

30 If the hawks' appearance explained how I got into birding, my satisfaction in discovering new birds and subsequently organizing them on my lists ought to explain the why in why I kept going. I suppose I didn't simply opt out after seasonal hawk watching because I found myself immersed in the activity
35 of birding. I certainly didn't fall in love with most birds at first, nor, to a large extent, did I appreciate their physical beauty. Rather, birding itself surpassed the label I'd assigned it earlier that year: "an exercise in boredom" and presented itself as an exercise in attention. I took incredible pleasure in
40 both the "hunt" and the "log." Perhaps there's something inherently carnal about me, but as I looked for smaller songbirds in the North Woods that spring, I began to feel more in touch with my primitive side; I loved stalking the bird to see it, take it down into my notes, and occasionally shoot it—
45 with my camera, that is. I even bought a camouflage hat. Camo in Manhattan! We didn't want to use bright colors to disturb the birds, especially if they might be migrating. Birding was like hunting without the bloodshed.

Passage B by Patrick Kennedy

I stop the car, and look briefly west. Beyond the power
50 lines, you might see a mottled form rise, dip, and rise again against the disappearing daylight. Like another means of marking the miles, Osprey roosts are spaced evenly along the highway. The white and brown of a mother osprey descends, gently, towards the mess of twigs platformed atop a wooden
55 beam, where young Ospreys anticipate their dinner.

Perhaps no raptor has ever intrigued me like the American Osprey (*Pandion haliaetus carolinensis*). Perhaps no other bird of any kind. You can find some variety of Osprey on every continent except Antarctica, which means that you can
60 find their terrible golden eyes staring at you, and perhaps into you, almost anywhere on the globe. Before the guidebooks and the road trips and the bird blinds start to dictate your life, that is where most of us ornithologists begin, with that one, fierce, invincible bird that haunted our attention.

65 Could that explain why New Jersey plants these roosts? Did someone else see their first Osprey take wing, decades ago, and want to perpetuate that sight, roost by roost. And there are so many of these roosts, too many: you would only need about a third of them to keep the actual
70 Osprey population intact. There is a mania here, an overbuilding as deep and maniacal as an Osprey's eye. But I digress. There is another entry to write, another site that lies just ahead. **GO ON TO THE NEXT PAGE.**

Questions 1-4 ask about Passage A.

1. It can be reasonably inferred that the reference to "key species" in lines 1-2 is ironic because at this point in the narrative the narrator:

   A. does not understand exactly what a "key species" is.
   B. has never been birdwatching on any previous occasion.
   C. does not appear to find birdwatching an important activity.
   D. has wrongly classified the Cooper's Hawk as a "key species."

2. Details in the passage most strongly suggest that the Cooper's Hawk:

   F. hunts actively during the winter months.
   G. is not usually found in Manhattan.
   H. is much smaller than most other hawks.
   J. forms large cooperative groups to survive.

3. It can be reasonably inferred that at the end of the passage the narrator finds birding to be:

   A. an absorbing pursuit.
   B. an artistic endeavor.
   C. a social responsibility.
   D. an unimportant pastime.

4. As it is used in line 22, the word *dwell* most nearly means:

   F. obsess.
   G. muse.
   H. creep.
   J. reside.

Questions 5-7 ask about Passage B.

5. In Passage B, the narrator uses all of the of the following writing devices EXCEPT:

   A. visual description.
   B. speculative questions.
   C. personification.
   D. simile.

6. Passage B indicates that, at the time when the narrator is observing the Ospreys, it is:

   F. morning, and the narrator is in the middle of a conflict.
   G. evening, and the narrator is driving to a new destination.
   H. morning, and the narrator feels relaxed and reassured.
   J. evening, and the narrator is near his house.

7. As it is used in line 70, the word *mania* in Passage B is best understood to refer to:

   A. the uncontrollable growth of the Osprey population.
   B. the creation of a considerable number of roosts.
   C. the narrator's lifelong fixation on the Osprey.
   D. the unusual beliefs of ornithologists.

Questions 8-10 ask about both passages.

8. The descriptions of Cooper's Hawk in Passage A and the American Osprey in Passage B are similar in that each passage describes:

   F. the relevant bird's full habitat range.
   G. the noises made by the relevant bird.
   H. the eyes and plumage of the relevant bird.
   J. the author's first sighting of the relevant bird.

9. An element of Passage A that is not present in Passage B is a reference to what aspect of birding?

   A. The classification names given to birds
   B. The activities of conservationists
   C. Clothes worn for birding
   D. Documents used by birders

10. A general similarity of the two passages is that they both:

   F. use an encounter with a single bird species to introduce some of the narrator's ideas about birding or the study of birds.
   G. acknowledge that the reader may be uninterested in birding and use colloquial language to address this difficulty.
   H. feature short sentences that are meant to communicate the narrator's sense of self-doubt.
   J. explain how the narrator's ideas about birding shifted from negative to positive.

GO ON TO THE NEXT PAGE.

Passage II

SOCIAL SCIENCE: This passage is adapted from the essay "Executive Overreach: Case Studies in Balance of Power." *Habeas corpus* (capitalized throughout for emphasis) is Latin a term that translates literally to "you have the body."

The President of the United States is granted a tremendous amount of power under the Constitution. Such power is by no means unlimited: as the framers of the Constitution intended, the President must work with the
5 American Congress (Senate and House of Representatives) in order to actually create laws. Yet the President is permitted to issue executive directives or orders, which often carry much of the same influence as federal laws. According to the Congressional Research Service, since there is no direct
10 "definition of executive orders, presidential memoranda, and presidential proclamations in the U.S. Constitution, there is, likewise, no specific provision authorizing their issuance." Despite the legal gray area that executive orders inhabit, it has been argued that Article II of the Constitution does indeed
15 give the President such executive powers.

In some form, individual executive power has been used by every President since George Washington. However, the widespread and widely-accepted use of such power has not always been a safeguard against controversy. No less a
20 President than Abraham Lincoln was forced to use his executive privileges in a divisive manner—incurring much criticism, and many charges of executive overreach, in the process.

It was 1861: a tumultuous time in America, since the
25 Civil War had just begun. So, how did President Lincoln use his executive power? He suspended the "writ of Habeas corpus," the legal procedure that keeps the government from holding individuals indefinitely without showing cause. In other words, by suspending Habeas corpus, a government
30 could keep a person locked up without explaining to a neutral judge the justification for holding that person.

Habeas corpus first appeared in the British tract of rights known as the Magna Carta (1215) and is the oldest human right in the history of English-speaking civilization.
35 As such, Habeas corpus is viewed as a fundamental tenet of English common law. Some say that, without this foundational right, the significance of all other rights crumbles.

The Framers of the Constitution believed strongly in Habeas corpus. They were even familiar with its operations
40 (and suspended operations) from personal experience, since they had been labeled enemy combatants, imprisoned indefinitely, and denied opportunities to appear before neutral judges. They saw such a pervasive departure from due process as an instrument of tyranny and became determined
45 to protect Americans from such government abuses.

For Lincoln, the possible suspension of Habeas corpus first arose in the case of John Merryman, a state legislator from Maryland. Merryman was arrested for attempting to hinder Union troops from moving from Baltimore to
50 Washington and was held at Fort McHenry by Union military officials; after learning of these events, Merryman's attorney immediately sought a writ of Habeas corpus so that a federal court could examine the charges. President Lincoln intervened, suspended the right of habeas corpus, and
55 continued to detain Merryman.

President Lincoln's executive action was so controversial that it was ruled unconstitutional by Roger Taney, Chief Justice of the Supreme Court. Yet rather than change course, President Lincoln simply ignored Taney and
60 the other Justices. Then, he defied their ruling completely. During a speech to the Senate, President Lincoln insisted that he needed to suspend certain legalities in order to put down the rebellion in the South. President Lincoln defended his action by citing a provision in the Constitution—Article I,
65 Section 9, Clause 2: "The Privilege of the Writ of Habeas corpus shall not be suspended, unless when in Cases of Rebellion or Invasion the public Safety may require it." Ultimately, Congress did not contest President Lincoln's suspension of Habeas corpus—a tacit way of expressing
70 support for the President's decision.

In 1865, the year that the Civil War came to an end, another sensitive case came before the Supreme Court. Lambdin P. Milligan, a member of a paramilitary outfit that plotted to overthrow the government, was captured and tried
75 by a military commission; he was sentenced to death by hanging. Lincoln delayed the sentence so that the Supreme Court could weigh in on the case. In their ruling, the Justices officially restored Habeas corpus and declared military trials illegal in areas where civilian courts were able to function.

80 The handling of the Milligan case helped to balance out Lincoln's earlier decision: it showed that Lincoln assumed extraordinary powers out of necessity. According to government scholar Michael Burlingame, "most historians believe that Lincoln did not violate the Constitution in
85 suspending the writ." Instead, "arrests were overwhelmingly justified by the circumstances of the war."

So the President does indeed have tremendous power, and it is imperative that he use that power to protect the country and to support its best interests. As Lincoln and the
90 historians who have studied him would argue, supporting those best interests may mean temporarily removing cherished rights.

GO ON TO THE NEXT PAGE.

11. According to the passage, Habeas corpus is defined as:

   A. the Congressional power that allows the appointment of military courts.
   B. the privilege that allows enemy combatants to negotiate directly with hostile governments.
   C. the legal right that prevents a government from holding an individual for an unlimited time.
   D. the ability of the President to suspend otherwise cherished rights during a time of war.

12. One of the author's main points about Lincoln's suspension of Habeas corpus is that:

   F. Lincoln was not the first President to suspend Habeas corpus in a time of crisis.
   G. Habeas corpus was called upon most frequently in the last few years of the Civil War.
   H. Lincoln's actions were vigorously disputed in the 1860s, but have been received favorably by later historians.
   J. Lincoln allowed the American Congress to decide whether Habeas corpus should be suspended.

13. It can be reasonably inferred that the "executive orders, presidential memoranda, and presidential proclamations" mentioned in lines 10-11 of the passage are:

   A. often incompatible with Congressional policies.
   B. not subject to strict procedures and regulations.
   C. overseen by the Congressional Research Service.
   D. the only substantial powers that the President enjoys.

14. As it is used in line 41, the word *labeled* most nearly means:

   F. publicized.
   G. belittled.
   H. classified.
   J. analyzed.

15. It can be reasonably inferred from the passage that one similarity between John Merryman and Lambdin P. Milligan was that both men were:

   A. directly connected to United States legislatures.
   B. ultimately sentenced to death for their actions.
   C. apparently hostile to Lincoln's government.
   D. unwilling to deal directly with the Supreme Court.

16. The passage indicates that Congress reacted to Lincoln's suspension of Habeas corpus in the Merryman case by:

   F. deciding not to dispute Lincoln's intervention.
   G. referring the case to Taney's Supreme Court.
   H. publicizing a relevant section of the Constitution.
   J. encouraging public criticism of Lincoln's decision.

17. The main function of the sixth and seventh paragraphs (lines 46-65) is to explain how:

   A. Lincoln took part in an important legal case and responded to those who opposed his decisions.
   B. Congress follows the advice of the President in matters of national security.
   C. the Union government became aware of Merryman's actions and brought charges against him.
   D. Justice Taney and the Supreme Court improperly assessed a sensitive legal matter.

18. The author of the passage states that the Framers of the Constitution were strong supporters of Habeas corpus in part on account of their:

   F. unwillingness to negotiate with the British military.
   G. fear that the government they created would fail.
   H. expertise in the history of English government.
   J. own direct experience of suspended legal rights.

19. According to the passage, Lincoln's handling of the Milligan case most strongly indicates that Lincoln wanted to:

   A. demonstrate that Habeas corpus should only be suspended under extreme circumstances.
   B. undermine the power of the Supreme Court by making a divisive decision.
   C. compromise in order to earn Congressional support for new military policies.
   D. encourage his contemporaries to re-interpret a neglected section of the Constitution.

20. The author of the passage states that Habeas corpus is notable for all of the following EXCEPT:

   F. its initial appearance in the Magna Carta.
   G. its status as one of the foundational principles of English and American legal practice.
   H. the fact that it cannot be altered or influenced by new amendments to the Constitution.
   J. its privileged place as an idea valued by the Framers of the Constitution.

GO ON TO THE NEXT PAGE.

Passage III

HUMANITIES: This passage is adapted from the essay "The Ancients and Their Tragedies." W.H. Auden was a twentieth-century poet and critic; "*musée des beaux arts*" is a French phrase that means "museum of fine arts."

Among the most famous Greek myths is the story of Icarus, the son of Daedalus. It was Daedalus who designed for King Minos of Crete a twining, prison-like maze known as the Labyrinth. Then, when Minos turned against him,
5 Daedalus designed an ingenious escape plan from Crete. For both himself and his son, the inventor created working wings using wax and feathers: the two men would fly to freedom. Icarus, once in the air, was overcome with the thrill of this invention. He ignored his father's warnings, and flew too
10 near the sun. The sun's rays melted the wax that held the artificial wings together. Icarus plummeted to his death.

There is a famous sixteenth-century painting entitled *Landscape with the Fall of Icarus*. Until recently, it was thought to have been painted by a Flemish artist, Pieter
15 Bruegel the Elder, although this attribution is now questioned. Matters of attribution aside, the painting remains one of its era's masterpieces. It also remains an oddity. To begin with, the title announces that the painting is a landscape, yet three quarters of the canvas depict a sea, sparkling under the sun
20 and crowded with ships plying their trade, sails full blown and flags fluttering confidently. Behind this seascape rises a steep, neat, prosperous, civilized town. In the foreground, a self-absorbed farmer guides his horse, tilling the rich soil. Nearby, a small flock of sheep is supervised by a young
25 shepherd, the only figure in the painting who does not seem to be completely preoccupied. He is looking upward, towards some point high in the heavens. If you follow the direction of his gaze, you can just make out, in the topmost corner of the painting, a minuscule figure that appears to be tumbling from
30 the heavens. This is Icarus falling to his death: give the painting merely a casual glance and you will miss him. Only the young shepherd appears to have glimpsed the falling figure, and the attitude that the shepherd assumes is one of thorough unconcern.

35 This may strike many of us as bizarre. Today, it is probable that the young shepherd would have taken a photo of the event and sold it to the tabloids. That shepherd boy would then be questioned, interviewed incessantly, and coerced to reveal exactly how he felt when he saw this
40 accident. He would probably be offered counseling, encouraged to work through his feelings so that he could achieve the healing calm of what we call "closure" after a disturbing event. Police would cordon off the spot where Icarus could be assumed to have crashed. An investigation
45 would be launched as to how this accident might have happened, research done to see what safety laws had been breached. Psychiatrists would attempt to discover the state of Icarus's mind before he set out on his final voyage. Headlines in the papers would exclaim, "Why did this have to happen?"
50 Social Services would become involved.

We pride ourselves on our compassion for the individual. Yet, if we compare ourselves to the individuals depicted in Bruegel's painting, we might find that our approach is not always as wise as we would like to think. One of the most
55 universal of all classical myths concerning life and death is that of the "Moirai," the god-like sisters of fate who spin the thread of each individual's life and can snip that thread at will. Death happens: searching for the reason why cannot change the situation. The people in the painting are not
60 indifferent to the fall of Icarus, but they accept its occurrence. They know that anything they say cannot change the boy's fate. As W. H. Auden writes in "Musée des Beaux Arts," a poem inspired by Bruegel's painting:

About suffering they were never wrong,
65   The old masters: how well they understood
Its human position; how it takes place
While someone else is eating or opening a window or
just walking dully along.

If one can accept Auden's (and Bruegel's) stance, then one
70 can begin to reconcile how we today react to catastrophe, and how older cultures did. Humans are mortal and, as such, limited in the appreciation of their roles in a more universal scheme. The invention of wings by Daedalus illustrates ingenuity. However, the myth of Daedalus's son shows that
75 human ingenuity can be so easily undone by ambition and self-importance. There are elements of the world that are simply beyond our influence; why not follow that sturdy farmer, and improve on what small patches of the world we can improve? It is necessary to know one's place.

21. One of the primary assumptions that is made by the author of the passage is that:

A. human tragedy was a topic that artists and storytellers have avoided until recent times.
B. it is impossible for a narrative and a work of art to communicate the same theme.
C. myths will be misinterpreted by people from cultures with well-developed technologies.
D. people from different eras are likely to respond to disaster in incompatible ways.

GO ON TO THE NEXT PAGE.

22. All of the following are factors that explain why Icarus plummeted to his death EXCEPT Icarus's:

    F. refusal to follow Daedalus's advice.
    G. desperation to escape King Minos.
    H. exhilaration once in flight.
    J. self-destructive feelings of pride.

23. The primary function of the first paragraph is to:

    A. help the reader understand the importance of storytelling in Greek culture.
    B. summarize a myth that the author interprets later in the passage.
    C. show why the Icarus myth would be an unexpected inspiration for a sixteenth-century painting.
    D. call attention to the three main figures depicted in *Landscape with the Fall of Icarus*.

24. As depicted in Bruegel's *Landscape with the Fall of Icarus*, the figure of Icarus is:

    F. unusually agitated.
    G. easily overlooked.
    H. especially prominent.
    J. elaborately drawn.

25. The passage states that most of the surface of the painting *Landscape with the Fall of Icarus* depicts:

    A. the sky.
    B. the sea.
    C. farmland.
    D. a city.

26. Which of the figures in *Landscape with the Fall of Icarus* observes Icarus falling to his death?

    F. A farmer
    G. A man on a ship
    H. A shepherd
    J. Daedalus

27. The author discusses W.H. Auden's "Musee des Beaux Arts" in order to emphasize the idea that:

    A. instances of human tragedy do not necessarily interrupt the course of everyday life.
    B. poetry and painting were once interpreted as incompatible forms of art.
    C. Auden identifies with Bruegel and other painters throughout his poetry.
    D. the figures in *Landscape with the Fall of Icarus* are unable to understand matters of life and death.

28. The author presents the myth of the Moirai in order to emphasize which of the following ideas?

    F. Art is a response to feelings of powerlessness.
    G. Some matters are beyond human control.
    H. Knowledge is a source of disillusionment.
    J. Great accomplishments are often forgotten.

29. One of the main functions of the third paragraph (lines 35-50) is to:

    A. provide a few reasons why *Landscape with the Fall of Icarus* remains a popular painting.
    B. justify a type of intervention that would normally be open to dispute.
    C. explain why so many individuals are interested in participating in media spectacles.
    D. present a manner of responding to tragedy that the author does not entirely endorse.

30. The final paragraph of the passage indicates the author's belief in the importance of:

    F. focusing on matters that directly affect our lives.
    G. avoiding difficult philosophical inquiry.
    H. understanding the source of intellectual greatness.
    J. valuing art that depicts individuals at work.

GO ON TO THE NEXT PAGE.

Passage IV

NATURAL SCIENCE: This passage is adapted from the essay "Close Encounters of a Statistical Kind: The Quest for Alien Life."

Are we alone in the universe? It is a question that, over the years, has fascinated Hollywood filmmakers, and which has yielded such blockbusters as *E.T.: The Extraterrestrial* and *Independence Day*. The result is that today's film
5 audiences are more familiar than ever with "visitors of another kind," to the point where we are perhaps inured to the idea that there might be life out there, other than ourselves. In fact, the majority of us may not even be aware that the search for life beyond our own spinning blue sphere is not
10 simply a matter of Hollywood special effects, but of very real, hard, and tangible science.

For years now, astrophysicists in California have been poring over satellite data and images in search of an "Earth twin"—a planet which is similar in size to our own, and
15 which orbits its star at a distance comparable to that at which our own Earth orbits the sun. Such a planet, if found, would have a reasonable chance of containing liquid water—a substance that, in the harsh conditions of outer space, is exceedingly rare, and is the basic condition for life as we
20 know it. (Leave it to the astrophysicists to show us just how lucky we are.) For years, however, the search for an Earth twin (also known as the "Goldilocks orb") has appeared to be in vain. The lack of evidence has even led some detractors to claim that the attempt to find an Earth twin is merely a
25 modern day reenactment of the quest for the Holy Grail, or the hunt for El Dorado—in short, a fool's errand.

But now, with new photographs and data collected from the Kepler telescope, these naysayers may find themselves backpedaling on their earlier pessimism. This is because the
30 Kepler telescope recently hit a milestone: in the course of an imaging mission that took place from 2009 to 2013, the Kepler unveiled and recorded over 1,000 new planets outside our solar system (known as "exo-planets"), including a large number of Earth twin candidates.

35 The most promising of these candidates is Kepler-186f, which is only 1.1 times the size of Earth. In addition to its comparable size, Kepler-186f orbits its star within its "habitable zone"—that is, at a distance where liquid water could potentially exist. Still, there are many unknowns
40 involved. For instance, in order to sustain liquid water, Kepler-186f would need to have an atmosphere containing enough carbon dioxide to trap heat energy, much as the atmosphere of Earth itself does. While this condition remains to be investigated, Elisa Quintana, an astronomer working at
45 NASA's Ames Research Center, is decidedly optimistic: "We definitely think this takes us one step closer to finding a true Sun-Earth analogue," she said in a recent interview.

The other main difference between our Earth and its potential twin is that Kepler-186f orbits an M-type dwarf
50 star, which is smaller and cooler than our own sun. As a result, Kepler-186f receives about one-third less heat than Earth receives, a fact that raises the likelihood that its surface temperatures might be too cold to sustain life.

Despite this, scientists are still excited about the new
55 data that the Kepler telescope continues to glean. Another astronomer, Christopher Burke of the SETI Institute, has begun to analyze the relationships between the numbers of planets that appear around stars of different temperatures. While his work is still in its preliminary phases, Burke has
60 found that planets with shorter revolution periods appear more frequently around cooler, M-type stars, such as the M-dwarf that Kepler-186f orbits. Most interestingly, when considering M-type solar systems, Burke has not found a single orbiting planet with a period that exceeds 150 days—
65 less than half the amount of time it takes Earth to orbit the sun.

While the significance of this finding is still unclear, it's both fascinating and encouraging to see that other solar systems, some as far away from our own as 150 parsecs (500
70 light-years), also have planets that orbit their stars at rates comparable to our own, 365-day orbit. Perhaps most striking is another potential Earth twin that is between 0.8 and 1.8 times the size of Earth, and which orbits its star every 376 days—only seven days more than our own solar year.

75 Nonetheless, the findings of the Kepler telescope are not nearly definitive. Much more remains to be discovered, and the Kepler itself, having suffered a malfunction in 2014, needs to be repaired. The search for an Earth twin will no doubt continue; for now, our best bet for finding extraterrestrial
80 life may still be down the street, at the local movie theater.

31. One of the main ideas established by the passage is that:

A. the different standards that have been used to determine potential Earth twins have changed in the recent past.
B. the search for an Earth twin planet has been met with enthusiasm, but has yet to produce definitive results.
C. a planet must orbit a star almost identical to our sun in order to be considered an Earth twin.
D. the public was uninterested in the Earth twin debate before the most recent data was gathered by the Kepler telescope.

GO ON TO THE NEXT PAGE.

32. As used in line 30, the word *milestone* refers to:

    F. the publication of new photographs of Earth twins.
    G. the refinement of the Kepler telescope technology.
    H. the acceptance of new Earth twin candidates.
    J. the discovery of new planets by the Kepler telescope.

33. According to the passage, one of the pieces of information that is NOT currently known about Kepler-186f is whether this planet:

    A. is situated within its star's "habitable zone."
    B. has been put forward as a potential Earth twin.
    C. is comparable in size to Earth.
    D. has an atmosphere that would sustain liquid water.

34. In the first paragraph, the author refers to the movies *E.T.: The Extra-Terrestrial* and *Independence Day* in order to emphasize the idea that:

    F. films treating life elsewhere in the universe raise philosophical points that few audiences appreciate.
    G. contemporary audiences are well acquainted with images of life forms from outer space.
    H. alien life forms have not always been a profitable subject for mainstream Hollywood movies.
    J. improved special effects have enabled viewers to learn more about conditions on other planets.

35. As used in line 13, the phrase *poring over* most nearly means:

    A. examining.
    B. criticizing.
    C. popularizing.
    D. validating.

36. The author of the passage defines an "exo-planet" as a planet that:

    F. orbits a dwarf star and might be too cold to sustain life.
    G. appears to be a convincing Earth twin candidate.
    H. has an atmosphere that is significantly different from that of Earth.
    J. lies outside the solar system that contains Earth.

37. It can be reasonably inferred that the passage compares the search for an Earth twin to the quest for the Holy Grail and the hunt for El Dorado in order to:

    A. indicate that the idea of an Earth twin is still rejected by most experts.
    B. demonstrate the resistance that greets innovative exploration technology.
    C. present a viewpoint that may turn out to be overly negative and ultimately incorrect.
    D. suggest that the term "Goldilocks orb" is slowly being replaced by different analogies.

38. The passage notes that an M-type dwarf star is:

    F. larger and colder than the Earth's sun.
    G. smaller and hotter than the Earth's sun.
    H. smaller and colder than the Earth's sun.
    J. larger and hotter than the earth's sun.

39. The final paragraph of the passage most strongly communicates the idea that:

    A. scientists may return to earlier views about the impossibility of an Earth twin.
    B. the technology used in the Kepler telescope is deeply flawed.
    C. the search for an Earth twin faces obstacles and uncertainties.
    D. most forms of extra-terrestrial life would disappoint movie-goers.

40. According to the passage, which of the following conditions would indicate that a planet is a potential Earth twin?

    F. An atmosphere with little carbon dioxide content
    G. An orbit distance comparable to Earth's orbit distance
    H. A distance from Earth greater than 150 parsecs
    J. A period that does not exceed 150 days

END OF TEST 4
STOP! DO NOT TURN THE PAGE UNTIL TOLD TO DO SO.
DO NOT RETURN TO A PREVIOUS TEST.

Answer Key: TEST 4

LITERARY NARRATIVE

1. C
2. F
3. A
4. J
5. C
6. G
7. B
8. H
9. C
10. F

HUMANITIES

21. D
22. G
23. B
24. G
25. B
26. H
27. A
28. G
29. D
30. F

SOCIAL SCIENCE

11. C
12. H
13. B
14. H
15. C
16. F
17. A
18. J
19. A
20. H

NATURAL SCIENCE

31. B
32. J
33. D
34. G
35. A
36. J
37. C
38. H
39. C
40. G

To see your scaled ACT Reading Score (1-36), determine
how many questions you answered correctly and consult
the Scoring Chart on Page 186 of this book.

Post-Test Analysis

This post-test analysis is essential if you want to see an improvement on your next test. Possible reasons for errors, both for the test overall and for each of the four reading passages, are listed here. Place check marks next to the types of errors that pertain to you, or write your own types of errors in the blank spaces provided.

GENERAL

◇ Spent too much time reading the passages
◇ Spent too much time answering the questions
◇ Did not attempt to finish all of the passages
◇ Did not create effective margin answers
◇ Did not use process of elimination
◇ Could not find evidence to answer the questions
◇ Could not comprehend the topics and ideas in the passages
◇ Could not understand what the questions were asking
◇ Interpreted the passages rather than using evidence
Other: _____

LITERARY NARRATIVE

◇ Spent too long reading the passage
◇ Spent too long answering the questions
◇ Could not identify the setting and characters
◇ Could not understand the plot or action
◇ Could not work effectively with tone and clues to tone
Other: _____

> **Use this form** to better analyze your performance. If you don't understand why you made errors, there is no way that you can correct them!

SOCIAL SCIENCE

◇ Spent too long reading the passage
◇ Spent too long answering the questions
◇ Could not understand the author's position or arguments
◇ Used outside knowledge rather than using evidence
Other: _____

HUMANITIES

◇ Spent too long reading the passage
◇ Spent too long answering the questions
◇ Could understand the themes and organization of the passage
◇ Could not understand the author's ideas and uses of evidence
Other: _____

NATURAL SCIENCE

◇ Spent too long reading the passage
◇ Spent too long answering the questions
◇ Found the concepts and ideas in the passage confusing
◇ Found the questions confusing
◇ Could not effectively work with the inference and logic questions
Other: _____

TEST 4 Answer Explanations

LITERARY NARRATIVE

1. Correct Answer: C

The reference to "key species" indicates that these species are important, yet at this point in the narrative the narrator notes that "my interest didn't grow much" (line 2). It is ironic that the species are described as "key" or "important" when the narrator's interest in birding is so low. Thus, choice **C** is an effective answer. **A** is problematic because the idea of a "key species" (and the narrator's knowledge of such species) is never really analyzed, **B** is apparently true but does not introduce an irony, and **D** is inaccurate because the Cooper's Hawk does not appear at all until later in the narrative.

2. Correct Answer: F

In Passage A, the narrator describes his excursions "during the winter months to look for Cooper's Hawks hunting in the late afternoon" (lines 20-21). Thus, the Cooper's Hawk is expected to hunt during the winter, so that **F** is the best answer. **G** is inaccurate: the Cooper's Hawk is found in Manhattan, but how often it is found there is not one of the narrator's main concerns. **H** wrongly compares the Cooper's Hawk to other hawks (which are never discussed at length), while **J** makes faulty assumptions about why the Cooper's Hawks form groups (when in fact the narrator only mentions in passing that they do form groups, not WHY).

3. Correct Answer: A

At the end of Passage A, the narrator describes birding as "an exercise in attention" (line 39) and notes that he "loved stalking the bird to see it" (lines 43-44). This information supports **A**, which rightly reflects the narrator's high interest in birding, and can be used to eliminate the negative answer **D** (which would only be relevant to the OPENING of the passage). **B** and **C** are both positive, but wrongly introduce topics (art and society, respectively) that are irrelevant to the narrator's idea of birding as a private and absorbing form of "hunting" (line 48).

4. Correct Answer: J

The word *dwell* describes the action of the "hawks" that can be found in "heavily wooded areas" (line 22). Thus, *dwell* means *live* or *reside* in this context, making **J** the best answer. **F** and **G** both refer to mental activities (as in "dwell over an idea" or "dwell on an issue"), while **H** is problematic in context: a hawk would fly, not creep, in order to move from place to place.

5. Correct Answer: C

In Passage B, the narrator describes the actions of a "white and brown" (line 53) Osprey, wonders why "New Jersey" plants Osprey roosts (line 65), and notes that the overbuilding of the roosts is "as deep and maniacal as an Osprey's eye" (lines 70-71). This information indicates that visual description (**A**), speculative questions (**B**), and simile (**D**) are all present in the passage. **C** describes a form of comparison that is absent: personification involves speaking about non-human things as though they are human, and the Osprey is never explicitly made to seem human in this manner.

6. Correct Answer: G

Early in the passage, the narrator refers to the "disappearing daylight" (line 51) in the scene that he is observing; later, he mentions that there is "another site that lies just ahead" (line 72) on his journey by car. This information indicates that **G** is an accurate answer: **F** and **H** both wrongly assume that the passage describes a morning scene, while **J** relies on a faulty inference. The narrator never mentions how far from home he is: in fact, because he is traveling, he may be driving farther and farther away from where he lives.

7. Correct Answer: B

The word "mania" occurs in the context of a discussion of Osprey roosts: the narrator notes that "there are so many of these roosts, too many" (line 68) and directly mentions that the mania involves "overbuilding" (line 70). Thus, **B** is the best choice. **A** is somewhat in context, because it does mention the Osprey, but does not directly define the "mania" as the excessive creation of Osprey roosts. **C** and **D** both relate to ornithology, but also fail to mention the "roosts" as the form taken by the "mania".

8. Correct Answer: H

In Passage A, the narrator explains that the Cooper's Hawk has "bright orange eyes", along with "a long tail streaked with black and brown, and a white and copper colored breast" (lines 13-14). In Passage B, the narrator explains that an Osprey is "white and brown" (line 53) and has "terrible golden eyes" (line 60). Thus, both passages refer to the eyes and plumage of the birds that are their points of focus. **H** is an effective answer, while only Passage B defines its bird's full range (eliminating **F**) and only Passage A refers to the noises made by the relevant bird (eliminating **G**) or the author's first sighting of the relevant bird (eliminating **J**).

9. Correct Answer: C

While the narrator of Passage A notes that he "even bought a camouflage hat" (line 45) and "didn't want to use bright colors to disturb the birds" (lines 46-47), the narrator of Passage B never describes his own appearance in any respect. (The most we learn is that he is driving to a new destination.) Thus, **C** is the best answer. **A** (the classification name in line 57), **B** (the emphasis on creating the roosts to preserve the Osprey), and **D** (the "guidebooks" mentioned in line 61) all refer to elements of Passage B. These answers should all be eliminated.

TEST 4 Answer Explanations

10. Correct Answer: F

While Passage A uses the narrator's encounter with Cooper's Hawk to lead up to the conclusion that "Birding was like hunting without the bloodshed" (line 48), Passage B uses the narrator's observations of the Osprey to examine how "most of us ornithologists begin" (line 63) to be fascinated by birds. Because the passages begin with single, individual birds to consider broader ideas, choice **F** is correct. Only Passage A discusses the possibility of being uninterested in birds (**G**) or a shift in the narrator's ideas (**J**). Moreover, in Passage A, short sentences are used to make clear points and for dramatic effect (as in lines 10 and 48): **H** wrongly attributes a negative tone to such sentences and must be eliminated.

SOCIAL SCIENCE

11. Correct Answer: C

The author describes *Habeas corpus* as, "the legal procedure that keeps the government from holding individuals indefinitely without showing cause" (lines 27-28). *Indefinitely* means "for an unlimited amount of time." Although *military trials* are mentioned in line 73, Habeas corpus is never defined as a Congressional power: thus, eliminate choice **A**. Choice **B** relies on similar confusion. Lines 41-43 state that the Founding Fathers "had been labeled enemy combatants, imprisoned indefinitely, and denied opportunities to appear before neutral judges," and elsewhere the passage discusses enemy combatants such as Lambdin P. Milligan. However, it is never noted that the right of Habeas corpus applies only to enemy combatants. **D** is a trap answer. The narrator does make mention of the suspension of "rights during a time of war" in lines 56-58, and further states that "President Lincoln insisted that he needed to suspend certain legalities in order to put down the rebellion in the South" (lines 61-63). However, Habeas corpus was a right that Lincoln suspended, not the ability to suspend such rights.

12. Correct Answer: H

In lines 56-57, the author writes that, "President Lincoln's executive action was so controversial that it was ruled unconstitutional by Roger Taney, Chief Justice of the Supreme Court." Here the narrator depicts the government's initial, negative feelings towards the suspension of Habeas corpus. Yet in lines 83-86, it is made clear that "'most historians believe that Lincoln did not violate the Constitution in suspending the writ.' Instead, 'arrests were overwhelmingly justified by the circumstances of the war.'" This evidence indicates that Lincoln's actions were justified in the public eye, or received favorably. Thus making answer choice H the correct answer. The passage does not explicitly state that "Lincoln was not the first President to suspend Habeas corpus" or even discuss other presidents by name, thus making answer choice F wrong. The author also makes no reference of Habeas corpus regarding its frequency of use during the Civil War, thus proving answer choice G to be incorrect. Only one suspension (Milligan) is discussed in

the passage, and this case occurred at the beginning of the Civil War. Lines 68-71 state that "ultimately, Congress did not contest President Lincoln's suspension of Habe-as corpus—a tacit way of expressing support for the President's decision." Answer choice **J**, contradicts with what the passage clearly states, since Lincoln (not the American Congress) too the initiative in suspending Habeas corpus.

13. Correct Answer: B

For this answer choice, you should use process of elimination because the question relies on logical inferences. Try to identify false words. In lines 9-11, the author writes that "there is no "direct definition" of executive orders, presidential memoranda, and presidential proclamations in the U.S. Constitution." In line 12, he goes on to say that these items inhabit a "legal gray area," which means that there are no "strict procedures and regulations in place," thus supporting choice **B**. The author makes no explicit linkage between the quotations in the question and *congressional policies;* although Congress is mentioned in the first paragraph, the line reference refers exclusively to presidential powers. This eliminates **A**. The author does not explicitly state that the Congressional Research Service, which simply provides a quotation, also oversees the president's powers; thus, eliminate **C**. Nor does the author mention that the powers in the line reference are the *only* "powers that the President enjoys." There could, indeed, be other powers, so eliminate **D**.

14. Correct Answer: H

Before the author introduces the word *labeled,* he writes that "The Framers of the Constitution believed strongly in Habeas corpus. They were even familiar with its operations (and suspended operations) from personal experience, since they had been labeled enemy combatants, imprisoned indefinitely, and denied opportunities to appear before neutral judges". Lines 38-39 directly indicate that *The Framers of the Constitution* had been labeled by the authorities or *classified* as *enemy combatants*, thus making answer choice **H** correct. Choices **F** and **J** misrepresent the specific context of the word labeled: although Lincoln's handling of Habeas Corpus was *publicized* and has been *analyzed* by Lincoln biographers, it is wrong to assume that the same actions apply to the Founding Fathers. (Explicit evidence, or a longer discussion of these figures, would be needed.) Answer choice **G** is wrong, since the strong negative tone of *belittled* makes it a poor synonym for the neutral word *labeled.*

TEST 4 Answer Explanations

15. Correct Answer: C

The author writes in lines 48-50 that "Merryman was arrested for attempting to hinder Union troops from moving from Baltimore to Washington," and in lines 73-74 that Lambdin P. Milligan was "a member of a paramilitary outfit that plotted to overthrow the government." Both were thus hostile to Lincoln's Union government, so that **C** is the best answer. Other answers refer to only one man or the other: Merryman alone was a legislator (lines 47-48, **A**) while Milligan alone was sentenced to death (lines 75-76, **B**). The Supreme Court did in fact play a role in both cases (lines 56-58 and 71-72), so that the facts of the passage contradict **D**.

16. Correct Answer: F

The author writes in lines 68-70 that "Congress did not contest President Lincoln's suspension of Habeas corpus—a tacit way of expressing support for the President's decision." Remember, in this context, *contest* means *dispute*. Thus, choose **F** and eliminate **J**, which wrongly indicates that Lincoln and the American Congress were at odds. The other answers misconstrue facts from the passage. The Merryman case came to the attention of Taney's Supreme Court (lines 56-58), but was not referred to the Court by Congress (**G**). And Lincoln, not Congress, cited the Constitution (lines 63-64) to justify suspending Habeas corpus (**H**).

17. Correct Answer: A

In the sixth paragraph, the author writes that "President Lincoln intervened, suspended the right of Habeas corpus, and continued to detain Merryman" (lines 53-55). This shows that the President "took part in an important legal case." Then, in the seventh paragraph, the author states that "President Lincoln defended his [executive] action by citing a provision in the Constitution—Article I, Section 9, Clause 2" (lines 63-65). This shows that the president "responded to those who opposed his decisions." Together, these pieces of evidence make **A** the best answer. The other answers place too much emphasis on small issues: Congress and Taney's Supreme Court are only important topics in the seventh paragraph (eliminating **B** and **D**) while Merryman's specific actions and the charges against him are only emphasized in the sixth paragraph (eliminating **C**).

18. Correct Answer: J

The author writes in lines 38-43 that "the Framers of the Constitution believed strongly in Habeas corpus. They were even familiar with its operations (and suspended operations) from personal experience, since they had been labeled enemy combatants, imprisoned indefinitely, and denied opportunities to appear before neutral judges." Thus, choose **J**, which describes the direct experiences of the Founding Fathers. **F** reverses the logic of the passage: if anything, the quoted evidence indicates that the British were unwilling to negotiate with the Founding Fathers over basic legal rights. Do not misinterpret the discussion of government in lines 32-37: this information provides background on Habeas corpus, but not a direct reason why the Founding Fathers supported Habeas corpus. Thus, eliminate **G** and **H**. Direct experience, not *fear* or *expertise* relating to government, explains the stances of the Founding Fathers.

19. Correct Answer: A

The author writes in the seventh paragraph that "President Lincoln defended his action by citing a provision in the Constitution—Article I, Section 9, Clause 2: The Privilege of the Writ of Habeas corpus shall not be suspended, unless when in Cases of Rebellion or Invasion the public Safety may require it." Yet in the case of Milligan, Lincoln acted in such a manner that "the Justices officially restored Habeas corpus" which "showed that Lincoln assumed extraordinary powers out of necessity" (lines 77-82). In other words, Lincoln only supported the suspension of Habeas corpus under *extreme circumstances* such as "Rebellion or Invasion." Thus, **A** is the best answer, while other answers misconstrue the content of the passage. The Milligan case shows that Lincoln wanted to let the Supreme Court "weigh in" (line 77) and that he respected the Court's authority: the passage thus contradicts **B**. Congress (**C**) and the Constitution (**D**) are important to the Merryman case (lines 46-70) but are never mentioned in relation to Milligan.

20. Correct Answer: H

The author writes in lines 32-33 that "Habeas corpus first appeared in the British tract of rights known as the Magna Carta (1215)," eliminating choice **F**. He then writes in lines 35-37 that "Habeas corpus is viewed as a fundamental tenet of English common law. Some say that, without this foundational right, the significance of all other rights crumbles," eliminating choice **G**. Finally, as the author writes in lines 38-39, "the Framers of the Constitution believed strongly in Habeas corpus." This final piece of information eliminates choice **J** and leaves choice **H**. The process of amending the Constitution is never addressed in this passage, and Lincoln in fact used "a provision in the Constitution" (line 64) to justify *suspending* Habeas corpus.

HUMANITIES

21. Correct Answer: D

The author explains that the reaction to tragedy depicted in the sixteenth-century painting *Landscape with the Fall of Icarus*, "may strike many of us as bizarre" (line 35). And in the last paragraph, the author writes that "one can begin to reconcile how we today react to catastrophe, and how older cultures did" (lines 69-70). Together, these pieces of evidence indicate that how we respond to *catastrophes* today and how people responded to *catastrophes* in other *eras* is *incompatible*, or sharply different. Thus, **D** is the strongest answer. **A** and **B** are both contradicted by the passage: the sixteenth-century artist Pieter Bruegel addressed tragedy in his painting (second paragraph) and *Bruegel's Landscape with the Fall of Icarus* and W.H. Auden's poem "Musee des Beaux Arts" treat similar themes (fourth paragraph). For choice **C**, different *technologies* are never among the passage's main preoccupations: at most, the third paragraph describes how cultures with different technologies respond to tragedy, not how such cultures interpret myths.

22. Correct Answer: G

In the first paragraph the author writes, "Icarus, once in the air, was overcome with the thrill of this invention" (lines 8-9), eliminating **H**. The author then writes, "He ignored his father's warn-

TEST 4 Answer Explanations

ings, and flew too near the sun" (lines 9-10), eliminating **F** and **J**. This leaves **G** as the best answer. Note that Icarus and Daedalus were trying to escape King Minos (line 3), but that *desperation* to escape is never explicitly cited as a reason for the death of Icarus.

23. Correct Answer: B

The author begins the first paragraph by writing, "Among the most famous Greek myths is the story of Icarus, the son of Daedalus" (lines 1-2). He then goes on to explain the *myth* in the first paragraph, and sketches out the chain of events that leads from Daedalus's captivity to Icarus's fall. This same *myth* is referred to in the second paragraph, where the author talks about the painting *Landscape with the Fall of Icarus*. Then, in the third paragraph, the author writes (with dark humor) about how this same *myth* would be received were the fall of Icarus to actually take place in today's society. The author's main argument, regarding the myth, is that it represents a view of fate that the contemporary world does not relate to: together, this evidence makes **B** the best answer. The first paragraph does not mention the cultural role of storytelling (**A**) and makes no reference to painting (which only appears in the second paragraph, **C**). However, as described in the second paragraph, *Landscape with the Fall of Icarus* only depicts one of the *main figures* from the first paragraph, Icarus himself: Daedalus and Minos, the other two, are never mentioned in connection with the painting. Thus, **D** must be eliminated.

24. Correct Answer: G

The author writes in lines 28-31 about what is depicted in the painting: "you can just make out, in the topmost corner of the painting, a minuscule figure that appears to be tumbling from the heavens. This is Icarus falling to his death: give the painting merely a casual glance and you will miss him." Since Icarus is *minuscule*, and missed if you give the painting a *casual glance*, this figure is *easily overlooked*. This information supports choice **G** and eliminates choice **H**. There is no direct justification for **F** or **J**, and the evidence also seems to disqualify these choices: an *unusually agitated* or *elaborately drawn* figure would probably command attention, and would probably not be missed at a *casual glance*.

25. Correct Answer: B

Describing the painting in lines 18-19, the author writes that "three-quarters of the canvas depict a sea." Make sure not to focus on the wrong element of the painting: Icarus falls from the sky (**A**), a working farmer is mentioned in line 23 (**C**), and an impressive town is mentioned in line 22 (**D**). Yet because of the earlier evidence, none of these elements can take up most of the space on the canvas.

26. Correct Answer: H

In the second paragraph, the author describes the painting in detail: "a small flock of sheep is supervised by a young shepherd, the only figure in the painting who does not seem to be completely preoccupied. He is looking upward, towards some point high in the heavens" (lines 24-27). It is soon explained that the "point" is "Icarus falling to his death" (line 30). Thus, **H** is the correct answer. As described in line 23, the farmer in the painting is *self-absorbed* and would thus not notice Icarus (**F**). A man on a ship (**G**) and Daedalus (**J**) are never explicitly mentioned as fig-

ures in the painting.

27. Correct Answer: A

The author writes about the apparent message of the *painting* and the *myth*, saying that, "The people in the painting are not indifferent to the fall of Icarus, but they accept its occurrence. They know that anything they say cannot change the boy's fate" (lines 59-62). He then introduces the poem which is "inspired by Bruegel's painting" (line 63) The poem is about how we must accept death and *suffering* because we cannot *change* it from happening. It will happen, as the author writes in the last quoted line of the poem, "While someone else is eating or opening a window or just walking dully along" (lines 67-68). Such "instances of human tragedy" are bound to happen, and these *instances* "do not necessarily interrupt the course of everyday life." Choices **B** and **C** mention issues that the passage never addresses: the historical connection between painting and poetry and the nature of Auden's other poems, respectively. The author would also disagree with **D**: because the people in *Landscape with the Fall of Icarus* "know that anything they say cannot change the boy's fate," they would in fact *understand* matters of life and death.

28. Correct Answer: G

The author presents the *myth* by writing in lines 54-59, "One of the most universal of all classical myths concerning life and death is that of the 'Moirai,' the god-like sisters of fate who spin the thread of each individual's life and can snip that thread at will. Death happens: searching for the reason why cannot change the situation." This quote emphasizes that "death happens" and that matters such as life and death "are far beyond human control." Thus, **G** is the best answer. Because the author never creates a direct link between the myth of the Moirai and *art* or *great accomplishments*, **F** and **J** should be eliminated quickly. The myth of the Moirai can itself seem bleak and disillusioning in the author's presentation, but the myth itself is about fate, not about knowledge and disillusionment: on account of this, eliminate trap answer **H**.

29. Correct Answer: D

In the third paragraph, the author describes heightened social and media involvement in tragedy. However, the author declares that "there are elements of the world that are simply beyond our influence" (lines 76-77) and asserts that "it is necessary to know one's place (line 79). It is reasonable to conclude that the author would not agree with modern and invasive approaches to tragedy, so that **D** is the best answer. The paragraph is about an imagined, hypothetical scenario involving Icarus, not about events that have happened in the real world: were are not given any information about the popularity of Landscape, with the Fall of Icarus (**A**) or actual media spectacles (**C**). Read the entire passage carefully, and you will see that the author is criticizing the kind of approach discussed in the third paragraph: the positive answer **B** misstates the author's attitude as one of justification.

30. Correct Answer: F

In lines 76-79 of the last paragraph, the author asserts that "there are elements of the world that are simply beyond our influence; why not follow that sturdy farmer, and improve on what small patches of the world we can improve?" The *sturdy farmer* is focusing on something that *directly affects* his life, and the author believes that people today should do the same. Thus, **F** is the strongest answer. Because this paragraph is about how to live life, not what kind of art to value, **J** should be readily eliminated. Both **G** and **H** can be tricky answers: however, they do not line up directly with the idea of improving what is closest to us. In fact, for some people, difficult philosophical inquiry may be a close concern (contradicting **G**), while intellectual greatness may be a distant issue (contradicting **H**).

NATURAL SCIENCE

31. Correct Answer: B

The author writes in the third paragraph, "the Kepler telescope recently hit a milestone: in the course of an imaging mission that took place from 2009 to 2013, the Kepler unveiled and recorded over 1,000 new planets outside our solar system (known as 'exo-planets'), including a large number of Earth twin candidates" (lines 29-34). The author also quotes a "decidedly optimistic astronomer named Elisa Quitana (line 45). These references show that there is some *enthusiasm* surrounding the *search for an Earth twin planet*. Then, in the last paragraph, the author writes, "the findings of the Kepler telescope are not nearly definitive" (lines 75-76), supporting the idea that no *definitive results* have been produced. Choices **A** and **D** both rely on factors that the author never addresses: the passage is focuses on present Earth twin standards and expert reactions the Earth twin search, not on changes in Earth twin standards and on public responses. Choice **C** is contradicted by lines 48-53, which describe a potential earth twin that orbits a star "smaller and cooler than our own sun" (line 50).

32. Correct Answer: J

After the author mentions the *milestone* (line 30), he explains what the milestone is: "in the course of an imaging mission that took place from 2009 to 2013, the Kepler unveiled and recorded over 1,000 new planets outside our solar system (known as 'exo-planets'), including a large number of Earth twin candidates" (lines 30-34). New planets have indeed been discovered, but to assume that photographs of these have been published (**F**) or that these new Earth twin candidates have been accepted (**H**) is to assume information that the passage never provides. Choice **J** also relies on a faulty assumption: though the Kepler technology is impressive, there is no indication that it was refined at the time of the *milestone*, or refined at all.

33. Correct Answer: D

In the fourth paragraph, the author writes, "The most promising of these candidates is Kepler-186f, which is only 1.1 times the size of Earth," which eliminates **B** and **C**. He then writes, "In addition to its comparable size, Kepler-186f orbits its star within its "habitable zone"—that is, at a distance where liquid water could potentially exist," eliminating **A**. And finally, the author writes, "Still, there are many unknowns involved. For instance, in order to sustain liquid water, Kepler-186f would need to have an atmosphere containing enough carbon dioxide to trap heat energy, much as the atmosphere of Earth itself does…this condition remains to be investigated" (lines 39-44),

pointing to choice **D**. While this planet is located "at a distance where liquid water could potentially exist" (line 38-39), the author does not say that water has definitively been found on Kepler-186f.

34. Correct Answer: G

After the author mentions these two films in the first paragraph, he writes, "The result is that today's film audiences are more familiar than ever with 'visitors of another kind,' to the point where we are perhaps inured to the idea that there might be life out there, other than ourselves" (lines 4-7). The word *inured* means to get used to something, so that **G** accurately describes audiences *well acquainted* with images of aliens. Other answers misrepresent the author's emphasis in this passage: the philosophical content (**F**), profits (**H**), and special effects (**J**) associated with movies are topics that lie outside this brief discussion of audiences that our now accustomed to the idea of extraterrestrial life. Eliminate these answers based on their false words. .

35. Correct Answer: A

In this sentence the author writes, "For years now, astrophysicists in California have been poring over satellite data and images in search of an *Earth twin*." There is no reason to assume a negative tone (**B**), since the scientists are searching under the assumption that the data is valid; however, the scientists are searching for an Earth twin itself, not seeking public approval for the idea (**C**). Also, the data is part of a search and is already valid itself: the presence of an earth twin, not the data, is what must be validated (**D**).

36. Correct Answer: J

The author tells us what an *exo-planet* is in the fourth paragraph by writing about "planets outside our solar system (known as "exo-planets")." All the other definitions are too narrow: an exo-planet may in fact orbit a dwarf star (**F**), be an Earth twin candidate (**G**), or differ radically from Earth (**H**). Yet planets that fulfill none of these conditions may still be found outside Earth's solar system, and none of these fits the explicit definition of an exo-planet.

37. Correct Answer: C

The author refers to the idea that "the attempt to find an Earth twin is merely a modern day reenactment of the quest for the Holy Grail, or the hunt for El Dorado—in short, a fool's errand" (lines 24-26). However, the author then notes that Earth twin "naysayers may find themselves backpedaling on their earlier pessimism" (lines 28-29). In other words, the negative analogies between an Earth twin and ideas such as the Holy Grail and El Dorado may be reversed, and may be too pessimistic: together, this information supports choice **C**. Other answers rely on faulty logic. The idea of an Earth twin is a divisive idea, but never makes it clear whether most experts accept or reject it (**A**). There is resistance to the Earth twin idea, but not necessarily to the innovative technology that has been used to examine earth twins (**B**). Finally, while analogies have been drawn between the search for an earth twin and the search for the Holy Grail or El Dorado, it should not be concluded from this that the terms "Holy Grail" and "El Dorado" are replacing the term "Goldilocks orb" (**D**).

TEST 4 Answer Explanations

38. Correct Answer: H

The author writes in lines 49-50 that "an M-type dwarf star…is smaller and cooler than our own sun." Use this data to systematically eliminate **F**, **G**, and **J**, leaving **H** as the only answer that fits both conditions.

39. Correct Answer: C

In this last paragraph the author writes, "Nonetheless, the findings of the Kepler telescope are not nearly definitive. Much more remains to be discovered, and the Kepler itself, having suffered a malfunction in 2014, needs to be repaired. The search for an Earth twin will no doubt continue" (lines 75-79). In the correct choice **C**, the *obstacles* are that the *findings* are not *definitive* and the Kepler has *suffered a malfunction*. And the *uncertainty* is that *much more remains to be discovered* and that the *search continues*. If the search will continue, it is unlikely that scientists will return to negative *earlier views* (**A**). And because the Kepler telescope has proven highly useful despite the mentioned malfunction, it is unlikely that the technology it uses is *deeply flawed* (**B**). In returning to the topic of movie-goers, the author only states that visions of extraterrestrial life are still confined to movies: we do not know enough about actual extraterrestrial life to decide whether it would disappoint movie-goers or not (**D**).

40. Correct Answer: G

The author describes an "Earth twin" as "a planet which is similar in size to our own, and which orbits its star at a distance comparable to that at which our own Earth orbits the sun" (lines 14-16). An Earth twin could also be found among "planets that orbit their stars at rates comparable to our own, 365-day orbit" (line 70-71). This information supports choice **G** and contradicts choice **J**. To eliminate **F**, note in lines 40-43 that high carbon dioxide would make a planet a more likely Earth twin and would help it to sustain liquid water. To eliminate **H**, note in the second-to-last paragraph that only *some* earth twins are more than 150 parsecs away from Earth; others may be much closer.

Test 5

READING TEST
35 Minutes—40 Questions

DIRECTIONS: There are four passages in this test. Each passage is followed by several questions. After reading a passage, choose the best answer to each question and fill in the corresponding oval on your answer document. You may refer to the passages as often as necessary.

Passage I

LITERARY NARRATIVE: This passage is adapted from the short story "The Map and the Mandala." The action is set in the southeast Asian country Myanmar (formerly Burma); Yangon was once the country's capital city.

When we were kids, Aung Ban and I used to get up early, and climb the evergreen trees that grew at the very edge of our village. Once at the top, we'd watch the sun rise, the faint hints of dawn creeping into the lower edges of the
5 sky. Sometimes, we would imagine that we could see all the way to China from up there. Aung Ban would say, "Hey, do you see the Great Wall over there?" And I would say no, because of course I had been told it's impossible to see that far.

10 "What's wrong with your eyes?" he would tease me. "It's right there!" I didn't know he was teasing me at the time, and I would always start crying and worrying about my poor eyesight. When we would get back to the village, grandmother would take one look at my red eyes and tears,
15 and I would explain how my eyes were so bad I couldn't even see the Great Wall of China from the top of the highest tree on the ridge.

"Your older brother is a cheeky little runt who's going to help me twice as long tomorrow picking tea," she would
20 say, and cook me a plate of fried banana leaves. All through my boyhood, grandmother always supported me, even as I got older and came to the decision to leave our small village, and to go to university in Mandalay—the second largest city in Myanmar, and some 350 kilometers from home.

25 My mother had not been pleased.

"Our family has lived here for generations," she said one evening at dinner, soon after I had received my acceptance letter to Parinya University. Mother said the words not so much to state a fact as to affirm a rule that was
30 not to be broken. I glanced up at her, feeling slightly hurt—why couldn't she be proud of my achievement?—but she quickly looked away.

Sitting around our unvarnished wooden table, we all ate in silence—me, Aung Ban, mother, father, grandmother,
35 and Uncle Bip. A few small candles illuminated the room: thatched walls, a rusted propane tank, a single burner, an old wok lying in the dirt. A bamboo ladder led up to our loft, where we all slept together on the floor. We were a family, an indestructible unit, unbroken for centuries—at least until
40 now. Before me, no one had ever left. No one had ever wanted to leave. At least, I didn't think so, until the next morning, when I was out in the tea fields with grandmother, counting down the days until I could pack my bags.

It was April, the very peak of the hot season in Myanmar.
45 As I worked, picking tea leaves and dropping them into the basket I held on my back, I had to keep wiping my brow with a rag, to keep the sweat from rolling into my eyes.

"There, there," said grandmother. I hadn't known she was right behind me. "Take a rest for a moment. You'll wear
50 yourself out!"

I stood up and turned. She stood with her hand outstretched, holding a cup full of cool water from the well. I took it, and drained it instantly, before thanking her.

"Don't worry about your mother," she said, taking the
55 cup from my hand, and it took me a moment to realize that she was talking about that dinner so full of tense silence. "Deep down, she's proud of you. We're all proud of you."

I tried to protest, but she shook her head.

"Did you know," she said, "that I once dreamed of
60 joining a dance troupe in Yangon?"

I shook my head no, feeling puzzled.

"I really did want to, when I was a girl, not much younger than you are now. Of course, I married your grandfather instead. But I still think about it sometimes.
65 What would my life have been like, had I left this place?"

She stopped speaking, and glanced around, out at the rolling green hills all around us. She sighed, looking back at me, and smiled once more.

GO ON TO THE NEXT PAGE.

"Make us proud," was all she said, before making her
70 way back to her basket, already half full with leaves.

When I was in my third year at the university,
grandmother passed away. I still think about that moment we
had in the tea fields. Does everyone dream of a bigger life,
outside the village? I'm not sure. But sometimes, when I'm
75 working very hard on my studies, I think about grandmother,
and how maybe I'm doing this for her just as much as I am for
me.

1. The passage states that Aung Ban is the narrator's:

   A. cousin.
   B. uncle.
   C. brother.
   D. classmate.

2. The details in the passage most strongly suggest that one
   consistency in the grandmother's character is that she:

   F. encouraged the other family members to support the
      narrator's plan to attend the university.
   G. showed the narrator support and compassion at
      different stages of his life in the village.
   H. turned down multiple opportunities to leave the
      village where her family lives.
   J. has tried to encourage her family members to share
      her interest in dance.

3. As stated in the narrator's account, all of the following
   were features of the narrator's family living space
   EXCEPT:

   A. candles to provide lighting.
   B. a propane tank.
   C. a worn and dirty rug.
   D. a bamboo ladder.

4. It can reasonably be inferred from the passage that the
   narrator's mother reacted to the narrator's university
   acceptance in a manner that:

   F. earned a harsh reprimand from the narrator's
      grandmother.
   G. persuaded the narrator to modify his educational
      goals.
   H. caused the narrator to wish for a different and less
      troubling response.
   J. reminded the narrator that he had been fundamentally
      unhappy in the village.

5. In the context of the passage, the narrator's family as a
   whole can best be described as:

   A. multi-generational and seemingly impossible to
      disrupt.
   B. incapable of understanding the narrator's desire to
      leave the village.
   C. distressed by the impoverished conditions of village
      life.
   D. intolerant of conflict but eager to make lifestyle
      changes.

6. It can be reasonably inferred from the grandmother's
   statement in lines 18-19 of the third paragraph that the
   grandmother intends to:

   F. feed the narrator to compensate for his family's
      negligence.
   G. punish Aung Ban for teasing the narrator.
   H. support the narrator in his desire to travel to China.
   J. report Aung Ban's behavior to other families in the
      village.

7. In context, the final paragraph (lines 71-77) serves all of
   the following functions within the passage EXCEPT:

   A. suggesting a possible motivation for the narrator's
      course of studies.
   B. raising a broad question about the individuals in the
      narrator's village.
   C. referring to an incident described at greater length
      earlier in the passage.
   D. outlining the narrator's plans for eventual travel to
      new countries.

8. It can be reasonably be inferred from the second
   paragraph (lines 10-17) that the narrator believed that he
   could not see the Great Wall of China on account of his:

   F. worrying personality.
   G. young age.
   H. flawed vision.
   J. position in the tree.

9. The passage suggests that "joining a dance troupe in
   Yangon" (line 60) can best be understood as:

   A. an objective that the narrator's mother has criticized.
   B. a sign of the grandmother's considerable knowledge
      of art and culture.
   C. a goal that many residents of the village share.
   D. an ambition that the narrator's grandmother never
      fulfilled.

GO ON TO THE NEXT PAGE.

10. According to the passage, the month of April is significant because it is:

F. a time when the weather is especially hot in Myanmar.
G. the month when the narrator first decided to attend the university.
H. the most busy time for picking tea leaves and performing other labor.
J. the month that the narrator and Aung Ban most enjoyed during childhood.

Passage II

SOCIAL SCIENCE: This passage is adapted from the article "The Major League Lifestyle."

Do you want a high paying job? Forget about law or medicine; instead, try professional baseball. The average Major League Baseball (MLB) player made over 3.3 million dollars in 2013, and the highest-paid player that year, Alex
5 Rodriguez, earned 29 million. In the 2014 season, the minimum salary for an MLB player was $500,000.

Baseball players did not always make enough money to pay off the national debt of a small country. As recently as the 1960s, many players needed jobs in the offseason for financial
10 reasons. However, the change in the state of affairs can be attributed, in large part, to only three baseball players: Curt Flood, Andy Messersmith, and Dave McNally. These men are certainly not as famous as the mythical Babe Ruth, the legendary Cy Young, and the estimable Willie Mays, yet
15 Flood, Messersmith, and McNally were instrumental in changing the rules that governed the financial side of baseball.

The outsized impact that Messersmith and McNally had upon the game of baseball can be traced to their action against a rule known as the Reserve Clause. According to this clause,
20 once a player signed on with a given team, that team "reserved" the rights to the player, at least until he was traded or released from his contract. Essentially, players were the property of their teams. Only through release from his original team could a player decide where to play. In practice,
25 though, a player's release usually signaled the end of his career.

Despite these rules, Messersmith and McNally went into the 1975 season on their respective teams without having signed new Reserve Clause deals. Their goal: free agency, the
30 right to decide where they played.

This was not the first time that baseball players had attempted to gain free agency. In the early 1970s, Curt Flood, an outfielder for the St. Louis Cardinals, had refused to accept a trade to the Philadelphia Phillies. Instead of reporting to the
35 Phillies, Flood sued to establish free agency and sought outside assistance.

That assistance came in the form of Marvin Miller. An economist by training, Miller had previously bargained on behalf of an America steelworkers' union. However, since
40 1965 Miller had been the leader of the labor union for the MLB players. At the time, the minimum salary for an MLB player was $6000, a figure that had not changed in two decades; the average salary for players was $19,000. Players with poor pension plans had no real venues for airing
45 grievances. Miller had been brought in to change all this.

The Curt Flood case was the opportunity Miller had been waiting for: he even described Flood as "a union-leader's dream." Despite this, Miller was under no illusions about Flood's slim chances of success. Flood was only the
50 third player to challenge the reserve clause, and success would require overturning a 1921 precedent by Supreme Court justice Oliver Wendell Holmes. Flood went forward nonetheless, convinced that his actions would benefit other players.

55 Ultimately, Miller's negative instincts were right. Flood did indeed lose the case. In 1972, the Supreme Court voted against Flood in a five-to-three split, with one justice withdrawing from the proceedings and one switching against Flood at the last minute. In reality, Flood's case was
60 undermined by a technicality: the court agreed that he had the right to serve as a free agent, but also asserted that collective bargaining was necessary for free agency negotiations. Baseball officials, however, got the message. The pressure on baseball owners that resulted from Flood's suit enabled
65 Miller to bargain for arbitration of grievances and release conditions.

In December of 1975, after Messersmith and McNally completed their season without official contracts, arbitrator Peter Seitz ruled the two players free agents. Thus, free
70 agency as we know it was created. While team owners have repeatedly tried to find ways to thwart free-agency rights, the practice appears to be here to stay.

Both players and owners have benefited from free agency. Naturally, the astronomical rise in salaries has been a
75 result of players' superior negotiating powers. The owners, for their part, have seen team values skyrocket. In 1975, Bill Veeck bought the Chicago White Sox for $10 million dollars. Today, the average value of an MLB team is $811 million. Baseball has become big business.

80 Only the fans, who have seen ticket prices skyrocket along with everything else, have really lost out. In the late 1970s, admission to watch the Philadelphia Phillies play was

GO ON TO THE NEXT PAGE.

a mere 50 cents; a standing room only ticket now costs $17. In addition, with the constant movement of players from team
85 to team, fans often feel less affection for athletes who seem to be in the game very much for the money.

11. The passage as a whole can best be described as:

    A. an argument in favor of free agency for baseball players.

    B. an overview of the acceptance of free agency in the sport of baseball.

    C. a condemnation of how baseball has become a multi-million dollar business.

    D. a nostalgic look at the earlier, simpler days of a professional sport.

12. It can reasonably be inferred from the statement "Baseball players did not always make enough money to pay off the national debt of a small country" (lines 7-8) that the author:

    F. is aware that high salaries were not always an essential part of baseball.

    G. believes that baseball players should donate more of their money to worthy causes.

    H. is envious of the salaries of baseball's biggest stars.

    J. is enthusiastic about baseball's recent financial trends.

13. The passage notes all of the following as changes that have occurred following the widespread use of free agency in baseball EXCEPT:

    A. an increase in salaries for players.

    B. an increase in ticket prices for consumers.

    C. an increase in the value of Major League teams.

    D. an increase in team loyalty among fans.

14. The passage states that, before taking on Curt Flood's case, Marvin Miller had bargained for:

    F. the Philadelphia Phillies.

    G. the Saint Louis Cardinals.

    H. an American steelworkers' union.

    J. Andy Messersmith and Dave McNally.

15. The author mentions Curt Flood, Andy Messersmith, and Dave McNally primarily in order to:

    A. give examples of three of baseball's famed players.

    B. list three of the most highly paid players in the history of baseball.

    C. present three players who had a significant impact on the economics of baseball.

    D. mention three players who have not been sufficiently recognized for their talents in business.

16. The main purpose of the third paragraph (lines 17-26) is to:

    F. show how players stayed active in the sport after being released from their teams.

    G. outline a problem that severely limited baseball players' freedom.

    H. discuss the origins of the Reserve Clause.

    J. highlight how bargaining players had significant advantages over team owners.

17. The main function of the eighth paragraph (lines 55-66) is to:

    A. present both the details of a Supreme Court ruling and this ruling's overall importance.

    B. depict Miller as idealistic in his attempt to win greater rights for baseball players.

    C. question the impact of a previous Supreme Court ruling.

    D. indicate that Miller felt a strong bond to his client Curt Flood.

18. The passage notes that all of the following were results of Flood's 1972 Supreme Court case EXCEPT:

    F. the justices ruled against Flood.

    G. Miller was able to bargain with baseball officials in order to gain expanded rights for all players.

    H. the Court ruled that the Reserve Clause was unconstitutional.

    J. the Court agreed that Flood had a right to free agency.

19. It can reasonably be inferred from the passage that by the end of December of 1975, Messersmith and McNally were:

    A. the first two free agents in the history of baseball.

    B. suspended without pay due to their attempts to gain greater bargaining rights.

    C. traded to other teams without having any say in the matter.

    D. frustrated with their contractual obligations.

20. The passage indicates that "the astronomical rise in salaries" (line 74) has primarily been a result of:

    F. economic inflation in various business sectors.

    G. an increase in the cost of attending baseball games.

    H. the increased bargaining abilities of baseball players.

    J. an increase in the overall number of talented and popular players.

GO ON TO THE NEXT PAGE.

Passage III

HUMANITIES: This passage is adapted from the personal essay "Writing Irish: Contemporary Literature and the Weight of the Past."

"You are an Irish author; therefore, you must write about Ireland." That is the unspoken standard that everyone, from colleagues to reviewers to the members of my immediate family, has always applied to my writing. There are good and
5 clear reasons why this is the case: if you are a college writing student, you will be instructed to "write what you know" when you are starting out. The same reasoning persists in writing MFA and PhD degree programs, and into the increasingly and self-consciously international world of
10 professional writing. Readers today want to be transported to Russia, and Uganda, and, yes, Ireland. Who better to whisk them to that far-off land than an actual Russian, or Ugandan, or—in my case—a light-skinned, red-haired, full-blooded Irishman?

15 All this makes sense, but all of it has very little to do with the kind of writing that most interests me.

Beyond a certain point, "writing what you know" can turn a creative writer into a tour guide. There is nothing wrong with sharing knowledge, yet other fields—
20 anthropology, history, cultural studies—are designed to do that and do it better. Creative writing at its highest level is often explained as serving a different purpose: as the theory goes, masterpieces of fiction and poetry help us to see universal human traits, urges, and forces, the ones that apply
25 to any and all cultures.

On occasion, it is possible for a writer to approach these universals while doing a little tour-guiding on the side. You can learn quite a bit about nineteenth-century Russian manners by reading Tolstoy—but who ever read Tolstoy
30 exclusively for that? We read him because he clearly saw the attractions of wealth, fame, romance, and religion. His primary characters were Russian aristocrats (like Tolstoy himself) but his themes are relevant continents away and centuries later.

35 My own quest for such universals has taken me along a different route. The last three books that I have written are (from least to most recent) a comical murder mystery set in contemporary New York, a satire of old-time vaudeville, and a crime saga that draws in characters from Australia, Japan,
40 and French Canada. Why did I write these stories? Part of me, first of all, has always been genuinely intrigued by these topics. (My mother always sang and whistled little snatches of show tunes; the vaudeville one was something I had to get out of my system, and something essential to who I have
45 always been.) But part of me has always been convinced that I could see universal themes more clearly if Ireland wasn't getting in the way. I stayed as far away as I could from local color to make the comedy, the tragedy, and the connections to the reader more vivid.

50 It would be dishonest of me, though, to deny the temptations of local color. Especially when writing short stories, I have forced myself to steer clear of Ireland, even the positive parts. And why? Would describing one rolling green field or one lithe dark-haired lass really hurt anyone that
55 much? Probably not, but it would probably come out as some tired commonplace. W.B. Yeats and James Joyce described all this first, and described it better than anyone could, and it is best to leave it at that—or to find some corner of Ireland that nobody has described. That is what, on occasion, I have
60 done; the traffic patterns in Dublin interest me more than the poetic lasses and the sunsets. I have no use for those. I doubt that the modern reader, ever fearful of books flooded with commonplaces, would either.

Yet could part of it also be that "writing what you know"
65 is really a stroke of unwelcome pride, not a gesture of wise humility?

To answer that, I always think back to one of my own favorite Irish authors, humorist Flann O'Brien. Now, O'Brien was writing at a time when the tour-guide approach to Irish
70 culture was very popular in fiction—sturdy peasants, beautiful landscapes, quaint old legends. It's an appealing picture of Ireland, but a simple and rosy one. O'Brien seemed to find all this amusing: instead of throwing out local color (as I have) he took these elements and exaggerated them to
75 the point of madness in novels like *At Swim-Two-Birds* and *The Poor Mouth*. Never will you read books with such ludicrously inappropriate "quaint and poetic" language, or with so many true-to-stereotype Irishmen wandering the countryside and eating potatoes.

80 O'Brien had a good laugh at the expense of "writing what you know," and left us all a cautionary lesson. "Writing what you know" often means "writing cultural clichés that everyone knows," while writing yourself into boredom. Better to write what you don't know and to keep the reader—
85 and yourself—always excited.

21. The passage is best described as being told from the point of view of a writer who is:

   A. recommending that all young writers read Tolstoy for inspiration.
   B. taking issue with the common saying "write what you know."
   C. composing novels primarily set in contemporary Ireland.
   D. lamenting the difficulties of earning one's living as a writer.

GO ON TO THE NEXT PAGE.

22. It can reasonably be inferred from the passage that the author feels a sense of frustration as a result of

   F. the expectation that he write about Ireland because he is Irish.
   G. the lack of a true literary culture in Ireland.
   H. his inability to accurately portray Irish culture in words.
   J. his inability to write more vividly than James Joyce or W.B. Yeats..

23. The author feels that in all of the following roles it is appropriate to write mainly "as a tour guide" EXCEPT as:

   A. an anthropologist.
   B. a social scientist.
   C. a novelist.
   D. a historian.

24. The passage indicates that, unlike some popular contemporary writings, "masterpieces of creative fiction and poetry"(line 23) tend to:

   F. appeal to only a small subset of readers.
   G. fade in popularity as time passes.
   H. appeal to audiences beyond a single culture
   J. be commercially unsuccessful when they appear.

25. It can be reasonably inferred from the passage that Flann O'Brien's novels *At Swim-To-Birds* and *The Poor Mouth* are works of:

   A. literary criticism.
   B. comedy.
   C. poetry.
   D. drama.

26. As described in the passage, the author's ideas about the use of "local color" and cultural details can best be summarized by which of the following statements?

   F. Local color is a narrative element that can seem attractive, but that can exert a negative influence if it is not consciously resisted.
   G. Highly educated writers have used local color, and have irresponsibly encouraged less accomplished authors to do so.
   H. Local color is used primarily by authors who hope to challenge their readers' expectations and create a broader market for satire.
   J. The use of local color is an aesthetically stimulating route for authors who are incapable of addressing universal themes.

27. The author discusses his three most recently written books primarily to show that:

   A. his work has largely been ignored by critics.
   B. he is widely published and respected.
   C. writers do not necessarily focus on their places of origin.
   D. only by appealing to a broad audience can one have success in the arts.

28. In the passage, the author implies that images of "sturdy peasants, beautiful landscapes, quaint old legends"(lines 70-71) are features of a movement in Irish writing that:

   F. was concerned with performing new research on Irish traditions.
   G. tried to accurately depict Ireland at its most prosperous.
   H. was much more popular when it first appeared than it is at present.
   J. offered a pleasant but ultimately unrealistic view of Ireland.

29. The author mentions "wandering the countryside" and "eating potatoes" as examples of activities that:

   A. were used in novels glorifying Ireland but have not been truly understood.
   B. are Irish stereotypes that appeared in the novels of Flann O'Brien.
   C. had fallen into disuse by the final decades of the twentieth century.
   D. would be considered strange and surprising by many people of Irish descent.

30. The last sentence of the passage can best be described as:

   F. an unexpected rejection.
   G. a tired commonplace.
   H. a constructive recommendation.
   J. a troubling warning.

GO ON TO THE NEXT PAGE.

Passage IV

NATURAL SCIENCE: Passage A is from *The Practice and Science of Drawing* (1913) by Harold Speed; Passage 2 is from "Optical Illusions, Demystified" (2015) by Paula Marino.

Passage A by Harold Speed

The pictures on our retinas are flat, of two dimensions, the same as the canvas on which we paint. If you examine these visual pictures without any prejudice, as one may with a camera obscura, you will see that they are composed of masses
5 of colour in infinite variety and complexity, of different shapes and gradations, and with many varieties of edges; giving to the eye the illusion of nature with actual depths and distances, although one knows all the time that it is a flat table on which one is looking.

10 Seeing then that our eyes have only flat pictures containing two-dimension information about the objective world, from whence is this knowledge of distance and the solidity of things? How do we see the third dimension, the depth and thickness, by means of flat pictures of two dimensions?

15 The power to judge distance is due principally to our possessing two eyes situated in slightly different positions, from which we get two views of objects, and also to the power possessed by the eyes of focussing at different distances, others being out of focus for the time being. In a picture the eyes can
20 only focus at one distance (the distance the eye is from the plane of the picture when you are looking at it), and this is one of the chief causes of the perennial difficulty in painting backgrounds. In nature they are out of focus when one is looking at an object, but in a painting the background is
25 necessarily on the same focal plane as the object. Numerous are the devices resorted to by painters to overcome this difficulty, but they do not concern us here.

The fact that we have two flat pictures on our two retinas to help us, and that we can focus at different planes, would not
30 suffice to account for our knowledge of the solidity and shape of the objective world, were these senses not associated with another sense all important in ideas of form, the sense of touch.

Passage B by Paula Marino

Some of the most famous optical illusions tempt us to see three dimensions when we are only seeing two. There is an old
35 story about a contest between two ancient Greek painters: Zeuxis, who painted grapes so realistic that birds flew down to peck at them, and Parrahasius, who painted a curtain so realistic that Zeuxis attempted to pull it open. (Needless to say, Parrhasius won.) More modern optical illusions appeal
40 similarly to sight, depth, and touch when, in reality, the only register of experience involved is a flat surface. The painters of

the late nineteenth and early twentieth century loved the "trompe l'oeil" (literally, "fool the eye" in French) effects that can attend hyper-realistic still lifes, complete with flawlessly
45 rendered surfaces and shadows. Today, there is even a vogue for three-dimensional tattoos, which make it look as though sculptured spines and flourishes are jutting right out of one's skin.

We're already pretty gullible from two dimensions into
50 three, but a three-dimension into three-dimension optical illusion is something else entirely. A few years ago, artist Johannes Stotter began circulating photographs of a large, red, perfectly three-dimensional parrot perched on a log. The parrot, however, wasn't a parrot: it was a woman in extremely
55 elaborate body paint, striking a precarious pose.

Stotter has repeated the trick by getting body-painted models to pose as chameleons and tree frogs—all of them completely true-to-life, at least at a glance. He is relying, of course, on the scrambling process that accompanies any optical
60 illusion, the fact that "our eyes skim and our brains tend to jump to conclusions," according to science journalist Michelle Castillo: "By arranging a series of patterns, images, and colors strategically, or playing with the way an object is lit, you can trick the brain into seeing something that isn't there. How you
65 perceive proportion can also be altered depending on the known objects that are nearby. It's not magic — it's an optical illusion."

Such optical illusions capitalize on the delay between when light rays initially bounce off an object, thus entering our
70 eyes, and when the brain fully makes sense of the information conveyed by those rays. That delay is roughly one tenth of a second. And in that tenth of a second, a clever two-dimensional composition can dupe is into believing that a painted image is subtly moving, that two dimensions have become three, or that
75 a woman in body paint is really a parrot.

> Questions 31-34 ask about Passage A.

31. According to Passage A, what difference between a real background and a painted background makes painting three-dimensional backgrounds so problematic?

A. A painted background is at a set distance from the eye; a real background involves different distances.

B. A painted background is static; a real background is often populated by moving people and foliage.

C. A painted background is normally a few colors; a real background involves many colors.

D. A painted background is seen through one retina; a real background is seen through both retinas.

GO ON TO THE NEXT PAGE.

32. As used in line 2, the word *examine* most nearly means:

F. interrogate.
G. inspect.
H. critique.
J. enable.

33. The author of Passage A develops his ideas about how humans perceive space and depth by:

A. making extended reference to a single well-known experiment.
B. offering general statements about the workings of the eyes.
C. arguing that it is easier to survive without sight than without touch.
D. describing several illusions that are in two dimensions but appear to be in three.

34. The main purpose of the fourth paragraph of Passage A (lines 28-32) is to:

F. contradict the ideas about sight presented in lines 1-2.
G. suggest an answer to the question posed in lines 10-12.
H. expand upon the parenthetical information in lines 20-21.
J. continue the topic that was introduced in lines 25-27.

Questions 35-38 ask about Passage B.

35. The primary purpose of Passage B is to:

A. develop a new theory of how optical illusions fool their viewers.
B. encourage greater respect for the work of Johannes Stotter and other contemporary illusionists.
C. argue that three-dimensional illusions are more sophisticated than two-dimensional illusions.
D. survey and explain optical illusions from both ancient and recent times.

36. The quotation from Michelle Castillo in lines 60-61, "our eyes skim and our brains tend to jump to conclusions," serves the purpose of:

F. criticizing anyone who has been fooled by an optical illusion.
G. explaining why Stotter's work is becoming popular.
H. showing how creators of illusions choose their topics.
J. clarifying how humans react to optical illusions.

37. As it is used in line 75, the word *parrot* is best understood as a reference to:

A. an artwork from ancient times.
B. an artwork made by the author.
C. a two-dimensional illusion mentioned earlier.
D. a three-dimensional illusion mentioned earlier.

38. As it is used in line 63, the phrase *playing with* most nearly means:

F. trifling with.
G. insulting.
H. manipulating.
J. enjoying.

Questions 39-40 ask about both passages.

39. A similarity between the two passages is that they both analyze:

A. two dimensional images that appear to be three dimensional.
B. three dimensional images that appear to be two dimensional.
C. two dimensional static images that appear to be moving.
D. three dimensional images that are not the items they initially appear to be.

40. Compared to Passage A's discussion of sight and optics, Passage B's discussion can be described as

F. more focused on experiments that have been carried out by the author.
G. more focused on specific named examples that the author considers at some length.
H. less focused on the role of three dimensional illusions in depicting the human body.
J. less focused on testimony from experts known to the author.

END OF TEST 5.

STOP! DO NOT TURN THE PAGE UNTIL TOLD TO DO SO.

DO NOT RETURN TO A PREVIOUS TEST

Answer Key: TEST 5

Test 5

LITERARY NARRATIVE

1. C
2. G
3. C
4. H
5. A
6. G
7. D
8. H
9. D
10. F

HUMANITIES

21. B
22. F
23. C
24. H
25. B
26. F
27. C
28. J
29. B
30. H

SOCIAL SCIENCE

11. B
12. F
13. D
14. H
15. C
16. G
17. A
18. H
19. A
20. H

NATURAL SCIENCE

31. A
32. G
33. B
34. G
35. D
36. J
37. D
38. H
39. A
40. G

To see your scaled ACT Reading Score (1-36), determine how many questions you answered correctly and consult the Scoring Chart on Page 186 of this book.

Post-Test Analysis

This post-test analysis is essential if you want to see an improvement on your next test. Possible reasons for errors, both for the test overall and for each of the four reading passages, are listed here. Place check marks next to the types of errors that pertain to you, or write your own types of errors in the blank spaces provided.

GENERAL

◇ Spent too much time reading the passages
◇ Spent too much time answering the questions
◇ Did not attempt to finish all of the passages
◇ Did not create effective margin answers
◇ Did not use process of elimination
◇ Could not find evidence to answer the questions
◇ Could not comprehend the topics and ideas in the passages
◇ Could not understand what the questions were asking
◇ Interpreted the passages rather than using evidence

Other: _____

LITERARY NARRATIVE

◇ Spent too long reading the passage
◇ Spent too long answering the questions
◇ Could not identify the setting and characters
◇ Could not understand the plot or action
◇ Could not work effectively with tone and clues to tone

Other: _____

> **Use this form** to better analyze your performance. If you don't understand why you made errors, there is no way that you can correct them!

SOCIAL SCIENCE

◇ Spent too long reading the passage
◇ Spent too long answering the questions
◇ Could not understand the author's position or arguments
◇ Used outside knowledge rather than using evidence

Other: _____

HUMANITIES

◇ Spent too long reading the passage
◇ Spent too long answering the questions
◇ Could understand the themes and organization of the passage
◇ Could not understand the author's ideas and uses of evidence

Other: _____

NATURAL SCIENCE

◇ Spent too long reading the passage
◇ Spent too long answering the questions
◇ Found the concepts and ideas in the passage confusing
◇ Found the questions confusing
◇ Could not effectively work with the inference and logic questions

Other: _____

TEST 5 Answer Explanations

LITERARY NARRATIVE

1. Correct Answer: C

In the passage, the narrator quotes his grandmother, who describes Aung Ban as the narrator's *older brother* in line 18. Be careful when answering this question; Aung Ban and the narrator appear to be roughly the same age, but *cousin* misstates the relationship (**A**) and *classmate* (**D**) is never substantiated. The only *uncle* (**B**) that the narrator mentions is Uncle Bip in line 35.

2. Correct Answer: G

The author writes about his grandmother saying, "All through my boyhood, grandmother always supported me, even as I got older and came to the decision to leave our small village" (lines 20-22). This directly illustrates that the grandmother "showed the narrator support," as stated in choice **G**. In the passage, the only family member that the grandmother is shown to interact with at length is the narrator: because of this, there is not sufficient context for either **F** or **J**. In addition, the grandmother is only mentioned as having turned down a single opportunity, the chance to join "a dance troupe in Yangon" (line 62). The idea of "multiple opportunities" makes **H** false.

3. Correct Answer: C

The author writes, "A few small candles illuminated the room: thatched walls, a rusted propane tank, a single burner, an old wok lying in the dirt. A bamboo ladder led up to our loft, where we all slept together on the floor" (35-40). This support eliminates choices **A**, **B**, and **D**, leaving **C**. An old and dirty *rug* may seem similar to the other objects, but you cannot assume that it is in the passage if it is not mentioned; in fact, because the wok lies "in the dirt," the family may not have rugs of any sort.

4. Correct Answer: H

The narrator writes how he felt about his mother's response to his university acceptance by saying, "I glanced up at her, feeling slightly hurt— why couldn't she be proud of my achievement?" The strong negative tone and the narrator's wish for his mother to be "proud" both substantiate **H**. Other answers are negative, but involve content that the passage contradicts: the grandmother says nothing in response (**F**), the narrator continues with his goal to attend the university (**G**), and the narrator never states that he had been unhappy in the village (**J**). Note that **J** is a trap answer. The family is not wealthy, and the narrator wants a different life, but the narrator is unhappy because of his mother's response, not because he finds his lifestyle miserable.

5. Correct Answer: A

In describing his family, the narrator writes, "We were a family, an indestructible unit, unbroken for centuries" (lines 38-39). *Indestructible* and *unbroken unit* points to *impossible to disrupt* in **A**. Consider specific family members to eliminate **B** and **D**; the grandmother understands why the narrator might want to leave, and the narrator is the only one who is eager to change his lifestyle. To avoid trap answer **C**, remember not to interpret the passage. You as a reader may be distressed by the impoverished conditions described in the passage, but the narrator's family accepts these conditions without distress or even complaint.

6. Correct Answer: G

In this line reference the grandmother says, "Your older brother is a cheeky little runt who's going to help me twice as long tomorrow picking tea," suggesting that Aung Ban will be *punished* for teasing the narrator about his *poor eyesight*. Simply focus on the content of the statement to eliminate false words; since the family at large (**F**), travel to China (**H**), and other families (**J**) are never mentioned, they cannot be connected to the statement. The narrator, Aung Ban, and the grandmother are the only factors or figures involved here.

7. Correct Answer: D

Here you must eliminate every answer choice that is mentioned in the passage. The author writes, "I still think about that moment we had in the tea fields," which eliminates **C**. He goes on to write, "Does everyone dream of a bigger life, outside the village?" which eliminates **B**. And finally, he writes, "maybe I'm doing this for her just as much as I am for me," which eliminates **A**, leaving **D** as your answer. For **D** to describe the narrator, you would need to know that travel beyond Malaysia is one of the narrator's goals, and should expect other countries or continents to be named.

8. Correct answer: H

In response to why he couldn't see the *Great Wall*, the narrator writes, "I would explain how my eyes were so bad I couldn't even see the Great Wall of China from the top of the highest tree on the ridge" (lines 15-19). At least in the narrator's own mind, he couldn't see the *Wall* on account of his poor eyesight or *flawed vision*, **H**. While the narrator may in fact have a worrying personality (**F**), young age (**G**), or poor position in the tree (**J**), the narrator himself does not believe that any of these factors explain why he cannot see the wall.

9. Correct Answer: D

The grandmother writes about her *aspiration* of "joining a dance troupe in Yangon" by saying to the narrator, "I really did want to, when I was a girl, not much younger than you are now. Of course, I married your grandfather instead," suggesting that this was an unfulfilled dream or *aspiration* of hers, **D**. The other answers involve misreading or misinterpretations of the passage's content: the narrator's mother responds negatively to the narrator's ambitions, not to the grandmother's (**A**), and the narrator even states that he is "not sure" (line 76) whether people dream of lives outside the village (**C**). Choice **B** is something of a trap: the grandmother had considered being a dancer, but whether she has considerable knowledge of dance or just a passing interest is an issue that the passage never addresses.

10. Correct Answer: F

The narrator describes the significance of the time of year by writing, "It was April, the very peak of the hot season in Myanmar" (line 44). This is the only direct description of April in Myanmar: the narrator never equates the hot season with a busy time of labor (**H**). April is also significant because this is the month when the concluding discussion between the narrator and the grandmother takes place. Be careful not to falsely assume that other important moments in the passage, such as the narrator's decision to attend the university (**G**) or the narrator's experiences with Aung Ban (**J**), occurred during this month.

TEST 5 Answer Explanations

SOCIAL SCIENCE

11. Correct Answer: B

The author starts the passage with a rhetorical question: "Do you want a high paying job?" He then suggests *professional baseball* as a possible profession. But then in the following paragraph the author writes that "Baseball players did not always make enough money to pay off the national debt of a small country," suggesting that in the past baseball was not as lucrative a profession. The author goes on to write, "the change in the state of affairs can be attributed, in large part, to only three baseball players," which he then lists. In the passage, the author explains how this *change* came about through the realization of *their goal*, which was "free agency, the right to decide where they played" (lines 29-30). Finally, before he gives an "overview of the acceptance of" this practice, he writes, "This was not the first time that baseball players had attempted to gain free agency" (lines 31-32), supporting choice **B**. Both **A** and **C** are too extreme: in the final two paragraphs, the author gives a balanced discussion of the positives and negatives of free agency. While the author refers to baseball's earlier days by naming famous players in the second paragraph, choice **D** avoids the central topics of free agency and baseball-related finances, placing emphasis instead on a time period that the author never depicts at length.

12. Correct Answer: F

The author writes in the sentence following the line reference that, "As recently as the 1960s, many players needed jobs in the offseason for financial reasons," suggesting that the high salaries of today are a new development, or, in other words, "high salaries were not always [a] part of baseball." There are no words surrounding this quotation that would indicate either a strong positive or a strong negative tone; because of this, both negative answers such as **G** and **H** and the positive answer **J** can be eliminated.

13. Correct Answer: D

In the second sentence of the passage, the author writes, "The average Major League Baseball (MLB) player made over 3.3 million dollars in 2013," eliminating choice **A**. In lines 80-83, the author writes, "Only the fans, who have seen ticket prices skyrocket along with everything else, have really lost out. In the late 1970s, admission to watch the Philadelphia Phillies play was a mere 50 cents; a standing room only ticket now costs $17," eliminating choice **B**. Finally, in lines 75-78 the author writes, "The owners, for their part, have seen team values skyrocket. In 1975, Bill Veeck bought the Chicago White Sox for $10 million dollars. Today, the average value of an MLB team is $811 million," eliminating choice **C**. Furthermore, in the last sentence of the passage, the author suggests the very opposite of choice **D**, stating "In addition, with the constant movement of players from team to team, fans often feel less affection for athletes who seem to be in the game very much for the money."

14. Correct Answer: H

The author writes that before he helped the players, "Miller had previously bargained on behalf of an America steelworkers' union" (lines 38-39). Other answers refer to Curt Flood, who was connected to both the Phillies (**F**) and the Cardinals (**G**) around

the time of his case; it would be inaccurate to assume a direct connection between either of these teams and Marvin Miller. Messersmith and McNally brought their case to court after Curt Flood did, but are never defined as Miller's clients, so that **J** can also be eliminated.

15. Correct Answer: C

Before the author introduces these players, he writes in the second paragraph that, "Baseball players did not always make enough money to pay off the national debt of a small country. As recently as the 1960s, many players needed jobs in the offseason for financial reasons. However, the change in the state of affairs can be attributed, in large part, to only three baseball players: Curt Flood, Andy Messersmith, and Dave McNally" (lines 7-12). In other words, it was these three players who *impacted* the economics of baseball. Do not confuse these three players with the three genuinely "famous" players mentioned in the second paragraph (**A**). And do not make faulty assumptions based on the information provided; although Flood, Messersmith, and McNally were influential, there is nothing indicate that they were among the most highly paid baseball players (**B**) or that they were talented businessmen (**D**). They are simply the figures associated with new free agency procedures.

16. Correct Answer: G

In this paragraph, the author describes the *Reserve Clause* by writing that "according to this clause, once a player signed on with a given team, that team 'reserved' the rights to the player, at least until he was traded or released from his contract. Essentially, players were the property of their teams" (lines 19-23). Given that based on this clause the players "were the property of their teams," we can assume that this clause "severely limited baseball players' freedom." The paragraph contradicts **F**, since release from a team typically meant the end of a player's career, and **J**, since team owners had advantages over players. **H** is something of a trap: the paragraph shows how the reserve clause functions, but never explains when or how the reserve clause originated.

17. Correct Answer: A

In this paragraph, the author writes, "Flood did indeed lose the case." He then goes on to describe the specifics of this loss, writing, "Flood's case was undermined by a technicality: the court agreed that he had the right to serve as a free agent, but also asserted that collective bargaining was necessary for free agency negotiations" (lines 59-61). Finally, the author ends by describing "the ruling's overall importance" by writing, "The pressure on baseball owners that resulted from Flood's suit enabled Miller to bargain for arbitration of grievances and release conditions" (lines 63-65). The passage contradicts the idea that Miller was idealistic (**B**), since Miller had "no illusions" about the possible success of the case (line 48) The paragraph mentions a 1921 Supreme Court ruling, but only as an obstacle Flood faced; the impact or importance of this ruling is never doubted (**C**). And although Miller worked with Flood, the details of their interactions are not clear, so that "strong bond" could easily be an overstatement (**D**).

TEST 5 Answer Explanations

18. Correct Answer: H

Your answer comes from lines 55-66, in which the author writes, "Flood did indeed lose the case. In 1972, the Supreme Court voted against Flood in a five-to-three split," eliminating **F**. He then writes, "the court agreed that he had the right to serve as a free agent, but also asserted that collective bargaining was necessary for free agency negotiations," eliminating **J**. And finally, the author writes, "Flood's suit enabled Miller to bargain for arbitration of grievances and release conditions," eliminating **G**. This leaves **H** as the answer. In fact, the Supreme Court is only mentioned in the passage as voting *against* Curt Flood and his free agency cause.

19. Correct Answer: A

The author writes in lines 67-72 that "In December of 1975, after Messersmith and McNally completed their season without official contracts, arbitrator Peter Seitz ruled the two players free agents. Thus, free agency as we know it was created." So, before this time, *free agency* was not an option. Therefore, they were "the first free agents" in baseball. Because the relevant paragraph describes a positive situation for the two players, you can readily eliminate **B**, **C**, and **D**, all of which are answers that take negative tones.

20. Correct Answer: H

The author writes that "the astronomical rise in salaries has been a result of players' superior negotiating powers" (lines 74-75). Another way to describe *negotiating* is *to bargain*. The passage only briefly refers to other business sectors in the first paragraph, and only briefly discusses the most talented and popular players in the second: neither of these issues is linked to the later discussion of rising salaries. Thus, **F** and **J** can be eliminated. Choice **G** is a trap: salaries and admission costs have risen at roughly be the same time, but the passage states that *both rises* are results of free agency: rising costs have not directly caused rising salaries.

HUMANITIES

21. Correct Answer: B

In the first three paragraphs of the passage, the author shows how the idea of "writing what you know" is a somewhat undesirable artistic practice. Then, in the last paragraph, the author explicitly reveals his point of view by writing, "O'Brien had a good laugh at the expense of 'writing what you know,' and left us all a cautionary lesson. 'Writing what you know' often means 'writing cultural clichés that everyone knows,' while writing yourself into boredom" (lines 80-83). Based on this, it can be concluded that the author doesn't like the adage "write what you know." The false answers can be eliminated for a variety of reasons. Tolstoy (**A**) is only mentioned briefly in the fourth paragraph and is set forward as an admirable author, but not as one who should necessarily be read by all young writers. The author indicates in the fifth paragraph that he has not primary composed novels set in Ireland (**C**) and is concerned with the problems that rules of writing present, not the financial problems writers face (**D**).

22. Correct Answer: F

In the first sentence, the author writes, "'You are an Irish author; therefore, you must write about Ireland.' That is the unspoken standard that everyone, from colleagues to reviewers to the members of my immediate family, has always applied to my writing." But then he gives his perspective on this by writing, "All this makes sense, but all of it has very little to do with the kind of writing that most interests me." Ultimately, we can infer from this reaction that the author feels negatively towards writing about Ireland "because he is Irish," choice **F**. The author cites writers such as Yeats, Joyce, and O'Brien as members of Ireland's literary culture, so that **G** can be eliminated, but is actually uninterested in recording Irish culture or mimicking these authors, so that **H** and **J** can be eliminated.

23. Correct Answer: C

The author writes in lines 17-21, that, "Beyond a certain point, "writing what you know" can turn a creative writer into a tour guide. There is nothing wrong with sharing knowledge, yet other fields—anthropology, history, cultural studies—are designed to do that and do it better." While the first sentence in this quotation supports **C**, the second sentence eliminates choices **A**, **B**, and **D**. Remember, a "social scientist" would naturally be involved in "cultural studies."

24. Correct Answer: H

In the larger line reference, the author writes that, "masterpieces of fiction and poetry help us to see universal human traits, urges, and forces, the ones that apply to any and all cultures" (lines 23-25). All of the other answers are negative in tone or construe "masterpieces" as narrow in scope, and can thus be eliminated. Do not use outside knowledge: though some real-life masterpieces may fulfill **G**, **H**, or **J**, the author does not explicitly discuss these traits. The author is concerned with standards that make art aesthetically and intellectually valuable, not with profits or popularity.

25. Correct Answer: B

As a writer, O'Brien took standard elements of Irish fiction "and exaggerated them to the point of madness in books like *At Swim-Two-Birds* and *The Poor Mouth*. Never will you read books with such ludicrously inappropriate 'quaint and poetic' language, or with so many true-to-stereotype Irishmen wandering the countryside and eating potatoes" (lines 74-79). The *exaggeration, ludicrously inappropriate language,* and *stereotypes* all suggest that his work is that of *comedy*, choice **B**. Also, because these books are described as fictional *novels* (line 75), they could not be described as literary criticism (**A**), poetry (**C**), or drama (**D**) in terms of format.

26. Correct Answer: F

In lines 47-49, the author notes that in his own writing he "I stayed as far away as I could from local color to make the comedy, the tragedy, and the connections to the reader more vivid." He also goes on to acknowledge the "temptations of local color" (line 51) and explains that giving into such temptations can lead to books "flooded with commonplaces" (lines 62-63). Thus, answer

TEST 5 Answer Explanations

F is the best summary of the author's ideas. The other answers rely on unsubstantiated assumptions about the kind of authors who have used local color: we know that local color is attractive, but whether it is a favorite device of highly educated authors (**G**) or writers of challenging satire (**H**) is never specified. The author would also be likely to disagree with **J**: the use of local color would be aesthetically stimulating only for a few highly talented and original authors, such as Yeats and Joyce (line 56). All other authors would be likely to produce the commonplaces that the author criticizes.

27. Correct Answer: C

The author writes in lines 35-36 that his "quest for such universals has taken [him] along a different route." This is the point when he introduces his three books. After which, he writes his reason for writing them by saying, "part of me has always been convinced that I could see universal themes more clearly if Ireland wasn't getting in the way. I stayed as far away as I could from local color to make the comedy, the tragedy, and the connections to the reader more vivid" (lines 45-49). So, by bringing up his books as examples, he is showing that it isn't necessary for authors to "focus on their places of origin" in their writing. Note that the author is here discussing a personal "quest for universals," not matters of literary reputation; because choices **A, B,** and **D** relate to matters of reputation, not to the author's inspirations and creative responses, they must be eliminated.

28. Correct Answer: J

The author describes the images of "sturdy peasants, beautiful landscapes, quaint old legends" as "an appealing picture of Ireland, but a simple and rosy one." Here *simple* can mean *pleasant* and *rosy* means the picture is better than the reality. Choices **F** and **G**, which mention research and accurate depiction, do not capture the defective quality that the author sees in simple and rosy writing. (In fact, the writing described is apparently based more on imagination and stereotypes than on research of any sort.) Choice **H** is a trap; the writing may in fact have decreased in popularity over time, but the passage does not provide any direct evidence for this conclusion.

29. Correct Answer: B

In the second-to-last paragraph, the author writes, "O'Brien seemed to find all this amusing: instead of throwing out local color (as I have) he took these elements and exaggerated them to the point of madness in books like *At Swim-Two-Birds* and *The Poor Mouth*." He then writes that O'Brien's work is rife with "true-to-stereotype Irishmen wandering the countryside and eating potatoes" (lines 74-77). The passage is concerned only with O'Brien's relation to these stereotypes; how well these stereotypes are understood (**A**), whether they are popular (**C**), and whether people of Irish descent would consider them strange (**D**) are issues that the passage does not address. In fact, because these are stereotypes (and are well-known by definition), it is unlikely that they would be baffling or strange to most observers.

30. Correct Answer: H

By encouraging writers to "write what you don't know" and give rise to "excited" responses (lines 84-85), the author takes a posi-

tive tone to provide advice on the art of writing—or provides a constructive recommendation (**H**). Choices **F**, **G**, and **J** are all negative in tone and can readily be eliminated. However, watch out for answer **G**: the author doesn't provide a tired commonplace, but transforms the commonplace "write what you know" into a wholly different piece of advice.

NATURAL SCIENCE

31. Correct Answer: A

In Passage A, the author notes that humans can detect distance because humans have "two eyes situated in slightly different positions" (line 16). However, the fact that "In a picture the eyes can only focus at one distance" (lines 19-20) is "one of the chief causes of the perennial difficulty in painting backgrounds" (lines 21-23). Thus, **A** is a correct response to the author's ideas. **B** wrongly focuses on the issue of motion (not the positioning of the eyes), **C** wrongly focuses on the issue of color, and **D** wrongly assumes that only one eye (with its retina) sees a painted background, when in fact BOTH eyes see it from the same distance.

32. Correct Answer: G

The word *examine* occurs in the context of "visual pictures" (line 3): somebody observing these pictures will "see that they are composed of masses of color in infinite variety and complexity" (lines 4-5). To examine in this context means to *inspect* in order to gather details such as these; thus, **G** is the strongest answer. **F** refers to the act of questioning a person, **H** is wrongly negative, and **J** is wrongly positive and (in most cases) would also refer to people, not to pictures.

33. Correct Answer: B

In Passage A, the author explains that "our eyes have only flat pictures containing two-dimension information about the objective world" (lines 10-11), and goes on to indicate the differences in how real distances and painted distances are perceived. Thus, **B** is a highly effective answer. **A** wrongly assumes that the author's information is taken from an experiment (when no such source is specified) while **C** distorts a point from the passage (that touch allows us to intuit solidity and shape, NOT that touch is more important than sight for survival). **D** is relevant mainly to Passage B: the only illusion that the author of Passage A mentions is a painted landscape, and no specific painted landscapes are described at length.

TEST 5 Answer Explanations

34. Correct Answer: G

In lines 10-12, the author asks how humans come by their "knowledge of distance and the solidity of things"; the final paragraph of Passage A explains that there is "another sense [beyond sight] all important in ideas of form, the sense of touch" (line 32). This information justifies **G**. The purpose of this paragraph is to shift emphasis to touch, not to offer new or different ideas about sight itself: thus, eliminate **F** and **H**. The final paragraph also departs from the discussion of "devices resorted to by painters," which the author even notes "do not concern us here" (lines 25-27); for this reason, eliminate choice **J**.

35. Correct Answer: D

Passage B begins by discussing the optical illusions developed by "two ancient Greek painters" (line 35), then goes on three dimensional still lifes and tattoos before focusing on the work of illusionist "Johannes Stotter" (line 52) and the optical mechanisms that Stotter uses to fool viewers. This information supports **D** and can be used to eliminate **B**, since Stotter's work is only one element of the author's larger discussion. **A** and **C** both wrongly assume that the author is writing an argumentative or persuasive essay: in fact, the author is simply stating facts about how various optical illusions work.

36. Correct Answer: J

The quotation from Michelle Castillo is part of the author's explanation of the "scrambling process that accompanies any optical illusion" (lines 59-60). Thus, choose **J**, which effectively sums up how Castillo's words build off the author's topic. Note that the author, at this point in the passage, is simply providing facts about the general workings of optical illusions: **F** is too negative in tone, **G** wrongly narrows the focus to Stotter (when in fact the quotation from Castillo applies to illusions generally), and **H** wrongly describes the creators of illusions, not the process by which a viewer reacts to an illusion.

37. Correct Answer: D

Earlier in the passage, the author describes an illusion developed by contemporary artist Johannes Stotter: a "perfectly three-dimensional parrot perched on a log" (line 53) that is really "a woman in extremely elaborate body paint" (lines 54-55). The parrot in the statement that "a woman in body paint is really a parrot" (line 75) is a reference back to this information. Thus, **D** is correct. **A** wrongly situates Stotter's work in ancient times, **B** wrongly assumes that the author is herself an artist (a possibility that is never explicitly raised), and **C** wrongly construes the three-dimensional woman as two-dimensional.

38. Correct Answer: H

The phrase *playing with* refers to "the way an object is lit" (line 63) in an optical illusion: the way an object is lit would thus be *modified* or *manipulated* to achieve a desired illusion effect. Thus, **H** is the best answer. **F** and **G** both introduce extreme and inappropriate negatives (since an optical illusion can be clever or pleasing), while **J** is a positive that does not directly fit the line in question. Viewers would *enjoy* the way an object is lit, but the way the object is lit would itself be *manipulated*.

39. Correct Answer: A

The author of Passage A offers a general analysis of how a "third dimension" can appear in "flat pictures of two dimensions" (lines 13-14); similarly, the author of Passage B begins her account by surveying famous optical illusions that "tempt us to see three dimensions when we are only seeing two" (lines 33-34). Thus, **A** correctly describes a major similarity between the passages. Neither passage describes three-dimensional images that appear to be two-dimensional (eliminating **B**) or consider images that appear to move (eliminating **C**). Only Passage B, in the discussion of Stotter's false parrot, raises the possibility of a three-dimensional object that is really another three-dimensional object (eliminating **D**).

40. Correct Answer: G

While Passage A considers the general sight mechanisms behind the perception of depth and space, the author of this passage does not provide any specific examples by name. In contrast, the author of Passage B discusses two "Greek painters" (line 35) and goes on to analyze the work of illusionist "Johannes Stotter" (line 52). **G** rightly sums up this difference and is thus correct. Neither passage directly explains that its author has carried out experiments (eliminating **F**) or focuses on depictions of the human body (since Passage A is mostly about landscapes, Passage B mostly about objects and animals, eliminating **H**). **J** is completely inaccurate: Passage B is in fact MORE focused on experts, since it quotes Michelle Castillo in order to explain optical illusions.

Test 6

READING TEST
35 Minutes — 40 Questions

DIRECTIONS: There are four passages in this test. Each passage is followed by several questions. After reading a passage, choose the best answer to each question and fill in the corresponding oval on your answer document. You may refer to the passages as often as necessary.

Passage I

LITERARY NARRATIVE: This passage is adapted from the short story "Not for Sale." The narrator, a woman of fifty-five named Luisa, lives with her husband Ramon in a suburb of Baltimore.

I am pretending to listen as Ramon tells me, for the millionth time this month, why the new restaurant is a bad idea. I know his arguments *and* I know the order he's set up for them. First, he reminds me of what I already know:
5 restaurants are fragile, the whole industry is fragile, just one stupid decision and you're done. Second, he lists off all the things we'll be competing with in our new location: seafood restaurants, steakhouses, the food court, and (holding up three fingers) three Chipotles. And what tourist (he asks this
10 slowly, almost angrily) will ever choose our tapas over Chipotle? Third, he tells me all about the costs. Fourth, he tells me all about the stress, the longer hours, the unreliable workers. Fifth, he looks at me and tells me that I haven't really been listening. And I haven't; I have been staring at
15 our aloe plant this whole time, wondering if it needs to be moved a little to the left.

Ramon takes a minute, waits for his voice to soften, and looks harder at me. "Listen, Luisa," he says, "we have a good restaurant, but we can't stretch it like this and keep it
20 good. Can we?" This is the argument he saves for last, because he knows it's the one that I can't knock away no matter how hard I swing.

I get up slowly and walk out to our deck, without a word, and Ramon doesn't follow me and doesn't say
25 anything. He doesn't need to, because he knows he's right. It took us twenty years to become the only Spanish restaurant that people think of when they think of Baltimore. I know, Spanish food in Baltimore. Making that combination work was a lot of the victory, for us. Keeping that combination
30 authentic was part of the victory, too. Ramon is afraid that a new location will have us selling crab tacos, trying to lure the eat-and-run Chipotle crowd. He also blames himself.

It was Ramon, after all, who first planted the idea in my head. A few years ago, when they were really cleaning up
35 Baltimore, building new hotels and restaurants in the Inner Harbor, Ramon called some friends of his, asked around about the prices for real estate, the ins-and-outs of downtown transportation, how many tourists wasted how many dollars at the Baltimore Aquarium. Then doubts began to set in. But
40 as the idea withered out in his head, the thought of a new location wound itself through me like a tough vine. The idea is always there, so much there that, sometimes, I feel I want our new, Inner Harbor restaurant for no other reason than to be rid of these thoughts.

45 We've done well. Decades ago we were a couple of confused, impossibly happy newlyweds, freshly arrived from Barcelona and—crazy as it all seems now—racing around Washington D.C. in a Mexican food truck. Now we have a restaurant where you can order any classic Spanish dish and
50 get it done right. In the room where we have the safe, we have a wall of newspaper clippings; in the safe itself, we have a copy of a three-star review that the *New York Times* gave us when we were starting out, when we were right at the bottom of our powers. The *Times* never, *never* gives three
55 stars. We have a son who will be going to Penn State University next year, two good cars, a comfortable house, the kind of life that should only be on sitcoms but by some miracle occasionally struggles its way into reality. I often tell myself that we have everything we've asked for, then extra.

60 I walk back inside and Ramon is watching a football game, and he doesn't even like football. I shut the door and stand a little away from him.

"You know I'm right," he says, without even turning his head from the television. This is how he talks when he is
65 watching television, no matter what mood he is in.

"No I don't," I say, but the truth is that I don't know if I'm right either. This isn't cooking: they tell you that cooking is an art, but cooking is also a system of right and wrong. Do this for this taste. Don't do this so you don't get that taste.
70 You set everything in place properly and you finish with something complete and pure. But we are beyond this now, and when I try to envision our new restaurant, I don't know if I see it as the ground of something new or as the ground that will make us stumble.

GO ON TO THE NEXT PAGE.

1. In the passage, Ramon's reasoning is based on the assumption that:

   A. extending the restaurant to a new location will undermine the entire business.
   B. earlier tapas restaurants have failed to compete and flourish in the Inner Harbor.
   C. long hours and unreliable workers are problems that he and Luisa have not faced before.
   D. Luisa is not listening because she does not want to understand his arguments.

2. It can be reasonably inferred that Ramon is especially troubled by Luisa's determination to build the new restaurant because:

   F. he believes that the tastes and habits of Baltimore tourists are extremely unpredictable.
   G. he is convinced that tourists save most of their money to spend at the Baltimore Aquarium.
   H. he waited too long to buy real estate and has watched the prices move much too high.
   J. he was the one who initially gave Luisa the idea of starting a new location.

3. As stated in the passage, one of the main reasons that Luisa wants to open a new restaurant with Ramon in Inner Harbor is that:

   A. Luisa believes that a fresh start would be good for their marriage.
   B. a location in the Inner Harbor will allow them to achieve greater publicity than they have so far.
   C. Luisa wants to rid herself of anxieties and troubling thoughts.
   D. the lack of authentic Spanish food in the Inner Harbor deprives tourists of an important source of world culture.

4. The passage as a whole is told from the point of view of a woman who:

   F. wants to find a more stable community in the wake of a disappointment in business.
   G. is longing for something new even though it could destroy the fulfilling life she has helped to build.
   H. is angry with her husband for belittling her plans as unrealistic.
   J. feels reassured about what the future holds because she believes that her husband will eventually support her.

5. In the first paragraph, Ramon makes all of the following points EXCEPT that:

   A. the restaurant industry is unstable.
   B. Luisa and he should be planning to retire.
   C. Luisa won't enjoy working longer hours.
   D. a new restaurant would entail new expenditures.

6. In the final paragraph, Luisa's references to cooking emphasize the idea that:

   F. a good cook will be comfortable with multiple recipes.
   G. cooking is difficult to compare to any other activity.
   H. leaving out key ingredients is risky but sometimes rewarding.
   J. cooking is highly systematic and has desired goals and outcomes.

7. As it is used in line 31, the word *lure* means:

   A. fascinate.
   B. deceive.
   C. attract.
   D. tempt.

8. According to the passage, what are the things Luisa feels lucky to have acquired in life?

   F. A husband, several children, and a lifestyle normally seen on sitcoms.
   G. A son who is going off to college, cars, and a house.
   H. A review in the *New York Times*, a husband, and real estate investments.
   J. A Spanish restaurant, a house in Baltimore, and contact with her family in Barcelona.

9. Based on the information provided in the passage, Ramon's attitude toward the televised football game can be described as:

   A. annoyed.
   B. uninterested.
   C. analytic.
   D. confused.

GO ON TO THE NEXT PAGE.

10. It can be reasonably inferred from the passage that Ramon and Luisa are:

   F. hardworking people who have built a successful restaurant from the ground up.

   G. a couple dealing with a conflict that will eventually undermine their marriage.

   H. individuals eager to return to the lifestyle they knew in Barcelona.

   J. members of a wealthy family that is trying to figure out how to enhance its reputation.

Passage II

SOCIAL SCIENCE: This passage is adapted from the essay "American Food Crises, Then and Now."

Before American settlers arrived in the Midwest, the native grasses of this area protected the soil from drying up and blowing away during droughts. But after farmers had established their homesteads, a process known today as the
5 "Great Plow-up" began: wheat was grown without either conscientious crop rotation or purposeful efforts to preserve the natural landscape. Essentially, this over-farming of the land destroyed the protective grasses and made the region extremely vulnerable to drought and drought-related
10 catastrophes. In the 1930s catastrophe known as the Dust Bowl, a drought in the Midwest destroyed millions of acres of farmland, and forced hundreds of thousands of farmers to leave their homes in search of new employment.

With this regional tragedy ever fresh in their minds, the
15 policymakers who had lived through the Great Depression decided to confront the problem of overproduction in the 1940s and 1950s. New federal food policies favored quantity controls on both the cultivation of crops and the storage of surplus grain. When food prices were high, the government
20 would add surplus grain to the market, so that food costs would remain moderate. When prices were too low, farmers cultivated less land, because smaller supply would increase prices and allow farmers to make a profit under conditions severely disadvantageous to consumers. In effect, federal
25 policies acted as counterweights to the ups and downs of a volatile food market.

But in the 1970s, federal inflation and a nationwide oil shortage led to a sharp rise in food prices. To ensure that food would be affordable for consumers, Earl Butz, the United
30 States Secretary of Agriculture, advocated a "get big or get out" policy that supported maximum production. Under Butz's conditions, farmers had to plant "fence row to fence row" and produce as much crop as possible in order to make a decent living. Small farmers were thus eliminated.
35 According to the Institute for Food and Development Policy,

the average farm size went from 200 to 400 acres, reflecting a steady shift to mega-farms. In addition to increasing the size of farms, federal policies discouraged biodiversity. After all, it was more profitable for a farmer to grow just one crop,
40 usually corn, than it would be for the same farmer to produce a variety of foods.

In one way, this mass-production of commodity crops has benefited Americans. According to the Economic Research Service of the United States Department of
45 Agriculture, middle-class Americans in 1929 spent about 23 percent of their disposable income on food. In 2011, the middle class only spent about 10 percent on food. While it is possible to argue that this decline is due to the rising costs of other needs, like housing and transportation, it is also
50 undeniable that food prices overall are lower than they once were. But while the proliferation of high-yield monoculture farms has led to a price drop for many of our food products, the lack of diversity in American harvesting practices has led to rises in the prices of fruits and vegetables.

55 And such pricing benefits may be offset by other disadvantages: an urgent problem related to the food system in America is the current obesity epidemic. The public health of the nation has deteriorated, and policy makers themselves are troubled by the long-term consequences of agricultural
60 overproduction. Indeed, according to a report by the Harvard School of Public Health, obesity rates in children ages 2 to 19 have more than tripled since the 1970s. Recent statistics do not simply reflect the nation's relative health; they also show just how expensive obesity can be. According to the Institute
65 for Food and Development Policy, the total cost of dealing with obesity-related diseases is $147 billion per year, and Medicaid and Medicare—funded by taxpayer dollars—are responsible for covering about half of these costs.

In short, federal policies since the 1970s have created a
70 dysfunctional food system, one in which farming is not a lucrative trade for most, in which cheap food is nutrient-poor and high in calories, and in which many people do not have access to the healthy foods that they require. Of course, federal policies do not exist in a vacuum. These problems
75 have been exacerbated by historical migration patterns, decreased investment in central cities, lack of coordination between urban and rural areas, and the influence of large businesses that benefit from an industrial food system. To really address such pervasive problems, people from all
80 points of the food system, from production to consumption to waste, must begin to develop collaborative, on-the-ground solutions to what often seem like hopelessly massive dilemmas.

In the face of a stubborn federal government, local
85 leaders have been trying to address food-related problems with food action plans, which set forth guidelines for

GO ON TO THE NEXT PAGE.

changing the current food system using positive and sustainable measures. Across North America, local governments have been adopting food action plans. The stakes
90 are as high for us as they were for the food policy reformers who witnessed the Dust Bowl, and time will tell if we can overcome our era's own agricultural and nutritional crisis.

11. In order to emphasize the problems in the American food system, the author creates an analogy between today's food crisis and:

A. the 1920s consumer market.
B. the 1930s Dust Bowl.
C. the 1950s food reforms.
D. the 1970s oil shortage.

12. One of the author's main points about American food policies from the 1970s on is that:

F. these policies have brought agricultural supply under control, but are insufficient for dealing with periods of high demand for food.
G. the popularity of these policies has dropped considerably as a result of America's obesity epidemic.
H. these policies have lowered food costs but are problematic for American consumers in other respects.
J. the American farming industry has become unable to compete in global markets as a result of the regulations created by Earl Butz.

13. The author points out the negative effects of obesity by calling attention to:

A. the financial burden that obesity places on America.
B. the social and psychological problems faced by obese children.
C. previously undiagnosed diseases related to obesity.
D. the link between obesity and life expectancy.

14. The main function of the first and second paragraphs (lines 1-26) is to:

F. dramatize catastrophes that are discussed using statistics later in the passage.
G. indicate that Americans in the 1940s and 1950s were willing to pay unusually high food prices.
H. imply that Butz's policies would have offended policymakers from the 1930s.
J. provide historical background that explains the food policies initiated in the 1970s.

15. Which of the following was NOT a consequence of the food and agricultural policies put in place by Earl Butz?

A. Decreases in food costs
B. Specialized single-crop agriculture
C. Disappearance of small farms
D. The founding of the Institute for Food and Development Policy

16. As it is used in line 68, the word *covering* most nearly means:

F. comprehending.
G. addressing.
H. concealing.
J. reporting.

17. According to the passage, the practices of the American agricultural system have resulted in higher consumer prices for:

A. farm equipment.
B. commodity crops such as corn.
C. obesity-related healthcare.
D. fruits and vegetables.

18. In line 84, the author refers to the federal government as *stubborn* most likely in order to emphasize:

F. obliviousness to nutrition problems on the part of national leaders and the need for publicity and letter-writing campaigns.
G. the government's inability to address major problems and the need for community-based solutions.
H. the standoff between reformers and food officials that led to an eventual victory for major agricultural corporations.
J. the unwillingness of government agencies to discuss the benefits of food action plans in official documents.

19. All of the following have worsened the already negative effects of federal food policies EXCEPT:

A. flaws in communication between urban and rural areas.
B. measures taken by large businesses that benefit from the current system.
C. negative publicity surrounding food action plans.
D. massive population movements throughout history.

GO ON TO THE NEXT PAGE.

20. In the fifth, sixth, and seventh paragraphs (lines 55-92), the author's attitude toward federal food policies can best be described as:

    F. harshly critical.
    G. reluctantly tolerant.
    H. ultimately optimistic.
    J. personally offended

Passage III

HUMANITIES: Both of these passages are taken from recent works of scholarship on the plays of William Shakespeare (1564-1616).

Passage A, from "Shakespeare's Maelstrom."

Imagine a young man, a student, approaching a play written by Shakespeare for the first time. It can be a little daunting. What approach does he need to take in order to understand what is going on? As an example of his dilemma,
5 how does he approach the first scene of a play like *The Tempest?*

The very first thing the student must do is to empty his mind of all preconceptions. As he begins to read, he should, in his mind's eye, imagine that he is standing in the Globe Theatre
10 watching the play for the first time. What does he see and what does he hear?

The Tempest begins with the following stage direction:

A tempestuous noise of thunder and lightning heard.

Here, the word "tempestuous" catches the attention - this
15 is a significant adjective, and a student might recall that, in literature, a storm can have both realistic and metaphorical significance. As the scene unfolds, we see two relatively unperturbed sailors, facing the dangers of the storm in a professional, competent and cheerful way; soon enough,
20 aristocratic characters appear on deck, worried about the weather and fearing for their lives.

Two groups of people, two starkly different reactions. However, the supposedly royal party is seen away from its familiar milieu, and appears to lack any sense of appropriate
25 behavior: one might say that the courtiers are out of their depth. We are aware of the lack of unity. So there is a cultural divide being observed here, in which the potential for longer-lasting forms of discord are suggested—in which the aristocrats may be fearing not only for their lives, but for their authority.
30 Tempestuous indeed.

Passage B, from "Miching Mallecho, or How Mischief Works."

Shakespeare enjoyed the use of alliterative phrases. One such phrase, "miching mallecho," comes from a scene in *Hamlet* and defines Hamlet's intentions for the travelling players he has invited to perform at Elsinore Castle, his home.
35 To a modern audience, neither of the two words is familiar outside this context, although the first word does still exist in certain dialects. In the North of England, "miching" refers to the stealing of small items, such as fruit from an orchard, without being caught. In Wales, there is the related phrase
40 "playing mwchms." This phrase is used to describe stealing time from school by playing hooky. In neither case is miching regarded as a serious crime: just a minor misdemeanor, nothing more. In all these examples, the word contains a spirit of mockery of the accepted order of society.

45 The word "mallecho" is no longer used at all. At first glance, it appears to be an imported Continental European word that Shakespeare is using. Scholars have searched for its derivation, and it is fairly clear that there are two root words here, presumably drawn from French or Italian: mal, meaning
50 "bad," and echo, meaning "repetition" of some kind. It is not known for certain whether the word was actually used in the English vernacular; in fact, it is believed that Shakespeare invented it himself; if the word is read in the context of the scene, it becomes clear that Hamlet himself feels the need to
55 explain the phrase: "Miching mallecho: it means Mischief." This elucidation would not be needed if the phrase were in general use.

Today, the word "mischief" is not regarded very seriously: a mischievous act is treated with leniency. Children get up to
60 mischief and adults smile indulgently and reminisce about the things they themselves used to do when they were young. However, in the seventeenth century, the word had more serious connotations. To begin with, it was accepted that there were two kinds of mischief. On the one hand, mischief could
65 be regarded as benevolent in intent. Prospero in *The Tempest* sends Ariel to "do that good mischief." This form of mischief was present on certain days of the year when the hierarchy at court was turned on its head and a "Lord of Misrule" was appointed, a comic figure whose wishes everyone, from the
70 highest to the lowest, had to obey.

Yet for the artists and the politicians of the Renaissance, miching mallecho was dangerous. Some might have said it was more than dangerous, a manifestation of evil where one would least expect to find it. "And some that smile have in their
75 hearts, I fear / Millions of mischief," says Octavius Caesar in that most political drama of the Shakespeare canon, *Julius Caesar*. The fear Shakespeare's contemporaries had of mischief involved never knowing to what ends it might lead.

GO ON TO THE NEXT PAGE.

Questions 21-23 ask about Passage A.

21. In analyzing *The Tempest*, the author of Passage A offers all of the following EXCEPT:

A. practical advice.
B. a quotation from the text.
C. comparison to other plays.
D. an interpretation of a single scene.

22. It can be inferred that the author of Passage A believes that:

F. students often have great difficulty with Shakespeare's language.
G. reading Shakespeare alone is more enjoyable than seeing Shakespeare's plays performed.
H. Shakespeare had a strong background in politics.
J. reading Shakespeare requires openness and imagination.

23. As it is used in line 22, the phrase *Two groups* is best understood as a reference to:

A. the sailors and the aristocrats.
B. the audience and the actors.
C. Shakespeare scholars and their students.
D. the tempest's noises and the other stage effects.

Questions 24-27 ask about Passage B.

24. According to Passage B, the word "miching" means:

F. "stealing," and was at one point in general use.
G. "stealing," and may have been invented by Shakespeare.
H. "mischief," and was at one point in general use.
J. "mischief," and may have been invented by Shakespeare.

25. The "Some" mentioned in line 72 have an opinion of mischief that most nearly resembles that of:

A. "Hamlet" (line 54)
B. "Children" (line 59)
C. "Prospero" (line 65)
D. "Octavius Caesar" (line 75)

26. As it is used in line 59, the word *treated* most nearly means:

F. depicted.
G. enjoyed.
H. responded to.
J. made available.

27. It can be reasonably inferred from Passage B that a lenient approach to childhood mischief:

A. was popular during Shakespeare's lifetime.
B. was condemned by Shakespeare's plays.
C. is popular in modern times.
D. is destructive in its effects.

Questions 28-30 ask about both passages.

28. Which of the following is an important consideration in both Passage A and Passage B?

F. Shakespeare's specific word choices
G. Shakespeare's reception among scholars
H. Shakespeare's use of comedy
J. Shakespeare's fluency in different languages

29. A scholar of Renaissance literature has written the following about Shakespeare:

"When the resources of English were not sufficient to his meaning, he would venture south, borrowing from the vocabularies of the European continent."

This quote substantiates ideas from:

A. Passage A, which talks about Shakespeare's aristocratic ideals.
B. Passage A, which considers Shakespeare's responses to non-English cultures.
C. Passage B, which indicates that the term "mallecho" might have been derived from Continental European languages.
D. Passage B, which indicates that most of Shakespeare's plays were set in the Continental European cities of the Renaissance.

30. Both Passage A and Passage B are written in tones that are best characterized as:

F. speculative and lighthearted.
G. observant and analytic.
H. impassioned and partisan.
J. instructive and overbearing.

GO ON TO THE NEXT PAGE.

Passage IV

NATURAL SCIENCE: This passage is adapted from the article "Upsurge: Episodes from the Mount Saint Helens Eruption."

Geologist David A. Johnston was camping in Washington State on the morning of May 18, 1980. At just past 8:30, he uttered his final words into a radio transmitter: "This is it!" Johnston's location on that spring morning was
5 Mount Saint Helens, the site of the most powerful volcano in the United States. The May 18 eruption removed nearly 15% of the volcanic mountain's summit.

This cataclysmic burst was accompanied by a massive earthquake, which registered at 5.1 on the Richter scale. (The
10 average earthquake measures in at 2.5 or less, a magnitude too small to be felt by most people.) Yet this was not the first earthquake that took place in the Mount Saint Helens area.

On March 20, 1980, an earthquake measuring 4.2 on the Richter scale took place deep beneath Mount Saint
15 Helens. Following this event, officials set up a round the clock watch that ultimately saved many lives. Just a week later, on March 27, the US Geological Survey issued an official Hazard Warning for Mount Saint Helens. This measure was prompted by three days of at least three quakes
20 a day, each quake measuring 4.0 or higher on the Richter scale, with smaller quakes occurring frequently.

The signs that Mount Saint Helens might erupt were right on the surface, yet we must travel below the earth to understand the physics of why such a volcano erupts.
25 Typically, there are three factors involved: the buoyancy of the molten rock, or magma; the pressure from the exsolved gases in the magma; and the injection of a new batch of magma into an already filled magma chamber.

When rock inside the earth melts, its mass remains the
30 same even though its volume increases, making it less dense than the surrounding rock. On account of its buoyancy, this lighter magma will naturally rise to the surface. If the density of the magma is less than that of the surrounding rocks, the magma reaches the surface and erupts.

35 Some forms of magma also contain dissolved volatile substances such as water, sulfur dioxide, and carbon dioxide. The amount of a dissolved gas in magma at normal atmospheric pressure is zero, but this amount rises with increasing pressure. When magma moves closer to the
40 surface, water is released as gas (or exsolved) from the magma; if the exsolved gas reaches a volume three times the volume of the magma, the magma will disintegrate and explode.

An eruption may also involve an injection of new
45 magma into a chamber that is already full. In this case, some of the magma in the chamber is forced to move through a fissure in the earth and will ultimately erupt at the surface.

On the basis of this information, one might suspect that volcanologists could predict a volcanic eruption. Yet this is
50 not the case. The character of an eruption is based on the natural history of the volcano in question and on its current volcanic composition. These can vary greatly from volcano to volcano, but at least volcanologists can figure out which of the three eruption factors is mostly responsible.

55 This is exactly what experts did after the March 20 earthquake at Mount Saint Helens. After the greatest tremors had settled, volcanologists set up reflective targets between the fissures to record changes. Volcanic tremors were measured by taking a record of rhythmic pulses; these pulses
60 indicated that magma was on the move. By late April, laser equipment had detected menacing signs: a bulge had emerged between the fissures and was growing at a rate of five cubic feet per day.

Yet gaseous forces were finally responsible for the
65 eruption. A cloud of burning gas and ash was created by the abrupt release of the pressure over the magma chamber, and the mountain face was blown out by rock debris and superheated gas. The blast was so powerful that everything within eight miles was wiped out within moments, while
70 subsequent shockwaves caused devastation over an area of 230 square miles. Then, a second, vertical explosion occurred at the summit of the volcano. Gas and ash shot more than 12 miles into the air and darkened the sky, affecting cities more than 300 miles away. Ash continued to erupt for more than
75 nine hours.

While Mount Saint Helens gave Americans a stark image of volcanic power, volcanoes continue to erupt all the time, all over the world. There are currently 1500 or so active volcanoes ("active" indicating that a volcano has erupted
80 once in the last 10,000 years) and there are roughly 50 eruptions every year. Many eruptions occur in Japan, which is home to 7% of the world's active volcanoes; one of these is Mount Ontake, which erupted to devastating effect in 2014.

31. The overall structure of the passage is:

   A. a rhetorical question followed by a description of a laboratory experiment.
   B. an account of an event followed by an explanation.
   C. a hypothesis followed by a series of counter-arguments.
   D. a theory followed by little-known scientific evidence.

GO ON TO THE NEXT PAGE.

32. According to the passage, which of the following is NOT typically a direct cause of volcanic eruptions?

F. The pressure from exsolved gases
G. The physical displacement of magma by other magma
H. High atmospheric pressure
J. The density of magma relative to the density of surrounding rock

33. According to the passage, why does water vapor dissolve in magma deep underground but not at ground level?

A. The solubility of water vapor decreases to zero as magma rises to ground level.
B. The solubility of water vapor increases quickly as magma rises to ground level.
C. Water vapor is classified as an exsolved gas.
D. Magma disintegrates and explodes at ground level.

34. Exsolving a substance is the opposite of:

F. melting the substance.
G. igniting the substance.
H. releasing the substance.
J. absorbing the substance.

35. As it is used in line 9, *registered at* could mean all of the following EXCEPT:

A. was measured to be.
B. was recorded as.
C. was signed up as.
D. had a magnitude of.

36. According to the information presented in the fifth paragraph (lines 29-34), rock beneath the earth's surface would do which of the following upon melting?

F. Stay in place
G. Be exsolved
H. Rise toward ground level
J. Sink to a lower depth

37. The author states that volcanologists did all of the following after the March 20, 1980 Mount Saint Helens earthquake EXCEPT:

A. set up reflective targets.
B. issue warnings to local townspeople.
C. record underground pulses.
D. use laser equipment to track the size of a magma bulge.

38. According to the passage, approximately how many active volcanoes are located in Japan?

F. 7
G. 50
H. 105
J. 1,500

39. As it is used in line 69, *wiped out* most nearly means:

A. cleansed.
B. polished.
C. repositioned.
D. destroyed.

40. According to the passage, the primary cause of the May 18, 1980 Mount Saint Helens volcanic eruption was:

F. the pressure from exsolved gases.
G. the growth of a magma bulge.
H. the injection of new magma into an already full magma chamber.
J. the creation of a cloud of burning ash.

END OF TEST 6
STOP! DO NOT TURN THE PAGE UNTIL TOLD TO DO SO.
DO NOT RETURN TO A PREVIOUS TEST.

Answer Key: TEST 6

Test 6

LITERARY NARRATIVE

1. A
2. J
3. C
4. G
5. B
6. J
7. C
8. G
9. B
10. F

HUMANITIES

21. C
22. J
23. A
24. F
25. D
26. H
27. C
28. F
29. C
30. G

SOCIAL SCIENCE

11. B
12. H
13. A
14. J
15. D
16. G
17. D
18. G
19. C
20. F

NATURAL SCIENCE

31. B
32. H
33. A
34. J
35. C
36. H
37. B
38. H
39. D
40. F

To see your scaled ACT Reading Score (1-36), determine how many questions you answered correctly and consult the Scoring Chart on Page 186 of this book.

Post-Test Analysis

This post-test analysis is essential if you want to see an improvement on your next test. Possible reasons for errors, both for the test overall and for each of the four reading passages, are listed here. Place check marks next to the types of errors that pertain to you, or write your own types of errors in the blank spaces provided.

GENERAL

◇ Spent too much time reading the passages
◇ Spent too much time answering the questions
◇ Did not attempt to finish all of the passages
◇ Did not create effective margin answers
◇ Did not use process of elimination
◇ Could not find evidence to answer the questions
◇ Could not comprehend the topics and ideas in the passages
◇ Could not understand what the questions were asking
◇ Interpreted the passages rather than using evidence
Other: _____

LITERARY NARRATIVE

◇ Spent too long reading the passage
◇ Spent too long answering the questions
◇ Could not identify the setting and characters
◇ Could not understand the plot or action
◇ Could not work effectively with tone and clues to tone
Other: _____

> **Use this form** to better analyze your performance. If you don't understand why you made errors, there is no way that you can correct them!

SOCIAL SCIENCE

◇ Spent too long reading the passage
◇ Spent too long answering the questions
◇ Could not understand the author's position or arguments
◇ Used outside knowledge rather than using evidence
Other: _____

HUMANITIES

◇ Spent too long reading the passage
◇ Spent too long answering the questions
◇ Could understand the themes and organization of the passage
◇ Could not understand the author's ideas and uses of evidence
Other: _____

NATURAL SCIENCE

◇ Spent too long reading the passage
◇ Spent too long answering the questions
◇ Found the concepts and ideas in the passage confusing
◇ Found the questions confusing
◇ Could not effectively work with the inference and logic questions
Other: _____

TEST 6 Answer Explanations

LITERARY NARRATIVE

1. Correct Answer: A

Ramon explains in the first paragraph that restaurants are "fragile" (line 5), and uses this as an argument against the new location. Later, the narrator explains the problem in greater depth in lines 28-32: "I know, Spanish food in Baltimore. Making that combination work was a lot of the victory, for us. Keeping that combination authentic was part of the victory, too. Ramon is afraid that a new location will have us selling crab tacos, trying to lure the eat-and-run Chipotle crowd." In the last sentence of this reference, the author insinuates that "selling crab tacos, trying to lure the eat-and-run Chipotle crowd" is not something Ramon wants and the *new location* might force him to do so, and thus "undermine the entire business" and compromise its identity. **B** misrepresents Ramon's objections: he is afraid that his restaurant will be unable to compete, but never names other, similar tapas restaurants that have failed. **C** misconstrues content from the passage: Ramon fears longer hours and unreliable workers (lines 12-13), but his fear could be based on earlier experiences with such drawbacks. **D** is contradicted by the passage's content: Luisa does not listen because she is in fact knows and understands Ramon's arguments too well (lines 1-4).

2. Correct Answer: J

The author writes in lines 32-34 that Ramon "also blames himself. It was Ramon, after all, who first planted the idea in my head." The *idea* referred to here, is that of opening a restaurant in *a new location*. Thus, **J** is the correct answer. Though Ramon does mention the Baltimore Aquarium (**G**) and real estate (**H**) in the third paragraph, both of these relate to Ramon's early enthusiasm for the new restaurant, not to his later, *troubled* reaction. For trap answer **F**, Ramon is unwilling to sell to tourists because doing so would compromise his business's identity (lines 30-32), not because he finds tourists unpredictable.

3. Correct Answer: C

As the narrator explains, the idea of the restaurant "is always there, so much there that, sometimes, I feel I want our new, Inner Harbor restaurant for no other reason than to be rid of these thoughts" (lines 41-44). Thus, **C** is the best answer; the thoughts can be understood as negative because they conflict between Luisa and Ramon, and because Luisa wants to *be rid* of them. As described in lines 45-60, Luisa's marriage and her business's publicity are both sources of contentment, so that negative answers **A** and **B** can be eliminated. Throughout the passage, Luisa and Ramon are primarily concerned with the impact of the new location on their own business, not on the cultural awareness of tourists, so that **D** is a trap answer.

4. Correct Answer: G

The narrator of the passage is a woman named Luisa, who has built a successful Spanish restaurant in Baltimore and who is considering the benefits and drawbacks of expanding her business. Her situation and state of mind are summed up in the final sentence of the passage: "When I try to envision our new restaurant, I don't know if I see it as the ground of something new or as the ground that will make us stumble." Together, this information supports **G**. The other answers can be eliminated quickly because they take faulty tones: Luisa has not experienced a business disappointment (**F**) and is unable to agree with her husband Ramon, but never gets angry at him (**H**). While **F** and **H** are too negative, **J** is too positive, since Luisa is still not certain of Ramon's support at the end of the passage.

5. Correct Answer: B

Luisa states in the first paragraph that, according to Ramon, "restaurants are fragile, the whole industry is fragile, just one stupid decision and you're done," eliminating **A**. She then describes Ramon's lines of argument further: "Third, he tells me all about the costs. Fourth, he tells me all about the stress, the longer hours, the unreliable workers," eliminating choices **C** and **D**. Retirement (**B**) is actually not mentioned anywhere in the passage: Luisa and Ramon are doing well in life but seem eager to continue running their business.

6. Correct Answer: J

In the final paragraph, Luisa states that "This isn't cooking: they tell you that cooking is an art, but cooking is also a system of right and wrong," supporting that "cooking is highly systematic." She then goes on to explain standard cooking rules: "Do this for this taste. Don't do this so you don't get that taste. You set everything in place properly and you finish with something complete and pure" (lines 67-71). Thus, **J** is the best answer, since cooking "has desired goals and outcomes." Since Luisa here considers cooking as a general activity, rather than presenting individual and specific recipes, **F** and **H** must be eliminated. The point of this paragraph is to contrast cooking with commerce: no other activities are considered, so that **G** is much too broad of a conclusion to draw from the text.

7. Correct Answer: C

The sentence that contains the word lure is as follows: "Ramon is afraid that a new location will have us selling crab tacos, trying to lure the eat-and-run Chipotle crowd" (lines 30-32). This sentence occurs in a discussion of business and commerce: to lure a crowd would be to draw it in or *attract* it for profit (**C**). Choice **B** is too negative for the context, while choices **A** (*fascinate*) and **D** (*tempt*) refer to emotional reactions, not to direct actions undertaken by paying customers.

8. Correct Answer: G

The author reveals in lines 55-58 that Luisa and Ramon "have a son who will be going to Penn State University next year, two good cars, a comfortable house, the kind of life that should only be on sitcoms but by some miracle occasionally struggles its way into reality." This information supports **G** as the best answer. **F** must be eliminated because only one child (the son) is mentioned. **H** and **J** refer to elements of the passage (real estate in line 37, links to Barcelona in line 47), but these elements are only mentioned briefly and in retrospect: they are never defined as things that Luisa feels *lucky* to have in the present.

TEST 6 Answer Explanations

9. Correct Answer: B

Describing Luisa's perspective, the author writes in lines 60-62, "I walk back inside and Ramon is watching a football game, and he doesn't even like football." Because Ramon *doesn't even like football*, we can assume he is not interested in what he's watching, which is why **B** is the correct answer. This information contradicts analytic (**C**), but does not provide support for either **A** or **D**. Both of these answers assume strong negative reactions and emotions, which Ramon never directs toward the televised football game.

10. Correct Answer: F

Beginning in line 45, Luisa explains her situation with Ramon by stating that "we've done well" and states that they began as "a couple of confused, impossibly happy newlyweds" and eventually became the owners of a Spanish restaurant. It can be inferred from this that they are *hardworking*. Luisa continues to describe their circumstances: "Now we have a restaurant where you can order any classic Spanish dish and get it done right" (lines 48-50). She also cites an extremely hard-to-get "three-star review that the *New York Times* gave" to her and Ramon when they were just starting out (lines 52-53). Thus, Ramon and Luisa are both hardworking and successful, justifying choice **F**. Choices **G** and **H** rely on false assumptions about the future and motives of the couple: it is not known for certain whether Ramon and Luisa's marriage will be undermined, and the characters nowhere express a desire to leave Baltimore and return to Barcelona. **J** attributes the wrong lifestyle (wealthy) and the wrong goal (an increase in family reputation) to Luisa and Ramon: the two characters are preoccupied mostly with a possible expansion of their small restaurant business.

SOCIAL SCIENCE

11. Correct Answer: B

The author starts out the passage by describing what happened in the 1930s: "In the 1930s catastrophe known as the Dust Bowl, a drought in the Midwest destroyed millions of acres of farmland, and forced hundreds of thousands of farmers to leave their homes in search of new employment"(lines 10-13) He then ends the passage by establishing a connection between the Dust Bowl and food crises today: "Across North America, local governments have been adopting food actions plans. The stakes are as high for us as they were for the food policy reformers who witnessed the Dust Bowl, and time will tell if we can overcome our era's own agricultural and nutritional crisis" (lines 87-92). Together, this information supports **B**. The other choices reference information from the passage, but not information that is used to create an analogy for today's food crisis. The 1920s were a time when Americans spent a larger portion of their income on food (lines 45-46), the 1950s were a period of successful food reform (lines 17-26), and the 1970s witnessed a rise in food prices (lines 27-28). These problems led up to today's epidemic of cheap food and poor health, but they are not similar or *analogous* to the epidemic. Thus, eliminate **A**, **C**, and **D**.

12. Correct Answer: H

As the author writes in the fourth paragraph, "In one way, this mass-production of commodity crops has benefited Americans.... food prices overall are lower than they once were" (lines 42-50). But then he goes on to explain that "such pricing benefits may be offset by other disadvantages: an urgent problem related to the food system in America is the current obesity epidemic" (lines 55-57). Choice **H** fits the author's argument, which combines some positive factors with strong negatives. Other answers can seem appropriately negative, but misrepresent the content of the passage. American food policies do control supply (lines 27-41), yet there is nothing to indicate that they are insufficient for periods of high demand, since food scarcity is not mentioned (**F**). The author sees America's obesity epidemic as a problem (lines 55-68), but focuses on the financial costs of obesity, not the negative publicity that obesity may or may not have brought to food policies (**G**). And the food policies have mostly hurt "small farmers" (line 34) and "biodiversity" (line 38): global competition is never mentioned, and large American farms may actually be ideally equipped to compete in *global markets* (**J**).

13. Correct Answer: A

The support for this answer can be found in the fifth paragraph; here, the author writes, "Recent statistics do not simply reflect the nation's relative health; they also show just how expensive obesity can be. According to the Institute for Food and Development Policy, the total cost of dealing with obesity-related diseases is $147 billion per year, and Medicaid and Medicare—funded by taxpayer dollars—are responsible for covering about half of these costs" (lines 62-68). Thus, answer **A** is correct. Although the author notes that the general "public health of the nation has deteriorated" as a result of the obesity epidemic (lines 58-59), the other answers refer to specific effects that the passage does not support. The psychology of obese children (**B**), newly diagnosed diseases (**C**), and life expectancy (**D**) are never mentioned.

14. Correct Answer: J

In the first two paragraphs of the passage, the author writes about events and circumstances that affected American food policies through the 1950s. As described in the second paragraph, "the policymakers who had lived through the Great Depression decided to confront the problem of overproduction in the 1940s and 1950s (lines 14-17). In other words, the government took a more active part in food regulation than it had before the Great Depression and the Dust Bowl crisis: this intervention-based approach to farming continued in the 1970s, when Earl Butz put in place measures that "supported maximum production" (line 31). Thus, **J** is the best choice, since the first two paragraphs gave *historical background* information that explains the *food polices* instituted in the 1970s. The other answers do not capture the function of both paragraphs together, and can be eliminated. **F** is incorrect because catastrophes such as the Dust Bowl are depicted primarily in the first paragraph, and are described in their historical context, not depicted using narrative scenes or *dramatized*. **G** is incorrect because food prices are only mentioned in the second paragraph, and are described as well-regulated. Finally, **H** must be eliminated because Butz is not mentioned or analyzed at all in these paragraphs, which simply set up context for a discussion of his policies. Thus, it cannot be assumed that 1930s policymakers (who are only mentioned in passing) would have disliked his ideas.

15. Correct Answer: D

The author writes in line 50, "food prices overall are lower than they once were," which was a direct result of Earl Butz's policy, so that choice **A** can be eliminated. He also writes, "federal policies discouraged biodiversity. After all, it was more profitable for a farmer to grow just one crop" (lines 39-40) so that choice **B** can be eliminated. And finally, he writes, "Small farmers were thus eliminated" (line 34), so that choice **C** can be eliminated. The Institute for Food and Development Policy (**D**) is only described in line 35: this organization studied the new food policies, yet it is not made clear whether the Institute was founded in response to Earl Butz's Policies.

16. Correct Answer: G

The word *covering* occurs in a sentence that deals with the costs of dealing with health problems: "According to the Institute for Food and Development Policy, the total cost of dealing with obesity-related diseases is $147 billion per year, and Medicaid and Medicare—funded by taxpayer dollars—are responsible for *covering* about half of these costs" (lines 64-68). Medicaid and Medicare would thus need to deal directly with these costs, or would need to *address* them. Other answers misrepresent the content of this sentence (costs and the policies that address costs). According to the passage, Medicaid and Medicare deal only financially with the costs: information-related tasks such as *concealing* (**H**) and *reporting* (**J**) are concerns of these agencies. Because the costs are already known, and because the sentence is about policy actions (not levels of comprehension), **F** must be eliminated.

17. Correct Answer: D

The author explains the effects of American agricultural policies in lines 50-54: "But while the proliferation of high-yield monoculture farms has led to a price drop for many of our food products, the lack of diversity in American harvesting practices has led to rises in the prices of fruits and vegetables." Thus, **D** is the best choice. Despite the passage's overall discussion of farming practices, the author never explicitly discusses the prices of farm equipment (**A**) or corn (**B**). In fact, because the author also states that food prices overall are "lower than they once were" (line 50), it is possible that prices for commodity crops such as corn have dropped, offsetting the price rise for fruits and vegetables. Choice **C** also misstates the logic of the passage: Americans spend a large amount of money on obesity-related healthcare, but it is never stated that healthcare prices are getting higher. It is possible that, over the years, *more Americans* are buying obesity-related healthcare at prices that have remained constant: thus, a growing overall cost does not necessarily involve rising individual prices.

18. Correct Answer: G

In the final paragraph, the author explains the significance of the "collaborative, on-the-ground solutions" mentioned earlier in the passage (lines 80-81): "In the face of a stubborn federal gov-

ernment, local leaders have been trying to address food-related problems" (lines 83-84). Thus, the author uses the word *stubborn* to *emphasize* that the federal government is not willing or able to solve food-related dilemmas; instead, individuals must work together and come up with on-the-ground, local, or *community-based solutions*. Thus, **G** is the strongest choice. **F** must be eliminated because the government could in fact be aware of the problems (but remain unwilling to address them) and because letter-writing campaigns are never mentioned in the passage. **H** must be eliminated because this answer misstates the author's analysis: the author does mention the power of "large businesses that benefit from an industrial food system" (lines 77-78), but never describes a standoff that increased the power of such businesses. **J** also misrepresents the author's logic: according to the author, government agencies seem unwilling to address food-related problems using practical measures. Whether or not such agencies discuss food-related problems in *official documents* is an issue that the author never raises.

19. Correct Answer: C

The author writes, "These problems have been exacerbated by historical migration patterns, decreased investment in central cities, lack of coordination between urban and rural areas, and the influence of large businesses that benefit from an industrial food system" (lines 74-78). This information eliminates choices **A**, **B**, and **D**. *Food action plans* are first mentioned in line 86 and are described as positive and productive measures by the author, so that **C** can be eliminated on account of its negative tone.

20. Correct Answer: F

In these paragraphs, the author describes food policy "disadvantages" to Americans (line 56) and the consequences of "a dysfunctional food system" (lines 64-65). Using this evidence, we can eliminate the positive answer choices, which are **G** (while *reluctantly* is negative, this is ultimately a positive answer choice on account of the word *tolerant*) and **H** (since the author is only optimistic about local reform efforts, NOT about federal food policies themselves). The author, who never refers directly to herself in the passage, cannot be described as *personally* taking offense. Thus, eliminate choice **J** and choose **F**, which accurately reflects the harshly critical tone of the author's discussion.

HUMANITIES

21. Correct Answer: C

In the course of Passage A, the author advises a student approaching Shakespearean drama to "empty his mind of all preconceptions" (lines 7-8), quotes a "stage direction" (line 12) from *The Tempest*, and argues that there is a "lack of unity" (line 26) that is discernible in the opening scene of *The Tempest*. This information can be used to eliminate **A**, **B**, and **D**, respectively. **C** is only present in Passage B, which offers a few comparisons involving the plays *Hamlet*, *The Tempest*, and *Julius Caesar*.

TEST 6 Answer Explanations

22. Correct Answer: J

In lines 7-11, the author of Passage A indicates that a student reading Shakespeare must "empty his mind of all preconceptions" and "imagine that he is standing in the Globe Theatre watching the play for the first time". These ideas align directly with the qualities of openness and imagination; thus, **J** is the most effective answer. Do not wrongly infer from the same information that Shakespeare is difficult (since there is no strong negative tone, eliminating **F**) or that Shakespeare performances are not enjoyable (since the passage focuses entirely on reading Shakespeare, eliminating **G**). **H** is a misinterpretation of the end of the passage: although *The Tempest* seems to address the political themes of class and unity, Shakespeare's own political knowledge is not a direct consideration.

23. Correct Answer: A

The author states that the "two groups" have "two starkly different reactions" (line 22): the reference would thus logically refer to the "competent and cheerful" (line 19) sailors and the "worried" (line 20) aristocrats mentioned immediately before. Thus, **A** is the correct answer. **B** and **C** refer to groups that are only considered (if at all) in earlier portions of the passage, while **D** refers to aspects of a production, not to people who could have "reactions".

24. Correct Answer: F

The author explains that "miching" was used in the North of England to refer to "the stealing of small items" (line 38); a similar term for stealing time from school was used in Wales. Eliminate **H** and **J** (which both mistake "miching" for "mallecho" or "mischief"), and eliminate **G** because "miching" was a generally used word, not a word that (like "mallecho" again) was invented by Shakespeare. Thus, **F** is the best answer.

25. Correct Answer: D

The "Some" mentioned in Passage B believed that "miching mallecho" was "more than dangerous, a manifestation of evil where one would least expect to find it" (lines 73-74). The opinion of this group is thus strongly negative, as is the opinion of Octavius Caesar, who expresses "fear" (line 75) on account of mischief. **D** is the best answer, while Hamlet (**A**) is a creator of mischief, children (**B**) are depicted as participating in mischief, and Prospero (**C**) appears to see mischief as benevolent or "good" (line 66). Eliminate all of these answers, since they introduce inappropriate positive tones.

26. Correct Answer: H

The word *treated* occurs in a discussion of how mischief "is not regarded very seriously" (line 58): if mischievous acts are not seen as serious, people would treat them with leniency or *respond* to them with leniency. Thus, **H** is the best answer. Other answers refer to the wrong elements of the passage: Shakespeare would *depict* mischief (**F**) and children would *enjoy* mischief (**G**) or have opportunities for mischief made available to them (**J**). None of these choices directly refer to the people who would observe and react to mischief.

27. Correct Answer: C

In Passage B, the author describes the approach to mischief that is prevalent "Today" (line 58): "Children get up to mischief and adults smile indulgently and reminisce" (lines 59-60). This evidence supports the idea that a lenient approach to mischief is now popular; thus, **C** is the best answer. Unlike society-wide adult mischief, childhood mischief is never a discussed as an element of Shakespeare's society (eliminating **A**) or as a topic in Shakespeare's plays (eliminating **B**). Nor does the author explicitly condemn such mischief, since the negative mischief that this passage discusses is a form of social unrest from Shakespeare's society (eliminating **D**).

TEST 6 **Answer Explanations**

28. Correct Answer: F

While Passage A calls attention to Shakespeare's use of the word "tempestuous" (line 14), Passage B focuses at length on the Shakespearean phrase "miching mallecho" (line 32) and its significance. Thus, choice **F** is an effective answer. While only Passage B mentions Shakespeare scholars (as opposed to the students in Passage A, eliminating **G**) and Shakespeare's comic figures (eliminating **H**), neither passage considers Shakespeare's fluency in different languages. Do not mistake the analysis of a few Welsh and Continental European terms in Passage B as a justification for **J**.

29. Correct Answer: C

In Passage B, the author mentions Shakespeare's word "mallecho", which "appears to be an imported Continental European word" (lines 46-47) and has root words "presumably drawn from French or Italian" (line 49). This information supports choice **C**, while the fact that Passage B only defines a single Shakespeare setting (Hamlet's Elsinore Castle, which is not placed geographically in the passage but is actually in Denmark) can be used to eliminate **D**. **A** and **B** both refer to Passage A, which does not directly consider ANY of Shakespeare's responses to Continental Europe: thus, eliminate these answers.

30. Correct Answer: G

While Passage A focuses intensively on the opening of Shakespeare's *The Tempest* and its possible social themes, Passage B discusses how Shakespeare used a single term ("miching mallecho") to address the theme of mischief. Both of these detailed passages can be described as "observant and analytic", making **G** the best answer. **F** introduces a mood ("lighthearted") that does not fit the passages' emphasis on social discord, **H** wrongly characterizes these composed and scholarly passages as "impassioned", and **J** applies a negative ("overbearing") that a student who dislikes Shakespeare may feel, but that does not relate directly to any evidence in the passages themselves.

NATURAL SCIENCE

31. Correct Answer: B

The author begins the passage by describing the events that surrounded the Mount Saint Helens explosion. As the author writes in the third paragraph, "On March 20, 1980, an earthquake measuring 4.2 on the Richter scale took place deep beneath Mount Saint Helens" (lines 13-15). Yet an important transition can be found in the fourth paragraph: "The signs that Mount Saint Helens might erupt were right on the surface, yet we must travel below the earth to understand the physics of why such a

volcano erupts" (lines 22-24). In the paragraphs that follow, the author illustrates how active volcanoes function (lines 37-54) and explains the geologic causes of the Mount Saint Helens eruption (lines 64-68). Thus, **B** accurately describes the passage as *an account* of the volcanic eruption *followed by an explanation* of why the eruption took place. **A** is incorrect because none of the sentences in the passage are actually structured as questions, and because the scientists in the passage were active at the site of Mount Saint Helens (lines 55-63), not in a laboratory. **C** is incorrect because the passage is explanatory in nature and does not entail either major arguments or counter-arguments: do not mistake the different reasons why volcanoes can erupt (lines 25-28) for hypotheses or counter-arguments. Finally, **D** is incorrect because the passage begins with a description of actual events, not a theory that must be held up to scrutiny. While it is true that the later stages of the passage involve scientific evidence, there is no direct indication that such evidence is *little-known*.

32. Correct Answer: H

The author reveals the forces that are responsible for volcanic eruptions: "Typically, there are three factors involved: the buoyancy of the molten rock, or magma; the pressure from the ex-solved gases in the magma; and the injection of a new batch of magma into an already filled magma chamber" (lines 25-28). **F** and **G** can be readily eliminated using this information, while **J** can be eliminated by factoring in another quotation from the passage: "when rock inside the earth melts, its mass remains the same even though its volume increases, making it less dense than the surrounding rock. On account of its buoyancy, this lighter magma will naturally rise to the surface. If the density of the magma is less than that of the surrounding rocks, the magma reaches the surface and erupts" (lines 29-34). Although the magma in a volcanic explosion may be put under pressure by exsolved gases, *atmospheric pressure* is mentioned only as a standard for measuring the amount of dissolved gas in magma (lines 37-38), not as a reason why a volcano may erupt. Thus, **H** is the correct choice.

33. Correct Answer: A

The author provides a direct answer to this question in lines 37-41: "the amount of a dissolved gas in magma at normal atmospheric pressure is zero, but this amount rises with increasing pressure. When magma moves closer to the surface, water is released as gas (or exsolved) from the magma." In other words, as magma approaches the surface, the solubility of water vapor in magma *decreases to zero* as the magma nears the ground. Thus, **A** is the correct choice. Choice **B** directly contradicts the evidence in the passage, while choices **C** and **D** both refer to irrelevant factors. The fact that water can be classified as an exsolved gas simply provides a categorization; it does not explain *why* water and magma react as they do (**C**). And the fact that magma explodes at ground level is does not directly account for the relationship between water and magma (**D**).

TEST 6 Answer Explanations

34. Correct Answer: J

The author tells us in line 40 that *releasing* a gas is also called *exsolving* a gas. The opposite of releasing is *absorbing*. Be careful not to loosely assume, based on the passage's discussions of liquid magma and the Mount Saint Helens explosion, that exsolving means *melting* (**F**) or *igniting* (**G**). Be careful also to find the opposite of exsolving, not the synonym *releasing* (**H**).

35. Correct Answer: C

The author tells us that the earthquake was *registered at* 5.1 on the Richter scale. Here, *registered at* must have something to do with a measurement or number, a concept that can be seen in **A**, **B**, and **D**. The only answer choice that does not have to do with measurement or numbers is choice **C**. To *sign up* would properly refer to a person, not to a quantity or a scientific observation.

36. Correct Answer: H

The author writes in line 32 that "lighter magma will naturally rise to the surface." Remember, *magma* is *melted rock*. This information supports **H** and allows **F** and **J** to be quickly eliminated. The exsolving process is discussed in the preceding and subsequent paragraphs, but not in the paragraph you are being asked to consider. As a result, **G** does not explain the activity of the magma.

37. Correct Answer: B

In lines 57-63 the author explains that volcanologists "set up reflective targets between the fissures to record changes," thus eliminating choice **A**. He goes on to state that "tremors were measured by taking a record of rhythmic pulses; these pulses indicated that magma was on the move," thus eliminating choice **C**. And finally, he writes that "by late April, laser equipment had detected menacing signs: a bulge had emerged between the fissures and was growing at a rate of five cubic feet per day," eliminating choice **D**. Considering the catastrophic power of Mount Saint Helens, **B** would seem to describe a reasonable precaution; however, since warnings to townspeople are nowhere described in the passage, **B** must be eliminated.

38. Correct Answer: H

In the last paragraph (lines 76-84), the author states that there are 1500 active volcanoes and that Japan is home to 7% of them. Using basic mathematics, you will find that 7% of 1500 is 105. This supports **H**, while the other numbers refer to other data: the 7 percent (**F**), the 50 eruptions every year (**G**), and the 1,500 or so active volcanoes (**J**).

39. Correct Answer: D

The author writes that "the blast was so powerful that everything within eight miles was wiped within moments, while subsequent shockwaves caused devastation over an area of 230 square miles." On account of the context of the word *wiped* (which can be given a strong negative tone), we can surmise that this word means something like *devastated* (as stated in the next clause). *Destroyed* (**D**) is the best answer: *cleansed* (A) and *polished* (B) are both positive and irrelevant, while the neutral *repositioned* (**C**) does not accurately refer to the idea of mass devastation.

40. Correct Answer: F

It is stated in lines 64-65 that "gaseous forces were finally responsible for the eruption" at Mount Saint Helens. Thus, **F** is directly supported by the passage. Moving magma (**H**) and a magma bulge (**G**) are both mentioned in lines 60-63, but the evidence in lines 64-65 establishes that gaseous forces were the final cause. "A cloud of burning ash" (**J**) is indeed mentioned in line 65, but is an effect of the explosion, not a cause.

Test 7

READING TEST
35 Minutes—40 Questions

DIRECTIONS: There are four passages in this test. Each passage is followed by several questions. After reading a passage, choose the best answer to each question and fill in the corresponding oval on your answer document. You may refer to the passages as often as necessary.

Passage I

LITERARY NARRATIVE: This passage is adapted from the short autobiographical essay "Vocation."

Sister Josaphat had an unusual arrangement for herself. Though she lived communally and owned virtually nothing of her own, it was understood that the convent farm was hers. These were her tidy rows of lettuce blooms, her orderly
5 tomato vines. At school she was our librarian, and while she wasn't stern she was certainly reserved, the imposing gatekeeper of a world of information. Yet on this little urban farm she was in her true element. When she stepped down onto her shovel, pushing it into the fresh-turned soil, she did
10 so with a certain air, one we weren't usually privy to. I could see that from the start.

The first time I worked on the farm was early on a cool, bright Saturday morning. The convent had bars and hair salons and of course our school as its nearest neighbors, but
15 it was situated on several acres of land that the nuns had owned since their order came to this country from Poland a hundred years before. All of this area was farmland once, or was at least undeveloped, but since that time the city had flourished in its ugly, boisterous way, turning the convent and
20 its bucolic grounds into a neighborhood oddity.

Some of us had decided to spend our community service hours helping out on the nuns' farm, which we had heard about but had never seen. I arrived with my friend Nina, driven there by her dad in his elderly blue sedan. Getting up
25 early on a Saturday, doing physical work, spending more time than usual with the nuns: all of these were things I could have complained about lustily. But the air that morning was fresh, and I was fifteen, and Nina's dad's car had a different scent than our car did. Everything about that day seemed
30 exciting somehow.

Sister Josaphat met us at the back of the prim white convent house. She looked different, which was the first surprise. You would only have suspected that she was a nun if you knew precisely what you were looking for: the crepe-
35 soled shoes, the wooden cross around her neck. Otherwise, she was dressed in comfortable jeans and a button-down

shirt, and her usual brown habit wasn't there, a change so startling it seemed almost like nudity. Her hair, though clipped short and tucked neatly behind her ears, was a rich
40 golden color, not too different from the color of mine. I realized for the first time that Sister wasn't very old. Nina and I shot each other a look. Sister Josaphat was pretty!

Sister began by breaking up the earth with her shovel, and when she hit a large rock she pulled it up and heaved it
45 onto the grass a few feet away. Some of us were given the rest of this job, which we continued by pulling a rake over the ground to expose the soil's tender, hidden underside. We then nestled seedlings down into the dirt where we hoped they would take purchase and grow. And we did hope. I did,
50 anyway. We were city kids and most of us had never done any of these outdoor things. This didn't feel like school; it seemed real, and if the plants died or failed to flourish I knew I would have felt sad and more than a little responsible. The girls who didn't do the planting helped Sister build a small
55 fence around the garden's perimeter to keep the deer and rabbits out. Deer and rabbits, there in the neighborhood? Sister said she'd often seen them.

We came back to the farm every Sunday for the next three months to help nudge the growing process along. Most
60 of our crops did do well, though I know now that luck and the weather have as much to do with gardening success as hard work and good wishes. At the time it felt like some combination of magic and our own diligence that made the carrots grow long, made the peas taste sweet when we popped
65 them into our mouths.

Nothing about my relationship with Sister Josaphat changed during that time, or afterward. She'd never been especially warm but she was always fair: no pets and, unlike some of the other teachers with their confusing prejudices,
70 no whipping boys. She was as professional as she'd ever been when I needed her help in the library, with its hard brown carpeting and trying-to-be-cheerful potted plants. But she looked like a different person, a woman, to me. When she handed me my books my eyes went to her hands, my mind to
75 the secret strength I knew lived there.

GO ON TO THE NEXT PAGE.

1. The narrator would most likely agree with which of the following statements about the experience of working in Sister Josaphat's garden?

   A. The experience caused the narrator to see Sister Josaphat in a new way, but did not noticeably alter the social interactions of the two women.
   B. The experience brought the narrator closer to her classmates, but alienated her from Sister Josaphat.
   C. The experience caused the narrator to doubt Sister Josaphat's authority, yet led to new forms of self-awareness.
   D. The experience helped the narrator to appreciate her surroundings and led to an enduring interest in gardening and nature.

2. The function of the third paragraph (lines 21-30) as it relates to the rest of the passage is to:

   F. explain the community service options available to the students.
   G. describe the past friendship of the narrator and her companion Nina.
   H. argue that the narrator's past complaints about the nuns are unjustified.
   J. establish feelings of anticipation and unexpected excitement.

3. Which of the following details is NOT mentioned in the passage as a dramatic alteration in Sister Josaphat's appearance?

   A. The comfortable jeans
   B. The button-down shirt
   C. The crepe-soled shoes
   D. Sister's short-clipped hair

4. The main point of the first paragraph of the passage is that:

   F. Sister Josaphat's possession of the convent farm has never been disputed by the other nuns.
   G. the narrator has trouble understanding certain aspects of Sister Josaphat's behavior.
   H. Sister Josaphat displays assurance and ownership in her connection to the convent farm.
   J. the narrator admires Sister Josaphat's sense of reserve and attention to detail.

5. At the time of the events of the story, the narrator is:

   A. an adult looking back on a pleasant experience in her early education.
   B. a teacher who is recounting events that explain her eventual career.
   C. a promising student who is in search of a positive role model.
   D. an adolescent who is in the process of fulfilling her community service requirement.

6. The narrator states that the successful cultivation of a garden is dependent on both:

   F. committed efforts and good weather.
   G. innovative planning and extraordinary luck.
   H. good land and high-quality tools.
   J. cooperation and mutual optimism.

7. It can be reasonably inferred from the passage that the children regarded the deer and rabbits in the neighborhood as:

   A. compensation for the more tedious parts of the gardening project.
   B. the primary danger to the successful cultivation of the garden.
   C. animals that would not normally be present in urban settings.
   D. wildlife for which Sister Josaphat feels a special affection.

8. The "area" mentioned in line 17 most nearly refers to:

   F. the nuns' original territory in Poland.
   G. the outskirts of the city.
   H. the acres of land occupied by the convent.
   J. the businesses that surround the convent.

9. In the final sentence of the passage, the narrator most likely mentions Sister Josaphat's "secret strength" in order to indicate that:

   A. Sister Josaphat's garden can be imagined as having magical properties.
   B. the narrator takes new pleasure in the library's books and decorations.
   C. Sister Josaphat can effectively resist the unfair teaching habits of the other nuns.
   D. the narrator's perception of Sister Josaphat has been changed by the Sundays on the farm.

GO ON TO THE NEXT PAGE.

10. The narrator states that Sister Josaphat's attitude toward her students in academic settings was:

F. reserved and selfish.
G. distant yet evenhanded.
H. good-natured and communicative.
J. unpredictable yet daunting.

Passage II

SOCIAL SCIENCE: This passage is adapted from the essay "How We All Went Automotive." Laurence Sterne was an eighteenth-century novelist and satirist; William Hazlitt was an early nineteenth-century essayist

What automobile counts as the "first" automobile remains an uncertain question even today. Many contemporary commentators agree that the Benz Patent Motor Car of 1885-1886 can claim the mantle of "first," even though much of the
5 engine and exhaust technology used by inventor Carl Benz had been kicking around at least since the late 1860s. The commentators of Benz's era, though, would certainly have agreed that the automobile would take some getting used to.

In appearance, the Patent Motor Car was not entirely
10 out of the ordinary on the streets of 1885: three-wheeled, two-seated, and without hoods or coverings of any sort, Benz's creation calls to mind the three-wheeled bicycles that were fashionable in Victorian England. But as cars began to incorporate features that are now regarded as indispensable—
15 headlights, bumpers, windshields, and door panels— European and American streets became disorienting places for their oldest inhabitants. A lifetime of horses, carriages, and occasionally bicycles—all gone in a few years. Attempts to gingerly adapt to the new order, rather than embrace it full
20 throttle, could be comically absurd. In 1899, inventor Uriah Smith conceived a car called the "Horsey Horseless," which featured the stuffed head of a once-living horse positioned right between its headlights. This animal head was designed to serve a multitude of purposes: it would store fuel, prevent
25 live horses from feeling out of their element, and prevent older, automobile-averse citizens from feeling out of theirs. Alas, the poor Horseless never saw production.

Both automobiles and automobile enthusiasts had proliferated by the early years of the twentieth century.
30 According to the 1907 book *The Automobilist Abroad*, composed by travel writer Francis Miltoun, "Anyone interested in automobiles should know something of the literature of the subject, which, during the last decade, has already become formidable." For its own part, *The*
35 *Automobilist Abroad* is both an entry in that growing literature and a relic of writing habits that can seem rather homely.

Miltoun begins by ushering in facts, figures, and data to prove that automobiles are the way of the future, the best means of navigating the French and English roads that
40 Miltoun—with his eye for data—tallies kilometer by kilometer. He has quite a bit to say about the ordeal of London traffic, which horses and carriages could only navigate at 11.3 miles per hour and with a high probability of collision. Cars, in contrast, are speed, luxury, and efficiency incarnate,
45 a point that Miltoun stresses in the remainder of *The Automobilist Abroad*.

Yet to genuinely drive this point home, Miltoun changes tactics in the later stages of his book. *The Automobilist Abroad* begins, after a time, to read less like an automotive
50 journal and more like a piece of quaint, classic travel writing from the late eighteenth or early nineteenth century—with automobiles thrown in, of course. Read far enough along, and you will encounter the kind of luxuriant run-on sentences that would be expected from a much older, leisure-loving
55 essayist, such as Laurence Sterne or William Hazlitt: "The town of Crépy has a delightfully named and equally excellent hotel in the 'Three Pigeons,' and one may eat of real country fare and be happy and forget all about the ham and eggs and bad whiskey of Chantilly in the contemplation of omelettes
60 and chickens and fresh, green salads, such as only the country innkeeper in France knows how to serve."

To sell a skeptical world on the idea of driving, Miltoun needed to appeal to both logic and excitement—faster speeds, fewer accidents, and fresh, green salads for all. He criticizes
65 the shortsightedness of the "average scoffer at things automobilistic," then asserts that "the great point in favor of the automobile is its sociability." And as it turns out, he figured out one of the seminal points of automobile advertising long before such marketing became its own industry.

70 Return to Benz, whose name lives on today in the hallowed Mercedes-Benz luxury brand. Cars at the top of the market—from six-figure Mercedes sports cars to seven-figure Rolls Royce limousines—promise their buyers both technical excellence and transforming emotions. Even cars at
75 much lower price points rely on a version of this magic equation: start with unquestionable efficiency, then add in fun, adventure, and maybe a racing stripe or some LED lights. Master the balance between technical innovation and time-tested human desires, and the 130-year Benz dynasty is
80 the result. If not, there is always the Horsey Horseless.

GO ON TO THE NEXT PAGE.

11. It can reasonably be inferred from the passage that the quotations from Miltoun's *The Automobilist Abroad* are presented primarily to:

    A. offer humorous diversions from the main topic of the passage.

    B. convey the opinions and writing style of an early automobile enthusiast.

    C. alert the reader to a series of changing standards in automobile-related journalism.

    D. situate the issue of automoble use as part of an ongoing controversy.

12. As presented in the passage, which of the following is NOT an advantage of automobiles that Miltoun considers in *The Automobilist Abroad*?

    F. Their relatively low cost

    G. Their speed and efficiency

    H. Their sense of luxury

    J. Their pleasant social influence

13. It can reasonably be inferred from the passage that the author regards the Horsey Horseless as:

    A. an idea too complicated to be successful.

    B. a sign of the shortcomings of early automobiles.

    C. an invention that deserves ridicule.

    D. a once-common sight in some American cities.

14. In line 15, the passage most strongly suggests that features such as "headlights, bumpers, windshields, and door panels" were:

    F. fashionable features of many vehicles in Victorian England.

    G. forms of technology that were pioneered by the Benz Patent Motor Car.

    H. not always included in the earliest automobiles.

    J. responsible for the proliferation of automobile enthusiasts.

15. The main function of the fifth paragraph (lines 47-61) in relation to the passage as a whole is to:

    A. encourage the reader to take up countryside driving as a leisure activity.

    B. illustrate the obstacles that Miltoun faced in promoting automobiles through his writing.

    C. show how Miltoun used specific writing tactics to present automobiles as appealing.

    D. introduce an extended comparison that involves Miltoun and two lesser-known authors,

16. The passage states that Miltoun's writing style was:

    F. based on the style of previous automobile enthusiasts.

    G. not reliant on firsthand accounts of automobile use.

    H. guided by skepticism about automobile technology.

    J. comparable to the style used by Sterne and Hazlitt.

17. According to the passage, the Benz Patent Motor Car did not seem out of the ordinary on account of its:

    A. usefulness both for countryside trips and for urban commutes.

    B. prominent role in automobile publications such as Miltoun's *The Automobilist Abroad.*

    C. adaptability to new and evolving automobile safety features.

    D. similarities in appearance to vehicles such as three-wheeled bicycles.

18. In context, the phrase "and fresh, green salads for all" (line 64) is best understood as:

    F. a direct reference to an observation made by Miltoun.

    G. a sarcastic dismissal of arguments against automobile usage.

    H. a description found in the writings of Laurence Sterne.

    J. an image that has been repeated in modern automobile marketing.

19. The author of the passage notes that there continues to be disagreement on the issue of:

    A. how easily Europeans and Americans adapted to the presence of automobiles in cities.

    B. whether Miltoun's ideas genuinely correspond to modern marketing principles.

    C. whether Miltoun's writings appealed to the readers in the early twentieth century.

    D. which automobile can most accurately be considered the first automobile.

20. The final two paragraphs of the passage are premised on the idea that:

    F. today's automobile buyers have some of the same motivations as much earlier consumers.

    G. automobile technology will continue to change and improve at a rapid pace.

    H. few consumers are willing to buy automobiles at relatively low price points.

    J. resistance to automobiles is a socially unacceptable viewpoint today.

GO ON TO THE NEXT PAGE.

Passage III

HUMANITIES: Taken from two recent travel essays that appeared in American publications.

Passage A by Gerald Leroux

Oscar Wilde once wrote that when good Americans die they go to Paris. One cannot vouch for the truth of that observation, but it would be fairly accurate to point out that ever since Benjamin Franklin became the first American
5 Ambassador to France, Americans have followed his trail with increasing ardor. Andrew Jefferson followed closely on Franklin's heels and spent a year in the city before returning to America and higher office. Later, Harriet Beecher Stowe stayed for a while, James Fennimore Cooper worked there,
10 Henry James passed some languid time there. American writers and artists, such as Edwin Hopper and F. Scott Fitzgerald, arrived in droves. Ernest Hemmingway et al, dubbed "The Lost Generation" by Gertrude Stein, roamed the Left Bank, throwing back the absinthe and generally living up to the title.
15 Two World Wars within the first fifty years of that century brought in an enormous number of Americans - plain, straightforward G.I. Joes, who passed through a misty and secretive Paris with little more knowledge of this foreign (in more than one meaning of the word) capital city other than the
20 phrase, "Je suis Américain."

The Parisians adored Americans then and have continued to welcome all Americans - and their dollars – ever since. In return, vacationing Americans have made Paris the first stop on their European tour. A morning up the Eiffel Tower, an
25 afternoon in the Louvre, a romantic (if chilly) evening dinner floating along the Seine are all on the list of "must-do": perhaps, a visit to Versailles (far too crowded with polite and eager groups taking photos) and a visit to the flea market (far too expensive but the vendors are charming) are determinedly
30 succeeded by a reverent tour of Notre Dame (an anxious eye cocked for the Hunchback who never appears) and an exhausting climb up all those steps from Montmartre to Sacre Coeur (sadly no longer full of French children dancing with Gene Kelly). Oh, how sophisticated are the shops and
35 boutiques! How charming are the pavement bistros! How so very, very Paris! And then the tourist mounts one of those incredibly sleek and comfortable French trains that hurtles them, at high speed, on to the next European capital. "Well!" the tourist exclaims, "Paris is simply wonderful, and that is
40 France. So long."

Passage B by Elaine K. Bellinger

For me, shopping is a necessity, and something to be accomplished in as short a time as possible: for the French, it is an art to be learned, taken seriously, and pursued with a critical

enthusiasm. I need bread for breakfast? My reaction is to dash
45 into the nearest boulangerie, give my order, pay, and leave. I warn you now: it is a mistake to attempt a quick sortie like that in the local shops of rural France. There is a ritual that must be followed.

As an American, I understand the necessity of queuing in
50 an orderly line should the shop be busy. Nobody in France has ever believed that standing in line is necessary. French shoppers group themselves in sets of two or three, blocking the passage between the counter and the door, and then settle down for a discussion – but only after first shaking hands or kissing one
55 another on both cheeks. Hands gesture vigorously, heads nod or shake; each participant makes a perfectly constructed speech. Interruptions are not permitted, but interjections of agreement are allowed to punctuate the progress of the argument. In a debate, this would be wonderful. In a shop, it is
60 infuriating, for the shopkeeper would not dream of stepping in to move the customers along.

After a time the discussion pauses, and one of the participants moves forward to be served; however, he or she does so not to present an order, but to segue into the next part
65 of the discussion. This is the elaborate greeting between shopkeeper and customer. A mere "Good morning!" is insufficient. The opening remark begins with a greeting, certainly, but is followed by an inquiry about the shopkeeper's health, a brief discussion of the weather, a rebuke over the
70 difficulties of parking the car, and sundry other matters. Eventually, the shopkeeper will ask about the requirements of the customer. It is true that any boulangerie in France will have a dazzling selection of boules and baguettes of various shapes, widths, and lengths; the shopkeeper is willing to cut large
75 items in half or to slice the loaf to measure while the customers – including the rest of the people in the shop - wait. To me, bread is bread. To a Frenchman, requesting bread is an exploration of complex tastes and health-giving properties.

> Questions 21-24 ask about Passage A.

21. The primary function of the first paragraph of Passage A is to:

    A. promote greater tolerance for foreign customs.
    B. enumerate Paris monuments for the reader to visit.
    C. provide a brief history of American travel to Paris.
    D. explain how Paris has inspired American writers.

GO ON TO THE NEXT PAGE.

22. It can reasonably be inferred that the "tourist" in line 36 regards Paris as:

  F. the most important city in Europe.
  G. a disappointment despite its reputation.
  H. only one destination in a larger trip.
  J. impossible to ever fully appreciate.

23. Which of the following is NOT mentioned in the first paragraph as a reason why Americans made their way to Paris?

  A. Art and leisure
  B. Business opportunities
  C. Military assignments
  D. Political duties

24. The long sentence in lines 24-34 serves to describe:

  F. Paris destinations that might be visited by American tourists.
  G. Paris landmarks that have been represented in modern literature.
  H. places in Paris that the author finds undesirable.
  J. customs that the French will soon abandon.

> Questions 25-28 ask about Passage B.

25. As it is used in line 46, the word *quick* most nearly means:

  A. inspired.
  B. efficient.
  C. rash.
  D. insignificant.

26. As it is used in line 59, the word *wonderful* most nearly means:

  F. surreal.
  G. famous.
  H. hilarious.
  J. praiseworthy.

27. Passage B presents the perspective of a writer who

  A. objects to the cynicism and materialism of French shoppers.
  B. has trouble comprehending the motives and habits of French shoppers.
  C. understands French shopping customs but has other priorities.
  D. finds French shopping customs elegant and desirable.

28. It can be reasonably inferred that the author of Passage B describes the greeting between shopkeeper and customer as "elaborate" (line 65) because the greeting involves:

  F. unusual word choices.
  G. a variety of topics.
  H. probable misunderstanding.
  J. interruptions and debates.

> Questions 29-30 ask about both passages.

29. Passage B differs from Passage A in all of the following ways EXCEPT that:

  A. Passage B focuses on a single everyday occurrence.
  B. Passage B does not focus exclusively on Paris.
  C. Passage B identifies the nationality of its author.
  D. Passage B offers general statements about a nationality.

30. The narrator of Passage A and the narrator of Passage B can both accurately be described as:

  F. detailed and dryly humorous.
  G. scholarly and reserved.
  H. eccentric and sentimental.
  J. sarcastic and irresponsible.

GO ON TO THE NEXT PAGE.

Passage IV

NATURAL SCIENCE: This passage is adapted from the essay "Where the Buffalo Thrive."

For many people who don't live in North America, the mention of United States wildlife calls up several images. Many of these visions are the result of our misspent hours of youth, which we passed in the darkest recesses of local
5 cinemas. As a result, the animal that we associate most nearly with the North American continent is the largest, grandest one that we encountered in those film clips—an animal not only revered by the Native American as both a spiritual and physical necessity of life, but also pursued and slaughtered
10 by frontiersmen for its hide and horns: the Buffalo. We watched these beasts charge across the plains, the earth trembling beneath their hooves. In our imaginations, we regarded them as the indestructible Lords of the Prairies. The truth, as always, is more prosaic.

15 Buffalo were originally referred to as American Bison, since it was once assumed that they were connected to the species of bison found in Europe and in Asia. Indeed there are similarities. However, it was the practical—though not especially poetic—French explorers of the seventeenth
20 century who gave them the name "buffalo." "Meat" in French is translated as *"boeuf."* In many ways, buffalo are related to cows and goats, and they, too, are herbivores. They are also, like these domestic mammals, classified as "ungulates."

When natural scientists began to explore the perceived
25 relationships between certain families of animals, they gave the title of "ungulate" to all those species related to one another by the fact that they have one thing in common: a form of hoof. It was felt that if any species were to survive and develop, then the arrival of fast-running predators was an
30 important milestone in evolutionary selection. It is true that buffalo do not prey on other animals, yet neither are they pursued by carnivores, although it is true that a pack of wolves might attempt to attack a buffalo calf. That would be a rather desperate maneuver. Until the calves reach about six
35 months, the herd looks after its own. After this period, the sturdy young buffalo's distinctive hump appears, as if to signify that the buffalo is now able to fend for itself.

Not naturally aggressive, buffalo are migratory animals; they search for fresh grasslands and water each morning and
40 evening. For over 30,000 years they covered the whole of Northern America, from what we now call Canada to Mexico and from the Eastern shoreline to, at least, the Rockies. It has been estimated that until the end of the fifteenth century there were over sixty million buffalo on the land. By 1900, their
45 number had fallen to around 700. To understand how this was brought about, it should be remembered that man, no less than the wolf or the mountain lion, is technically a predator. Most predators in nature kill for food: man is the only creature of this sort that kills for less immediate and less

50 necessary reasons. Indeed, it often seems that man kills and destroys simply for the reason that man has the power to do so.

In all fairness, the human species has recently tried to reverse this unique trend of destroying anything that is not
55 material to its own wellbeing. In 2000, the number of buffalo in North America was estimated at around 360,000 head, a five hundred-fold increase over the estimate from 1900.

Still, buffalo can no longer wander the country at will. It has been a long time since these animals were seen in the
60 region of New York, and many herds are restrained within the borders of National Parks. Such restrictions are human-imposed and are designed to guarantee the purity of the breed. Elsewhere, there have been attempts to "domesticate" buffalo through crossbreeding with cattle: buffalo meat is
65 extremely healthy for human digestion, low in both fat and cholesterol. The problem is that buffalo are not easily tamed. Although generally peaceful, they will attack humans if provoked, and in such cases they will exhibit wild, ungovernable tempers. It is almost impossible to control an
70 animal of this size, an animal that is also capable of leaping over six feet off the ground. A stampeding herd of buffalo makes more than the earth tremble; it is a sight that reminds us that the buffalo were here long before us and may well be here when we have long disappeared as a species.

31. In the passage, the author claims that Buffalo are:

    A. falsely represented by the images in movies and other forms of entertainment.
    B. unrelated to cows and goats.
    C. as numerous today as they were in the past.
    D. not naturally aggressive, but capable of fighting vigorously if provoked.

32. According to the passage, which statement best describes the current status of the American buffalo population?

    F. Buffalo herds are limited in range and continue to face the threat of extinction.
    G. Ranchers are increasingly successful in their efforts to tame and domesticate buffalo.
    H. Human efforts have helped to reverse the buffalo population decreases that took place before 1900.
    J. Buffalo have resisted attempts at domestication and thus continue to decrease in number.

GO ON TO THE NEXT PAGE.

33. The passage states that the word "buffalo" is derived from a word which means:

    A. bison.
    B. hoof.
    C. meat.
    D. prairie.

34. According to the passage, film clips have often portrayed the buffalo as a:

    F. species closely related to other large mammals.
    G. source of spiritual strength for frontiersmen.
    H. massive and seemingly invincible animal.
    J. species that is quickly approaching extinction.

35. The author mentions "the wolf" and "the mountain lion" (line 47) in order to emphasize the point that:

    A. humanity is another animal species that has been known to attack and destroy buffalo.
    B. these animals are primarily responsible for the decline in buffalo numbers.
    C. predators are animals that kill only for food.
    D. even hungry predators are unlikely to attack buffalo.

36. According to the passage, it would be a "desperate maneuver" for wolves to attack a young buffalo because:

    F. a buffalo calf would easily overpower a wolf.
    G. wolves do not normally feed on buffalo meat.
    H. buffalo are powerful animals that defend their young.
    J. wolves know not to attack if a buffalo has attained its distinctive hump.

37. The importance of the cinema images mentioned in the paragraph is that these images are responsible for:

    A. the widespread slaughter of thousands of buffalo.
    B. causing the buffalo to be the animal that is most closely associated with North America.
    C. the misconception that buffalo are naturally aggressive animals.
    D. generating public concern about the current problems faced by buffalo herds.

38. As used in line 58, the phrase *at will* most nearly means:

    F. without danger.
    G. without limitations.
    H. within set boundaries.
    J. without supervision.

39. As used in the passage, the term "ungulate" is understood to describe:

    A. any animal related to the cow.
    B. all species of buffalo, including those in Europe and Asia.
    C. an animal having a diet of only vegetables.
    D. a hooved animal, whether a buffalo or a member of another species.

40. The first and last paragraphs of the passage are similar in that both paragraphs:

    F. suggest that buffalo have valuable hides and horns.
    G. mention the emotional responses called forth by the image of a moving buffalo herd.
    H. call attention to the overall health benefits of buffalo meat.
    J. describe the difficulties involved in taming buffalo.

END OF TEST 7
STOP! DO NOT TURN THE PAGE UNTIL TOLD TO DO SO.
DO NOT RETURN TO A PREVIOUS TEST.

Answer Key: TEST 7

Test 7

LITERARY NARRATIVE

1. A
2. J
3. C
4. H
5. D
6. F
7. C
8. H
9. D
10. G

HUMANITIES

21. C
22. H
23. B
24. F
25. B
26. J
27. C
28. G
29. D
30. F

SOCIAL SCIENCE

11. B
12. F
13. C
14. H
15. C
16. J
17. D
18. F
19. D
20. F

NATURAL SCIENCE

31. D
32. H
33. C
34. H
35. A
36. H
37. B
38. G
39. D
40. G

To see your scaled ACT Reading Score (1-36), determine how many questions you answered correctly and consult the Scoring Chart on Page 186 of this book.

Post-Test Analysis

This post-test analysis is essential if you want to see an improvement on your next test. Possible reasons for errors, both for the test overall and for each of the four reading passages, are listed here. Place check marks next to the types of errors that pertain to you, or write your own types of errors in the blank spaces provided.

GENERAL

◇ Spent too much time reading the passages
◇ Spent too much time answering the questions
◇ Did not attempt to finish all of the passages
◇ Did not create effective margin answers
◇ Did not use process of elimination
◇ Could not find evidence to answer the questions
◇ Could not comprehend the topics and ideas in the passages
◇ Could not understand what the questions were asking
◇ Interpreted the passages rather than using evidence

Other: _____

LITERARY NARRATIVE

◇ Spent too long reading the passage
◇ Spent too long answering the questions
◇ Could not identify the setting and characters
◇ Could not understand the plot or action
◇ Could not work effectively with tone and clues to tone

Other: _____

> **Use this form** to better analyze your performance. If you don't understand why you made errors, there is no way that you can correct them!

SOCIAL SCIENCE

◇ Spent too long reading the passage
◇ Spent too long answering the questions
◇ Could not understand the author's position or arguments
◇ Used outside knowledge rather than using evidence

Other: _____

HUMANITIES

◇ Spent too long reading the passage
◇ Spent too long answering the questions
◇ Could understand the themes and organization of the passage
◇ Could not understand the author's ideas and uses of evidence

Other: _____

NATURAL SCIENCE

◇ Spent too long reading the passage
◇ Spent too long answering the questions
◇ Found the concepts and ideas in the passage confusing
◇ Found the questions confusing
◇ Could not effectively work with the inference and logic questions

Other: _____

TEST 7 Answer Explanations

LITERARY NARRATIVE

1. Correct Answer: A

The narrator states that "nothing about my relationship with Sister Josephat changed during that time" (lines 66-67), meaning that this experience "did not noticeably alter the social interactions of the two women." Furthermore, in the second to last sentence of the passage, the narrator states that Sister Josaphat, "looked like a different person, a woman, to me," supporting the idea that the narrator now sees "Sister Josephat in a new way." Thus, **A** is correct. Because the relationship between Sister Josaphat and the narrator did not change, both **B** and **C** can be readily eliminated: being "alienated from Sister Josaphat" and doubting "Sister Josaphat's authority" are negative changes that go against the mostly positive tone of the passage. Also, because the passage focuses entirely on a small stage of the narrator's childhood, answer **D** can be eliminated: it is impossible to tell whether the narrator's interest in gardening is "enduring" or not.

2. Correct Answer: J

In this paragraph, the author writes, "some of us had decided to spend our community service by helping out on the nuns' farm, which we had heard about but never seen," signaling *anticipation*. She then writes, "Getting up early on a Saturday, doing physical work, spending more time than usual with the nuns: all of these were things I could have complained about lustily... [But] everything about that day seemed exciting somehow," signaling *unexpected excitement*. Both community service and the narrator's friend Nina are mentioned, but not in ways that would justify answers **F** or **G**: we are not told about the different community service options or about the narrator's past friendship with Nina, only about the gardening option and about the friends' activities on a single day. Instead of making a case about the narrator's "past complaints about the nuns" **H**, the paragraph simply states that the narrator could have complained about spending time with the nuns. This answer also goes against the paragraph's largely positive tone.

3. Correct Answer: C

The author writes that "[Sister Josaphat] was dressed in comfortable jeans and a button-down shirt, and her usual brown habit wasn't there, a change so startling it seemed almost like nudity. Her hair, though clipped short and tucked neatly behind her ears, was a rich golden color, not too different from mine" (lines 36-40). Every answer choice is mentioned here as a "change" except *crepe–soled shoes* (lines 32-33), which Sister Josaphat wears every day and was simply wearing at the time.

4. Correct Answer: H

In the first paragraph, the author writes, "Though [Sister Josaphat] lived communally and owned virtually nothing of her own, it was understood that the convent farm was hers." This information supports the idea of "ownership in her connection to the convent farm." The author then goes on to write, "on this little urban farm she was in her true element," supporting the *assurance* that Sister Josaphat *displays* on the farm. Though this paragraph mentions the convent, the other nuns are never de-

picted explicitly here **F**. Both **G** and **J** misrepresent the narrator's response: although there is a disparity between Sister Josaphat's behavior on the farm and her behavior in the library, the narrator never voices confusion, or anything that indicates a strong negative tone. It may be possible to conclude that the narrator admires Sister Josaphat's sense of ownership of the farm, but attention to detail is never directly identified as one of Sister Josaphat's admirable qualities.

5. Correct Answer: D

For this answer choice, you must use process of elimination because the evidence is not explicitly written out. Try to identify and eliminate false words. In **A**, *education* is false because this story is primarily about the narrator's *community service*. In **B**, *teacher* is false because this passage is not from Sister Josephat's point of view. **C** is the trap answer because it involves an assumption that a test-taker might make; however, this interpretation is not supported by the passage. Despite the narrator's generally positive attitude toward Sister Josaphat, you can see that the narrator is not *in search of* Sister Josaphat as her *role model,* leaving **D** as your answer. It is clear from the third paragraph (and from the preceding questions) that this answer accurately describes the narrator's situation.

6. Correct Answer: F

As the narrator states, "I know now that luck and the weather have as much to do with gardening success as hard work and good wishes" (lines 62-64). This quotation justifies **F**. For the other choices, eliminate false words: the planning of a garden does not need to be *innovative*, just attentive and effective **G**; the quality of the efforts, not the quality of the *land* and *tools*, is important to the narrator (**H**); *cooperation* may be important to some types of gardening, but is never identified directly by the narrator as a key to gardening success (**J**).

7. Correct Answer: C

In the passage, the narrator writes, "Deer and rabbits, there in the neighborhood?" The question mark suggests that the presence of these animals comes as a surprise to the narrator, thus supporting the idea that deer and rabbits are "animals that would not normally be present" in the area. While **A** attributes a falsely negative tone to the gardening project (which the narrator regards positively), **D** attributes a falsely positive tone to Sister Josaphat's attitude toward the deer and rabbits (which is never explicitly defined, and could be negative since they seem to threaten the garden). Although the deer and rabbits could endanger the garden and require a precautionary fence, the narrator never defines these animals as the main or *primary* threat, since other factors such as weather can hurt the gardening efforts. Thus, **B** can be eliminated.

8. Correct Answer: H

Before the author mentions *this area*, she writes, "[The convent] was situated on several acres of land that the nuns had owned since their order came to this country from Poland a hundred years before" (lines 15-17), directly indicating that the *area* referred to in the following sentence is "the acres of land occupied by the convent." Do not simply focus on the word *Poland* and neglect the structure of this sentence, since this will result in the false answer **F**. The other false answers also misconstrue the content of the passage: the convent is in the city, but we are never told whether it is on the *outskirts* or not (**G**), and there are businesses that *surround* the convent, but they are not part of its territory (**J**).

9. Correct Answer: D

The author writes, "But she looked like a different person, a woman, to me. When she handed me my books my eyes went to her hands, my mind to the secret strength I knew lived there." This is another way of saying that "the narrator's perception" of the nun "has been changed" by her time spent on the farm. Notice that the other answers focus on elements of the narrative that the narrator does NOT discuss in the final few sentences of the passage: the books (**B**) and other nuns (**C**) are mentioned earlier, but are not directly linked to Sister Josaphat's "secret strength." For **A**, the narrator does mention magic (line 63) in reference to the garden—but as part of an earlier discussion of different issues.

10. Correct Answer: G

When describing Sister Josaphat, the narrator states, "She'd never been especially warm but she was always fair," in lines 67-68. This lines up with the adjectives *distant* and *evenhanded*, thus mak-ing G the correct answer choice. This description also contradicts words in the other answers: Sister Josaphat cannot be *selfish*, or take on other strong negatives, because she is *fair* (**F**); she cannot be *communicative* because she is not *warm* (**H**); she cannot be genuinely *unpredictable* because she is always *fair* (**J**).

SOCIAL SCIENCE

11. Correct Answer: B

Before the author introduces *The Automobilist Abroad*, he writes in lines 28-29 that "Both automobiles and automobile enthusiasts had proliferated by the early years of the twentieth century." (Remember, *proliferated* means *multiplied*.) Then, in the following sentence, the author introduces one such *enthusiast* and that enthusiast's book, *The Automobilist Abroad*. Only answer choice **B** is about an *automobile enthusiast*. Other answers misrepresent the content of the passage. **A** is a trap, since there are moments of humor in the passage; however, Miltoun's writing relates to the main topic of automobiles rather than diverting attention from it. Although the final paragraph does discuss contemporary issues, they do not discuss Miltoun and do not deal with automobile journalism or current controversies. Thus, **C** and **D** can be eliminated.

12. Correct Answer: F

The author writes, "Cars…are speed, luxury, and efficiency incarnate, a point that Miltoun stresses in the remainder of *The Automobilist Abroad*" (lines 44-46). This information eliminates choices **G** and **H**. Then the author quotes Miltoun as saying, "the great point in favor of the automobile is its sociability" (lines 56-57). This eliminates **J**, leaving **F** as the answer. Do not confuse low cost and efficiency: a car that is efficient can in fact be expensive, and the author provides examples of these in lines 67-68.

13. Correct Answer: C

In the passage, the author indicates that some responses to new automobile conditions were *comically absurd* (line 20), then goes on to discuss the Horsey Horseless as an example of such an absurd response. This is why the Horsey Horseless would deserve ridicule, as stated in **C**. Both **A** and **B** misrepresent the author's attitude; the Horsey Horseless was bizarre but not particularly complicated (since it can quickly and easily be described), and it was an invention with shortcomings of its own, NOT an indication that actual automobiles had shortcomings. **D** is directly contradicted by the passage, since the Horsey Horseless "never saw production" (line 27).

14. Correct Answer: H

The author writes that "cars began to incorporate features that are now regarded as indispensable— headlights, bumpers, windshields, and door panels" (lines 13-17). This suggests that, that before this time, these features were *not always included*, as stated in choice **H**. The passage does not specify that these features of cars were popular in Victorian England (only bicycles are mentioned in this relation, eliminating **F**), and does not draw a link between these features and automobile enthusiasts (who are mentioned only in the next paragraph, eliminating **J**). **G** contradicts the passage, since the Benz Motor Car is an example of a vehicle that did NOT include these features.

15. Correct Answer: C

The author starts this paragraph by writing, "Yet to genuinely drive this point home, Miltoun changes tactics in the later stages of his book" (lines 47-48), indicating that Miltoun used *specific writing tactics*. The "point" that is referenced is the just-offered idea that "Cars … are speed, luxury, and efficiency incarnate" (line 44). By quoting Miltoun and establishing the traits of his style, the paragraph shows exactly how Miltoun emphasized the above-mentioned ideas in his writing. Thus, **C** is the best answer. The paragraph does present the virtues of driving, but does not explicitly *encourage* the reader to take up such activities (**A**); the paragraph also presents the two authors Laurence Sterne and William Hazlitt, but only briefly compares them to Miltoun and does not provide context to indicate whether or not they are *lesser-known* (**D**). Answer **B** is problematic for other reasons: though Miltoun may indeed have faced obstacles in promoting automobiles, the paragraph says nothing about what these obstacles were, and instead describes Miltoun's writing tactics.

16. Correct Answer: J

The author describes Miltoun's writing style by saying, "Read far enough along, and you will encounter the kind of luxuriant run-on sentences that would be expected from a much older, leisure-loving essayist, such as Laurence Sterne or William Hazlitt" (52-55). Miltoun's style is thus comparable to theirs, justifying **J**. The passage does not quote or analyze any other writers who favored automobiles, so that **F** is automatically out of context. Both **G** and **H** are contradicted by the passage, since Miltoun used abundant firsthand accounts (as demonstrated in lines 47-62) and since Miltoun was enthusiastic about automobiles (not skeptical or doubting).

TEST 7 **Answer Explanations**

17. Correct Answer: D

The author writes, "In appearance, the Patent Motor Car was not entirely out of the ordinary on the streets of 1885: three-wheeled, two-seated, and without hoods or coverings of any sort, Benz's creation calls to mind the three-wheeled bicycles that were fashionable in Victorian England" (lines 9-13). The other answers distract from this direct comparison: the information in **A** (different settings) and **B** (Miltoun's writings) are only mentioned later, once the discussion has shifted away from the Patent Motor Car. Choice **C** is problematic for different reasons. Although features such as headlights and bumpers (line 15) may indeed be safety features, the Patent Motor Car is notable because it did NOT use features of this sort.

18. Correct Answer: F

Earlier in the passage, Miltoun describes "fresh, green salads, such as only the country innkeeper in France knows how to serve" (line 60). This is what the author is referring to when he writes, "and fresh, green salads for all." The tone of this re-quotation may be humorous, but the author of the passage does not genuinely take a negative tone to automobile usage, so that trap answer **G** can be eliminated. The image of "fresh, green salads" comes from Miltoun, not Sterne (**H**) and is being re-used only by the author of the passage, so that there is no context for attributing it to automobile marketers as well (**J**).

19. Correct Answer: D

The author starts out the passage by writing, "What automobile counts as the 'first' automobile remains an uncertain question even today" (lines 1-2). This directly justifies choice **D**. In the second and third paragraphs, the author indicates that Europeans and Americans, after some disorientation, eventually adapted quite well to automobiles. This line of reasoning eliminates choice **A**. Choices **B** and **C** both misrepresent Miltoun's writings, which appeared at a time of debate about automobiles but are never defined as subject to debate today.

20. Correct Answer: F

The author describes Miltoun's notion (in favor of cars) that what is most appealing about the car "is its sociability" (lines 56-57). The author then writes that "as it turns out, [Miltoun] figured out one of the seminal points of automobile advertising long before such marketing became its own industry" (lines 68-69). This *sociability* is one of the *time-tested human desires* the author is describing in the last paragraph, suggesting people who buy cars today "have some of the same motivations as much earlier consumers." Other answers use faulty logic or ideas from elsewhere in the passage. **G** can be eliminated because, though some forms of automobile technology are discussed, how rapidly these technologies will *change and improve* is never explained. **H** can be eliminated because effective marketing for automobiles at lower price points is discussed, and because the author never establishes which price bracket consumers will buy most often. **J** can be eliminated because resistance to automobiles is a topic that occurs much earlier and is not condemned or even discussed here.

HUMANITIES

21. Correct Answer: C

The relevant paragraph begins by mentioning Benjamin Franklin and goes on to describe the "Americans" (line 5) who have followed him in visiting Paris; this group includes writers, artists, and the "enormous number of Americans" (line 16) who passed through as soldiers during the World Wars. Thus, **C** is a correct answer. This paragraph mainly states facts, rather than presenting an argument, so that **A** indicates the wrong approach. **B** indicates the wrong kind of facts (about monuments, not about individuals), while **D** assumes a different kind of analysis: the author only notes that American writers visited Paris, but does not describe the effects of Paris on their writing. In any event, writers are only a few of the individuals that the author names in this paragraph.

22. Correct Answer: H

The author of Passage A describes the "tourist" as traveling "on to the next European capital" (line 38); in doing so, the tourist observes that "Paris is simply wonderful, and that is France. So long" (line 40). This information supports **H**, since the tourist is traveling to another European capital and would naturally see Paris as only a single destination. While **F** overstates Paris's importance for the somewhat dismissive tourist, **G** is contradicted by the tourist's moderately positive response. **J** is irrelevant to the reactions of the tourist, who is less interested in "fully appreciating" Paris than in simply enjoying the city and moving on.

23. Correct Answer: B

In the first paragraph, the author explains that Paris attracted self-indulgent "writers and artists" (lines 10-11), "G.I. Joes" (line 17) during the World Wars, and ambassadors such as "Benjamin Franklin" (line 4). This information can be used to eliminate **A**, **C**, and **D**. Because no businessmen or even business pursuits are explicitly mentioned, choose **B** as an answer that is not directly relevant to the author's discussion.

24. Correct Answer: F

The long sentence is prefaced by a reference to "vacationing Americans" (line 23); in terms of its own content, the sentence in the line reference describes Paris sites such as the Eiffel Tower, the Louvre, Notre Dame, and Sacre Coeur. It can be reasonably inferred that an American tourist would have the opportunity to visit these sites in Paris, so that **F** is the best answer. **G** refers to an issue that is presented in the first paragraph (literature) but never raised here. **H** and **J** wrongly assume that the author is clearly negative about the Paris sites: although tourists are subjected to light criticism in the final sentences of the passage, the sentence for the line reference is mostly factual and does not contain strong negatives.

25. Correct Answer: B

The word *quick* describes the narrator's typical "sortie [or trip]" (line 46) to obtain breakfast: normally, the narrator will "dash into the nearest boulangerie, give my order, pay, and leave" (lines 44-45). These actions should be performed with little trouble, so that the sortie is efficient; thus, **B** is the best answer. **A** wrongly indicates that the narrator exhibits strong emotion or ingenuity (when in fact the sortie is an everyday occurrence), while **C** and **D** both apply incorrect negatives to an action that the narrator describes approvingly.

26. Correct Answer: J

The word *wonderful* refers to the "interjections of agreement" (lines 57-58) that might be *appropriate* and *effective* in a debate argument, but that are "infuriating" (line 60) in a shopping context. Because the author is talking about a positive possibility during a debate, *praiseworthy* is an effective choice. Thus, **J** is the best answer. **F** (*surreal*) and **H** (*hilarious*) might refer to the tone of the passage as a whole, but do not directly fit the context of this sentence. **G** is out of scope: how positive the debate tactic is, not how well known or *famous* it is, is the author's concern.

27. Correct Answer: C

The author of Passage B is mainly concerned with describing the elaborate "ritual that must be followed" (lines 57-58) in French shopping: this ritual is described in great detail, although the author ultimately concludes that "To me, bread is bread" (lines 76-77). Thus, **C** is an effective answer. **A** misstates the purpose of the author's critique (since the author objects to the time that the French spend shopping, not to their cynicism), **B** wrongly assumes that the author does not understand French customs, and **D** wrongly assumes that the author speaks positively of French shopping customs.

28. Correct Answer: G

In explaining how the greeting proceeds, the author states that the opening remarks are "followed by an inquiry about the shopkeeper's health, a brief discussion of the weather, a rebuke over the difficulties of parking the car, and sundry [various] other matters" (lines 68-70). These different topics make **G** the best answer. **F** misconstrues the author's ideas (since the length of the greeting, not its word choices, is strange), while **H** wrongly attributes an overall negative to a greeting that involves only a few negatives ("rebuke") and that does not actually involve misunderstandings. **J** is a tempting answer, yet "interruptions" and "debates" are topics that occur earlier in the passage, not in the direct context of the greeting.

29. Correct Answer: D

Unlike Passage A (which offers a survey of American travel to Paris), Passage B discusses a specific conversation that can be observed in a French shop, indicates that its content is relevant to French life generally (not simply to Paris, which is never directly mentioned), and identifies its author as "an American" (line 49). This information can be used to eliminate **A**, **B**, and **C**. Both passages offer general statements about a nationality: while the conversation in Passage B is typical of French shopping habits, the author of Passage A states that "The

Parisians adored Americans and have continued to welcome all Americans" (lines 21-22). Thus, **D** is the correct answer.

30. Correct Answer: F

While the author of Passage A begins with a detailed account of American travel to Paris and ends with an ironic depiction of a typical American tourist, the author of Passage B describes French shopping rituals in a manner meant to call attention to how over-elaborate and subtly ridiculous they are. **F** is the best answer. **G** (*scholarly*) neglects the strong and occasionally humorous tones of the passages, **H** (*sentimental*) wrongly depicts these analytic authors as more emotional than they are, and **J** (*irresponsible*) involves a strong negative that would serve to condemn the authors themselves, not to characterize their critical styles.

NATURAL SCIENCE

31. Correct Answer: D

The author writes that" it is true that buffalo do not prey on other animals, yet neither are they pursued by carnivores" (lines 30-32). He then goes on to write that buffalo are "not naturally aggressive," and that, "although generally peaceful, they will attack humans if provoked, and in such cases they will exhibit wild, ungovernable tempers" (lines 67-69). The passage contradicts **B**, because buffalo are related to cows and goats, and **C**, because buffalo were once much more numerous. The author would also disagree with **A**, because the movies described by the author rightly depict buffalo as physically powerful animals.

32. Correct Answer: H

The author describes the American buffalo population, stating that for "over 30,000 years they covered the whole of Northern America… By 1900, their number had fallen to around 700" (lines 40-45). However, "the human species has recently tried to reverse this unique trend of destroying anything that is not material to its own wellbeing. In 2000, the number of buffalo in North America was estimated at around 360,000 head, a five hundred-fold increase over the estimate from 1900" (lines 53-57). Since the buffalo population is not decreasing, answers **F** and **J** can be eliminated, since both are premised on the idea that the number of these animals is getting smaller. Line 66, which states that buffalo "are not easily tamed" and supports a larger argument about the current problems faced by those who hope to domesticate buffalo, contradicts **G**.

33. Correct Answer: C

When describing how the buffalo got its name, the author writes, "it was the practical—though not especially poetic—French explorers of the seventeenth century who gave them the name "buffalo" (lines 18-20). As noted in the passage, "meat" in French is translated as "*boeuf.*" Of the other answers, **A** is another name for buffalo, **B** is the important feature of most ungulates, and **D** is the

TEST 7 Answer Explanations

natural habitat of the buffalo. None, however, explain the direct origins of the word "buffalo."

34. Correct Answer: H

In describing how we envision buffalo, the author writes, "the animal that we associate most nearly with the North American continent is the largest, grandest one that we encountered in those film clips…We watched these beasts charge across the plains, the earth trembling beneath their hooves. In our imaginations, we regarded them as the indestructible Lords of the Prairies" (lines 5-13). Words such as grandest and indestructible indicate that **H** is the correct answer. **F**, **G**, and **J** all refer to traits of the buffalo mentioned elsewhere in the passage, and of these, buffalo are no longer approaching extinction (**J**). However, none of these are explicitly connected to the film clips mentioned in the first and last paragraphs.

35. Correct Answer: A

In the line reference in which the author mentions *the wolf* and *the mountain lion*, the author states that it "should be remembered that man, no less than the wolf or the mountain lion, is technically a predator" (lines 46-48). Through this information, the author helps us to better understand why the number of buffalo had fallen in the 1900s. He goes on to write, "Most predators in nature kill for food: man is the only creature of this sort that kills for less immediate and necessary reasons" (lines 48-50). In other words, we are "another animal species" that, in the past, "has been known to…destroy buffalo." **B** is incorrect because humanity has been responsible for the buffalo's decline; **C** is incorrect because humanity, a predator species, does not always kill for food. While the passage contradicts these two answers, the author never specifies whether the wolf and the mountain lion would be hungry predators; the danger of attacking buffalo is mentioned earlier, when the author is not focusing on the interactions of buffalo and humans. As a result, **D** can be eliminated.

36. Correct Answer: H

The author writes that "it would be a rather desperate maneuver" for carnivores "to attack a buffalo calf" because, "until the calves reach about six months, the herd looks after its own" (lines 32-35). Eliminate **F** and **G** using false words: based on the passage it is unclear whether a buffalo calf could easily overpower a wolf and whether wolves normally feed on buffalo meat. Be cautious of the faulty logic in **J**: the buffalo's hum signifies that the buffalo can fend for itself, not that wolves will cease to attack it. In fact, the wolves may be willing to attack even a dangerous opponent.

37. Correct Answer: B

The author writes that, "For many people who don't live in North America, the mention of US wildlife calls up several images. Many of these visions are the result of our misspent hours of youth, which we passed in the darkest recesses of the local cinema. As a result, the animal that we associate most nearly with the North American continent is the largest, grandest one that we encountered in those film clips … : the Buffalo" (lines 1-10). Thus, **B** is correct because it describes the *association* between Buffalo and North America. **A**, **C**, and **D** all refer to aspects of the passage, but are not directly linked to the cinema images. The slaughter

of buffalo was caused by hunting, the buffalo are depicted as powerful but not as naturally aggressive or destructive in the film clips, and the reasons for the increased *public concern* about buffalo (as described in lines 53-67) are never linked to the films.

38. Correct Answer: G

Here, if you look at the sentence, in context the words *at will* refer to how buffalo wander. The definition of wandering is to walk leisurely in an aimless way, or to go about freely and *without limitations*. Thus, **G** is the best answer. While **J** looks like an appealing answer to choose, it is in fact an assumption, given that one can wander at will while still being supervised. For **F**, the buffalo could have faced dangers even when they wandered more broadly; for **H**, *within set boundaries* is the direct opposite of *at will*.

39. Correct Answer: D

The author defines the word *ungulate* by writing, "they gave the title of "ungulate" to all those species related to one another by the fact that they have one thing in common: a form of hoof." Cows (**A**), buffalo species (**B**), and animals that eat vegetables (**C**) can all be ungulates, but only choice **D** calls attention to the primary criterion for defining an ungulate. Certain ungulates may be unrelated to cows or may not eat vegetables, and the group of ungulates is much larger than the group of all buffalo species.

40. Correct Answer: G

In the first paragraph, the author writes that he and other film viewers "watched these beasts [buffalo] charge across the plains, the earth trembling beneath their hooves. In our imaginations, we regarded them as the indestructible Lords of the Prairies" (lines 10-13). This sentence mentions how we respond to the image "of a moving herd of buffalo" in our *imaginations*. Similarly, in the last paragraph the author describes buffalo on the move: "A stampeding herd of buffalo makes more than the earth tremble; it is a sight that reminds us that the buffalo were here long before us and may well be here when we have long disappeared as a species" (lines 71-74). Once again, the author talks about what this same image *reminds us* of or presents "the emotional responses called forth" by this *sight*, which inspires awe in those who witness it. Only the first paragraph discusses **F** ("hide and horns," line 10), while only the final paragraph discusses **H** (lines 64-66) and **J** (lines 66-69).

Test 8

READING TEST

35 Minutes—40 Questions

DIRECTIONS: There are four passages in this test. Each passage is followed by several questions. After reading a passage, choose the best answer to each question and fill in the corresponding oval on your answer document. You may refer to the passages as often as necessary.

Passage I

PROSE NARRATIVE: Adapted from *A Princess of Mars* (1917) by Edgar Rice Borroughs and *Marsland* by Thomas Thorley (1958). The first passage is narrated by a man from Earth who has been transported to Mars, while the second depicts a shady real estate tycoon who intends to open a theme park on the planet.

Passage A by Edgar Rice Borroughs

I opened my eyes upon a strange and weird landscape. I knew that I was on Mars; not once did I question either my sanity or my wakefulness. I was not asleep, no need for pinching here; my inner consciousness told me as plainly that I
5 was upon Mars as your conscious mind tells you that you are upon Earth. You do not question the fact; neither did I.

I found myself lying prone upon a bed of yellowish, mossy vegetation which stretched around me in all directions for interminable miles. I seemed to be lying in a deep, circular
10 basin, along the outer verge of which I could distinguish the irregularities of low hills. It was midday, the sun was shining full upon me and the heat of it was rather intense upon my body, yet no greater than would have been true under similar conditions on an Arizona desert. Here and there were slight
15 outcroppings of quartz-bearing rock which glistened in the sunlight; and a little to my left, perhaps a hundred yards, appeared a low, walled enclosure about four feet in height. No water, and no other vegetation than the moss was in evidence, and as I was somewhat thirsty I determined to do a little
20 exploring.

Springing to my feet I received my first Martian surprise, for the effort, which on Earth would have brought me standing upright, carried me into the Martian air to the height of about three yards. I alighted softly upon the ground, however, without
25 appreciable shock or jar. Now commenced a series of evolutions which even then seemed ludicrous in the extreme. I found that I must learn to walk all over again, as the muscular exertion which carried me easily and safely upon Earth played strange antics with me upon Mars. Instead of progressing in a sane and
30 dignified manner, my attempts to walk resulted in a variety of hops which took me clear of the ground a couple of feet at each step and landed me sprawling upon my face or back at the end of each second or third hop. My muscles, perfectly attuned and accustomed to the force of gravity on Earth, played the mischief
35 with me in attempting for the first time to cope with the lesser gravitation and lower air pressure on Mars.

I was determined, however, to explore the low structure which was the only evidence of habitation in sight, and so I hit upon the unique plan of reverting to first principles in
40 locomotion, creeping. I did fairly well at this and in a few moments had reached the low, encircling wall of the enclosure.

Passage B by Thomas Thorley

Not so extreme that you'd go bouncing off. Not so subtle that you wouldn't notice. Perfect, thought Lewin, bouncing gingerly up and down one last time, just to make sure he
45 wasn't getting carried away, thinking too much of his own judgment. The kids will love it. The adults won't mind it. Perfect.

So the gravity on Mars was exactly what the science people (and, more importantly, the marketing people) had
50 predicted. But what about the rest of it, the cold, empty, reddish expanses? You'd freeze to death without a suit. Lewin had also heard (from the science people) about the freak sandstorms that could sweep the planet and had determined (based on two different focus groups) that these might be a
55 problem. If one hit during construction, everything would be halted for days. Everything would have to be repainted or at least touched up. People could get killed. And that would only set back the construction even more.

But even in the midst of all these qualms (signs of a good
60 businessman, though, always thinking things through), Lewin allowed himself to scan his surroundings. That gulch, over there: fill it with water, set up a flume for the kids to ride, set up an old man with a balloon stand and an old woman selling soft pretzels right near the exit. That outcrop, just above: that's
65 for the big metal rollercoaster and the giant swings. Then that long, ominous plain: there's your parking lot, food court, budget motel, shopping center, and "luxury resort" for the people with the really spoiled kids and, of course, morons on honeymoons. "It's like the wild west," said Lewin to himself.
70 Take a desert, take cheap food and ramshackle buildings and empty pleasures, take a bunch of suckers, mix them all together, and turn it all into money.

GO ON TO THE NEXT PAGE.

Questions 1-4 ask about Passage A.

1. The narrator of Passage A, in his attempts to understand his new surroundings, does which of the following?

   A. Draws an analogy between his new location and a location on Earth
   B. Endeavors to scientifically classify the forms of plant life that he encounters
   C. Tries to figure out how and why he was transported away from Earth
   D. Observes the sky in order to figure out whether the weather will improve or worsen

2. In Passage A, the narrator is uncertain about:

   F. whether he is awake.
   G. whether he is truly on Mars.
   H. what time of day it is.
   J. what is within the enclosure.

3. As it is used in line 11, the word *irregularities* most nearly means:

   A. disruptive tendencies.
   B. random events.
   C. dissimilar shapes.
   D. strange behaviors.

4. In the final paragraph of Passage A, the narrator decides to adopt a "creeping" form of locomotion because:

   F. he wants to take a more precise measurement of the strength of the gravity on Mars.
   G. his earlier attempts to walk upright resulted in inconvenience.
   H. he wishes to escape detection.
   J. he has been seriously injured.

Questions 5-7 ask about Passage B.

5. The statement about the "plain" in lines 65-69 is typical of Passage B in the way that it:

   A. indicates that Lewin's scheme is so elaborate that it will probably fail.
   B. quickly relates conditions on Mars to Lewin's construction project.
   C. reveals Lewin's lack of scientific and geographical knowledge.
   D. ultimately suggests that Lewin wants to do more in life than succeed in business.

6. What is one purpose of the parenthetical statements that occur in the second paragraph of Passage B?

   F. They summarize conflicts from Lewin's life on Earth.
   G. They clarify some of Lewin's sources of information.
   H. They reveal Lewin's lack of success in business.
   J. They provide details about the landscape of Mars.

7. It can be reasonably inferred from Passage B that Lewin views the prospective visitors to his theme park with:

   A. hatred.
   B. pity.
   C. indifference.
   D. contempt.

Questions 8-10 ask about both passages.

8. In what way do Passage A and Passage B differ in their descriptions of Mars?

   F. Passage A indicates that there is much animal life on Mars; Passage B indicates that Mars is unpopulated.
   G. Passage A indicates that Mars has stronger gravity than Earth; Passage B indicates that Mars has weaker gravity than Earth.
   H. Passage A indicates that Martian soil is yellow; Passage B indicates that Martian soil is red.
   J. Passage A indicates that Mars is relatively hot; Passage B indicates that Mars is relatively cold.

9. Which statement most effectively compares the protagonists of the two passages?

   A. The narrator of Passage A is observant and meticulous, while Lewin is cynical and materialistic.
   B. The narrator of Passage A is whimsical and poetic, while Lewin is selfless and hardworking.
   C. The narrator of Passage A is optimistic and adventurous, while Lewin is cautious and fearful.
   D. The narrator of Passage A is eager and idealistic, while Lewin is determined and vengeful.

GO ON TO THE NEXT PAGE.

10. An important element of Passage B that is not present in Passage A is:

F. precise observation of the amount of gravity exhibited on Mars.

G. writing that indicates the main character's thoughts and observations

H. direct reference to individuals other than the main character.

J. a clear goal that the narrator hopes to accomplish.

Passage II

SOCIAL SCIENCE: This passage is adapted from the article "Reach Across, and They Reach Back: Life in the Modern Classroom."

In the United States we take education for granted; in Africa, it has often been necessary to fight for good schooling. No one understood this better than Hastings Banda, the first President of the nation of Malawi. When he was in his early
5 teens, Banda left his native village and set off, on foot, to South Africa. Most Malawian males did this, seeking work in the mines, for work was scarce in Malawi in the early twentieth century. Banda was lucky. Through the help of a member of the Methodist church whom he met while he was
10 working in South Africa, he was given the chance to go to school in Wilberforce, Ohio. Once in America, he seized every opportunity, and ruthlessly used his charm and intelligence to get ahead. In 1937, he graduated with a degree in medicine; his original intention had always been to return
15 to Malawi and become a doctor. However, because his own country was a British territory, Banda was required to earn a further medical degree in the United Kingdom before he could do that. It was a long haul, but it explains why education became such a priority when Banda rose to the Presidency.

20   Once in office, Banda moved immediately to tackle the problems created by the widespread illiteracy of the native Malawian population. Under British rule, education in general was confined to the European expatriates who had settled in the country: where native Malawians were
25 concerned, education was left to the mission schools, which lacked the means to take education much beyond the level of village infants chanting rhymes under a Baobab tree— charming for the tourists, no doubt, but hardly likely to advance a fledgling country. Banda needed to build a
30 Malawian civil service for his nation. In terms of advanced education, his own background told him what was needed. He thus created the scenic Kamuzu Academy, where "the brightest and the best" children from every village could be educated up to university level at no cost to their families: the
35 state provided everything from imported teachers to living quarters and uniforms. To be accepted at K.A. was to earn

yourself a chance at a prosperous future. If you did not make it in, you had few other opportunities to move beyond your village.

40   The establishment of Kamuzu Academy was a tremendous acknowledgment of the importance of education. This academy was an elite institution, but it was still a symbol of hope in a country trying to build post-imperial infrastructure. In its early days, Kamuzu Academy did
45 succeed in producing what Banda wanted: it accepted outstanding students, and gave all Malawians something to aspire to. Later, rumors and criticisms emerged: some claimed that family connections became more important than test scores in determining admission to Kamuzu. Yet the most
50 pressing criticism was that the entire education budget for the country was expended on the needs of K.A.

I arrived in Malawi in 1994 to teach English, not at Kamuzu but at one of the two schools that Banda had designated for non-native children in Malawi, the sons and
55 daughters of the Indian community and expatriates from Zimbabwe and elsewhere. In his nineties at the time, Banda had finally agreed to open elections and had lost. The new president, Bakili Muluzi, withdrew some of the academy's money in order to provide wider education in the country.
60 Kamuzu had to begin to fend for itself: it had to shed some of its pupils and send them to the expatriate schools. The school where I was employed had a new, energetic principal, who agreed to take in advanced Kamuzu students—the first native Malawians in the school's history.

65   I have never had pupils so fiercely determined to seize the chances that they had been given. They wrote essays. I checked these essays and sent them back to be redone again and again, and the students smiled and laughed and willingly undertook revision after revision. They involved themselves
70 in the school sports, the local choir, the drama club, the school festivals. They all passed their exams with flying colors.

The fact remains that Hastings Banda created a legacy of hope for the youth of Malawi. Throughout the country, he generated the determination to know something beyond a life
75 of growing coffee and tea and corn and waiting each year for the rains to arrive. Today, if you travel almost anywhere in the world, it is highly probable that you will meet a Malawian working as a lawyer, a doctor, a scientist, or an engineer, and sending money home every month to help the rest of this
80 optimistic nation. I know. I taught some of them.

GO ON TO THE NEXT PAGE.

11. The point of view from which the passage is written is that of:

A. a school reformer encouraging American institutions to imitate Kamuzu Academy.
B. an American educator with direct experience of the schooling system in Malawi.
C. an instructor of history explaining why Hastings Banda deserves greater respect than he receives.
D. a British journalist documenting the most important effects of the 1994 election in Malawi.

12. One of the main arguments that the author is trying to make in the passage is that:

F. Banda adopted an American model for Kamuzu Academy, but dramatically improved upon foreign practices.
G. Banda's educational reforms improved the lives of many Malawians, but were not necessarily immune to criticism.
H. Banda's reputation as a reformer was undermined by his unwillingness to promote younger politicians.
J. the work of Kamuzu Academy deserves greater international publicity than it has received.

13. The author describes the Kamuzu Academy as:

A. an elite institution that covered the education expenses of its students.
B. an outstanding school that inspired similar educational projects throughout Africa.
C. a policy measure that Malawi's citizens greeted with unwavering support.
D. the source of a political dispute that Malawians are eager to forget.

14. According to the passage, in which countries did Banda receive his education in medicine?

F. The United States and the United Kingdom
G. The United States and South Africa
H. The United Kingdom and South Africa
J. Malawi and South Africa

15. In line 27, the narrator mentions "village infants chanting rhymes under a Baobab tree" in order to:

A. introduce a larger discussion of the day-to-day conditions faced by Malawian villagers.
B. call attention to the primary reason why tourists visit Malawi.
C. highlight an ultimately defective educational practice.
D. present an important event from Banda's childhood.

16. It can be reasonably inferred from the passage that Banda's determination to improve education in Malawi was a direct result of his:

F. winning and agreeable personality.
G. lifelong desire to study a variety of subjects.
H. discussions with other Malawian workers who had relocated to South Africa.
J. experiences within the American and British educational systems.

17. All of the following are reasons why Banda created the Kamuzu Academy EXCEPT a need to:

A. combat illiteracy in Malawi.
B. build a Malawian civil service.
C. establish connections with British schools.
D. provide educational resources for gifted children.

18. When teaching at the school in 1994, the narrator discovered that the native Malawian pupils were:

F. especially drawn to jobs in literature and the arts.
G. cheerful and eager to succeed.
H. not aware of economic hardships.
J. optimistic yet harshly competitive.

19. What characteristics of contemporary Malawians does the author emphasize in the final paragraph?

A. Family connections and knowledge of history
B. Strong education and dislike of menial labor
C. Prestigious professions and underlying insecurities
D. International travel and loyalty to Malawi

20. The transfer of Kamuzu students to other Malawian schools can be explained by:

F. the new admissions standards favored by Kamuzu school administrators.
G. the education funding policies of Bakili Muluzi.
H. the arrival of new expatriates from India and Zimbabwe.
J. Hastings Banda's resignation from the Malawian presidency.

GO ON TO THE NEXT PAGE.

Passage III

HUMANITIES: This passage is adapted from the philosophical study "The Polar Universe."

One of the central tenets of the ancient Chinese traditions of Taoism is the concept of *wu-wei*—a word often translated into English as "non-action." Far from its ostensible meaning of simply "doing nothing," *wu-wei* implies
5 something far more nuanced. In the *Tao Te Ching*, Lao-tzu, the father of Taoist doctrine, writes that "One does nothing [*wu-wei*], yet nothing is left undone." And yet, how can this be? In our hectic modern world, readers across cultures might see this sentence and view it as the height of absurdity. If we
10 don't go to work, we don't get paid. But what if Lao-tzu is driving at something to which, in our tireless quest to achieve, we have all become blind?

Act, but through non-action.
Be active, but have no activities.
15 Taste, but have no tastes.

So writes the sage in Chapter Sixty-Three of the *Tao Te Ching*. Lao-tzu's book is filled with seeming paradoxes such as this one, which have perhaps thickened the air of inscrutability that can surround so much Asian philosophy, at
20 least as seen by Americans and Europeans. In order to understand the truths behind these apparent contradictions, to unveil the meaning of *wu-wei*, it is first necessary to look at a few Taoist ideas about our world and our universe that run quite contrary to popular convention. The first is that of *yin*
25 and *yang*, a concept that has been popularized shamelessly but seldom fully understood; the second is that of the Tao itself.

"Oh, East is East, and West is West, and never the twain shall meet," wrote Rudyard Kipling at the beginning of his
30 famous "The Ballad of East and West". It is a sentiment that, had Lao-tzu been around to read it, he would probably have rejected. For how can we even speak of an East without a West? Or, for that matter, of a West without an East? The two concepts depend upon one another for their distinction, for
35 their very existences, and thus they are inextricably linked. "At the very roots of Chinese thinking and feeling," writes scholar and lecturer Alan Watts in his book *Tao: The Watercourse Way*, "there lies the principle of *polarity*, which is not to be confused with the ideas of opposition or conflict.
40 In the visualizations of other cultures, light is at war with darkness, life with death, good with evil … and thus an idealism to cultivate the former and be rid of the latter flourishes throughout much of the world."

From a Taoist point of view, which looks at the world
45 through the lens of polarity, such metaphors are utterly flawed because they are based upon the fundamental misconception that it is possible to preserve the good while eliminating the bad entirely. "To the traditional Chinese way

of thinking," writes Watts, "this is as incomprehensible as an
50 electric current without both positive and negative poles." Or, as Lao-tzu puts it:

To have and to lack generate each other.
Difficult and easy give form to each other.
Long and short off-set each other.
55 High and low incline into each other.
Note and rhythm harmonize with each other.
Before and after follow each other.

Thus, we have a picture of the universe in which all opposites are paradoxically intertwined, simultaneously
60 depending upon one another, one waxing while the other wanes, one ebbing while the other flows, existing much more like two children at play than like two enemy combatants striving for supremacy. This is the real, underlying principle behind the Chinese conceptions of *yin* and *yang*, which are
65 seen as the two archetypal poles of cosmic energy. Together, they are associated with the feminine and the masculine, the yielding and the firm, the dark and the light, the weak and the strong, to name but a few of the limitless polarities that exist in nature. *Yin* and *yang* can thus be seen as the two contending
70 forces within any pair of opposites, and to embrace one at the expense of the other is, for the Taoist, an exercise in self-defeat. "Thus the art of life is not seen as holding on to *yang* and banishing *yin*," writes Watts, "but as keeping the two in balance, because there cannot be one without the other." This
75 is an unsettling proposition for the Westerner, who likes to believe in the idea of progress from era to era, and of steadily making the world a better place.

At first glance, the Taoist perspective might seem to imply an almost fatalistic outlook in which we are powerless
80 to "rid the world of evil," as some present-day American politicians have sought to do. But Taoist doctrine emphasizes just how closely all humans are connected to one another, and to the rest of the cosmos. To be ignorant of or indifferent to the rest of that creation is, thus, to strike a blow against one's
85 true nature.

GO ON TO THE NEXT PAGE.

21. The author's intention in writing this passage is most likely to:

    A. analyze a system of belief that can seem incompatible with American and European ways of understanding the world.

    B. argue against the interpretation of Taoism that has been popularized by Alan Watts in *Tao: The Watercourse Way*.

    C. encourage the adoption of Taoist methods of managing conflict in fields as different as politics and business.

    D. capture the disorienting nature of the Taoist universe using a series of unusual and incompatible metaphors.

22. The passage presents contrasts between all of the following EXCEPT:

    F. the principle of polarity and the principle of conflict.

    G. Lao-tzu and Rudyard Kipling.

    H. the *Tao Te Ching* and *Tao: The Watercourse Way*.

    J. Taoist beliefs and current political ideals.

23. It can be reasonably inferred that the author believes that the concept of *yin* and *yang* has been promoted in a manner that is:

    A. inaccessible.

    B. irresponsible.

    C. insignificant.

    D. illegal.

24. One major assumption made by the author of the passage is that:

    F. the popularity of Taoism is steadily increasing in Europe and America.

    G. the modern Western world values intense activity and positive change.

    H. the *Tao Te Ching* is incomprehensible without knowledge of Lao-tzu's biography.

    J. Taoism is not the only Asian belief system that relies on a principle of polarity.

25. The author includes a substantial quotation from the *Tao Te Ching* in lines 52-57 in order to:

    A. demonstrate that the use of metaphor is a significant feature of ancient Chinese writing.

    B. help the reader to appreciate Lao-tzu's command of poetic rhythm.

    C. directly present Lao-tzu's ideas about the order of existence.

    D. compensate for flawed earlier translations of Lao-tzu's writing.

26. As it is used in line 73, the word *keeping* most nearly means:

    F. maintaining.

    G. isolating.

    H. preventing.

    J. stockpiling.

27. A follower of Taoist doctrine would be most likely to DISAGREE with the idea that:

    A. non-action can be a path to fulfillment.

    B. good depends on evil in order to be expressed.

    C. contrasting forces can be brought into harmony.

    D. each human being is fundamentally isolated.

28. Throughout the passage, the quotations from Alan Watts serve to:

    F. defeat the assumption that Westerners have not studied or written about Taoism.

    G. summarize and clarify some of the important principles of Taoist thought.

    H. offer viewpoints that simultaneously intrigue and upset the author.

    J. help to strengthen Watts's reputation as a major defender of Taoist thought.

29. According to the passage, which of the following would NOT be an appropriate way of envisioning the Chinese concepts of *yin* and *yang*:

    A. Light and darkness

    B. Two poles of energy

    C. Two children at play

    D. Two enemies in combat

30. As quoted in the fourth paragraph, Watts most likely discusses the "visualizations of other cultures" (line 40) in order to:

    F. illustrate the thinking of individuals who do not adhere to a Taoist concept of polarity.

    G. criticize the followers of Lao-tzu for misrepresenting standard Taoist beliefs.

    H. indicate that the metaphors used to explain Taoism have not yet been sufficiently analyzed.

    J. demonstrate that the worldwide influence of Taoism is neglected by Western readers.

GO ON TO THE NEXT PAGE.

Passage IV

NATURAL SCIENCE: This passage is adapted from "The Lives of Large Marine Mammals in Domesticity," a research article that considers the conditions of a variety of dolphin species that have been placed under human supervision.

The killer whale, also referred to as the orca whale or simply the orca, is a marine mammal that is both iconic and widespread. These animals are classified as members of the salt water dolphin family and can be found in every ocean in
5 the world. Their capacity to survive in various temperatures and their ability to hunt and reproduce in differing oceanic environments both ensure their longevity. In fact, orcas have an average life expectancy of 30 to 50 years in the wild; the maximum in especially healthy orca populations can range
10 anywhere from 60 to 70 years. Female orcas generally live longer than males and can live as long as 100 years in the wild.

And there are few real threats to these animals in such conditions. Both male and female orcas are considered apex
15 predators, meaning that they are an alpha species, one little threatened by the other species in their environment. They have remained at the top of the aquatic food chain, and will probably continue to reside there as long as evolution stays its oceanic course.

20 In sharp, sad contrast, orcas that have been removed from their native habitats and placed in captivity rarely live beyond the median age of nine.

All of this cuts sharply against what was once thought— that orcas could adapt to captivity, and even flourish under
25 human supervision. According to Dr. Susan Tranchard of the International Marine Mammal Conservancy, "Captivity can greatly impact both an orca's lifespan and its behavior. While killer whales are known to eat fish, seals, and even other large whales, they are unlikely to ever seek out human flesh
30 as a food source; this is even true for those orcas living in captivity. Although these orcas are trainable and are often displayed prominently at aquariums, it is important to remember that they are, still hunters and killers by biological design. Captivity redirects and worsens their aggression."

35 To date, there has been only one reliable report of an orca in the wild attacking a human, even though humans have been pressing farther and farther into orca territory. In contrast, orcas have been known to attack humans when kept in water tanks; zoologists and scientists are increasingly
40 convinced that this aggression is the result of the great mental and emotional stress that captive killer whales experience. They will only attack during what is described as a "breakdown," a burst of frustration explained by the absence of everything that a killer whale instinctively considers
45 natural and important.

While only three human beings have been killed by captive orcas since 1991, many others have been injured. Often, the whales have lashed out at their trainers, the very people with whom these creatures have built working
50 relationships. Unfortunately, the handlers are often unprepared for these unprovoked attacks.

Yet there is a positive side to human interaction with whales, as Tranchard and her colleagues at the Conservancy have acknowledged. At the very least, scientists "now
55 understand the complex social life of killer whales—the native conditions that captive orcas are desperate to experience."

There are four types of killer whales known to marine biologists and zoologists, and these types are categorized by
60 living condition: residential, transient, offshore, and captive. Residential orcas are the orcas most commonly spotted by the human eye, since they live, feed, and hunt within one general area. These killer whales are typically found in the northeastern Pacific Ocean. Transient orcas travel in small
65 groups and mainly communicate vocally while living and hunting. Their diet is comprised of a large variety of food sources since they are often on the go—hence their "transient" classification. Offshore orcas are found in the northeastern Pacific as well, and have been actively observed by scientists
70 and researchers since first being discovered in this particular habitat in 1988. They often are discovered to have large scars and cuts, presumably the results of individual encounters with larger mammals or sharks. These offshore orcas have been observed in sizable groups of anywhere from 20 to 75
75 adults.

The last classification of orca whales is the captive group. This unfortunate group is made up of orcas that are caught and captured in the wild and transported to facilities at zoos, aquariums, and theme parks, each new habitat
80 designed to recreate marine life environments for the benefit of the general public. These orcas have been known to give birth in captivity, yet seldom live long enough to fully nurture their young.

Despite human encroachments, killer whales have one
85 of the most stable family and living environments of all the mammals found in marine ecosystems today. Due to their large range, their strength in numbers, their ability to hunt vigorously and effectively, and their overall adaptability, it is unlikely—despite their difficult history with humans—that
90 they will become endangered at any time in the near future.

GO ON TO THE NEXT PAGE.

31. The passage states that the median age for an orca that has been placed in captivity is:

   A. 100 years.
   B. 60 years.
   C. 30 years.
   D. 9 years.

32. One of the main points that the author seeks to make in this passage is that captive orcas:

   F. are placed in conditions that make their quality of life inferior to that of wild orcas.
   G. are being returned to the wild as a result of the efforts of animal rights groups.
   H. will become resistant to training after only a few generations.
   J. exhibit psychological behaviors that have few clear parallels among human habits and emotions.

33. The author uses the quotation from Susan Tranchard in lines 26-34 to emphasize the idea that:

   A. a captive orca will instinctively see aquarium visitors as threats to its safety.
   B. orcas living in captivity have a relatively small range of food sources.
   C. aquariums have not been responsive to attempts to release orcas back into the wild.
   D. captivity can distort an orca's natural behaviors in ways that have destructive consequences.

34. As described in the eighth paragraph (lines 58-75), residential, transient, and offshore orcas differ primarily in terms of:

   F. level of aggression towards humans.
   G. diet and size when mature.
   H. habitat and patterns of travel.
   J. ability to communicate and cooperate.

35. As it is used in line 20, the word *sharp* means:

   A. evident.
   B. angry.
   C. abrupt.
   D. expressive.

36. It can be reasonably inferred that the large scars found on some offshore orcas are the result of:

   F. collisions with ships and motorboats.
   G. fights with other large marine animals.
   H. competition between different orca groups.
   J. storms at sea that destroy smaller and weaker marine mammals.

37. The author of the passage would agree with all of the following statements regarding orcas EXCEPT that:

   A. orcas could become an endangered species despite their ability to adapt.
   B. scientists have developed clear standards for classifying orcas.
   C. both wild and captive orcas are unlikely to attack humans.
   D. wild orcas often live much longer than captive orcas.

38. The function of the fifth paragraph (lines 35-45) is to:

   F. list a few of the most deadly orca attacks.
   G. explain why captive orcas lash out at humans.
   H. depict the different stages of an orca breakdown.
   J. show why wild orcas are likely to flee from humans.

39. According to the passage, one of the few beneficial effects of keeping orcas in captivity is that doing so has enabled scientists to:

   A. keep orcas from invading areas with much human activity.
   B. prevent the injuries that many offshore orcas would experience in the wild.
   C. figure out how to prevent wild orcas from attacking humans.
   D. gain a new perspective on the living conditions that orcas favor.

40. Which of the following is NOT one of the negative effects of keeping an orca in captivity?

   F. Possibility of violence against humans
   G. Inability to nurture offspring
   H. Sickly and upsetting appearance
   J. Decreased life expectancy

END OF TEST 8
STOP! DO NOT TURN THE PAGE UNTIL TOLD TO DO SO.
DO NOT RETURN TO A PREVIOUS TEST.

Answer Key: TEST 8

Test 8

LITERARY NARRATIVE

1. A
2. J
3. C
4. G
5. B
6. G
7. D
8. J
9. A
10. H

HUMANITIES

21. A
22. H
23. B
24. G
25. C
26. F
27. D
28. G
29. D
30. F

SOCIAL SCIENCE

11. B
12. G
13. A
14. F
15. C
16. J
17. C
18. G
19. D
20. G

NATURAL SCIENCE

31. D
32. F
33. D
34. H
35. A
36. G
37. A
38. G
39. D
40. H

To see your scaled ACT Reading Score (1-36), determine
how many questions you answered correctly and consult
the Scoring Chart on Page 186 of this book.

Post-Test Analysis

This post-test analysis is essential if you want to see an improvement on your next test. Possible reasons for errors, both for the test overall and for each of the four reading passages, are listed here. Place check marks next to the types of errors that pertain to you, or write your own types of errors in the blank spaces provided.

GENERAL

◇ Spent too much time reading the passages
◇ Spent too much time answering the questions
◇ Did not attempt to finish all of the passages
◇ Did not create effective margin answers
◇ Did not use process of elimination
◇ Could not find evidence to answer the questions
◇ Could not comprehend the topics and ideas in the passages
◇ Could not understand what the questions were asking
◇ Interpreted the passages rather than using evidence

Other: _____

LITERARY NARRATIVE

◇ Spent too long reading the passage
◇ Spent too long answering the questions
◇ Could not identify the setting and characters
◇ Could not understand the plot or action
◇ Could not work effectively with tone and clues to tone

Other: _____

> **Use this form** to better analyze your performance. If you don't understand why you made errors, there is no way that you can correct them!

SOCIAL SCIENCE

◇ Spent too long reading the passage
◇ Spent too long answering the questions
◇ Could not understand the author's position or arguments
◇ Used outside knowledge rather than using evidence

Other: _____

HUMANITIES

◇ Spent too long reading the passage
◇ Spent too long answering the questions
◇ Could understand the themes and organization of the passage
◇ Could not understand the author's ideas and uses of evidence

Other: _____

NATURAL SCIENCE

◇ Spent too long reading the passage
◇ Spent too long answering the questions
◇ Found the concepts and ideas in the passage confusing
◇ Found the questions confusing
◇ Could not effectively work with the inference and logic questions

Other: _____

TEST 8 Answer Explanations

LITERARY NARRATIVE

1. Correct Answer: A

In Passage A, the narrator observes that the heat on Mars is "no greater than would have been true under similar conditions in an Arizona desert" (lines 13-14). This information supports **A** as the best answer choice. The other answer choices are incorrect because they distort the significance of actual details from the passage: the narrator encounters "vegetation" (line 8) but does not attempt to scientifically classify it (eliminating **B**), realizes that he is definitively "upon Mars" (line 5) but does not actually try to figure out how he got there (eliminating **C**), and observes that "It was midday" (line 11) but does not make any conjectures about the weather (eliminating **D**).

2. Correct Answer: J

In describing the enclosure, the narrator notes that he is "determined to do a little exploring" (lines 19-20) and approaches the "low, encircling wall of the enclosure" (line 41) in order to figure out what is within. This information indicates that the narrator is not sure what is within the enclosure; thus, **J** is the best answer choice. Elsewhere in the passage, the narrator expresses certainty that he is awake (line 3), that he is on Mars (line 2), and that it is midday (line 11): this information can be used to eliminate choices **F**, **G**, and **H**, respectively.

3. Correct Answer: C

The irregularities are a feature of "low hills" (line 11) that the narrator can observe or distinguish: the word *irregularities* should thus refer to a physical *shape* that would catch attention. Thus, **C** is the correct choice. While choices **A** and **D** both wrongly refer to actions instead of to shapes, **B** fits the context of the passage (which depicts random *events* overall) but not the context of the sentence (which calls for a description of unchanging hills).

4. Correct Answer: G

In describing his attempts to move from place to place on Mars, the narrator notes that his muscles "played the mischief with me" (lines 34-35) when he attempted to walk upright: to avoid inconvenience, he adopted a creeping approach and "did fairly well at this" (line 40). Thus, **G** is an effective answer choice. **F** misstates the narrator's priorities (since the narrator is trying to deal with the decreased gravity, not trying to measure it), while **H** (escape) and **J** (injury) introduce negatives that are not relevant to the narrator's true situation. He does not know if there are any other people in the area, and was inconvenienced, not "seriously injured", by his other attempts to move.

5. Correct Answer: B

Before discussing the "plain", Passage B mentions a "gulch" (line 61) and an "outcrop" (line 64) that Lewin envisions as specific sites in his amusement park. The plain is similarly and quickly designated as the site of a parking lot, food court, budget motel, and other structures related to Lewin's overall construction project. Thus, **B** is the best answer choice. The sentence about the plain only explains details of Lewin's plans: it does not predict a negative outcome (eliminating **A**) or deal at all with Lewin's desires beyond business (eliminating **D**). Choice **C** may offer a true statement, since Lewin is not revealed as a scientific expert, but must be eliminated because the statement about the plain does not deal with scientific knowledge in any explicit way.

6. Correct Answer: G

In Passage B, parenthetical statements are used to indicate that Lewin has obtained facts about Mars from "the marketing people" (line 49), "the science people" (line 52), and "two different focus groups" (line 54). Thus, **G** is the correct answer. Note that the groups are simply designated as sources of information: although some of Lewin's ideas may seem unusual, these statements do not involve negatives such as conflict (eliminating **F**) or a lack of success in business (eliminating **H**). Note also that choice **J** distorts the function of the parenthetical statements, which cite sources for the details provided OUTSIDE the parentheses.

7. Correct Answer: D

Near the end of Passage B, Lewin describes the prospective visitors to his amusement park as "people with really spoiled kids", "morons on honeymoons", and "a bunch of suckers" who enjoy low-quality diversions (lines 68-72). This information supports **D**, *contempt* or "extreme disrespect", and can be used to eliminate choice **C**, which is neutral. While both **A** and **B** are negative overall, they do not accurately describe how Lewin feels: hatred would indicate an unwillingness to deal with the prospective visitors or an insecurity about them, while pity would indicate that Lewin feels bad for them (when he expresses nothing of the sort).

8. Correct Answer: J

In describing Mars, the narrator of Passage A mentions the midday sun and notes that "the heat of it was rather intense upon my body" (lines 12-13); in contrast, the narration of Passage B indicates that on Mars "You'd freeze to death without a suit" (line 51). This information indicates a clear difference in relative temperature, so that **J** is the correct choice. **F** is incorrect because Passage A describes plant life on Mars but never mentions animal life, **G** is incorrect because Passage B does not rigorously compare the gravity on Earth and on Mars (and if anything suggests that the gravity on Mars is weaker), and **H** is incorrect because Passage A describes the vegetation on Mars, not the soil, as "yellowish" (line 7).

TEST 8 Answer Explanations

9. Correct Answer: A

While the narrator of Passage A is preoccupied with the conditions of gravity and atmosphere on Mars, and wants to explore a "low structure which was the only evidence of habitation in sight" (lines 37-38), Lewin in Passage B wants to attract "suckers" (line 71) to Mars for the purpose of making money. This information makes **A** the best answer, while **B** ("selfless") and **C** ("fearful") apply incorrect adjectives to the money-oriented and mostly confident Lewin. **D** describes both characters incorrectly, since the narrator of Passage A is objectively observant (not "idealistic") and Lewin simply harbors negative opinions (but does not seek revenge).

10. Correct Answer: H

The narrator of Passage A is interested primarily in how Mars appears and how he is affected by its gravity: the closest he comes to describing another individual is describing vegetation and a structure that may be "evidence of habitation" (line 38). Lewin, in contrast, refers at length to the specialists he works with and to the prospective visitors to his amusement park. Thus, **H** is an extremely effective answer. Both passages contain some reference to the gravity on Mars (eliminating **F**), record the thoughts of the main character (even though Passage A is first-person and Passage B is third-person, eliminating **G**), and involve a clear goal (exploration for Passage A, money for Passage B, eliminating **J**).

SOCIAL SCIENCE

11. Correct Answer: B

In line 1, the author writes that "in the United States we take education for granted," so that the author groups herself with other Americans as *we*. Then in lines 52-54, the author writes that, "I arrived in Malawi in 1994 to teach English, not at Kamuzu but at one of the two schools that Banda had designated for non-native children in Malawi." This information indicates that the author is an American educator well acquainted with Malawi's schooling system, and justifies **B**. Although the author is reporting throughout on history and culture, it would be wrong to infer that the author is a history instructor (**C**) or a journalist (**D**), since the author only identifies herself generally as a teacher. Nor does the author see Kamuzu academy as a model for American education: if anything, the author recognizes the academy's flaws and most admires the work ethic of Kamuzu students (**A**).

12. Correct Answer: G

The author describes the "rumors and criticisms" (line 47) that surrounded Kamuzu Academy, but concludes her discussion by striking a positive note and declaring that "Hastings Banda created a legacy of hope for the youth of Malawi" (lines 72-73). Thus, **G** is the correct answer, while other choices misstate the content and intent of the passage. Choice **F** would require a more detailed and sustained analysis of the American model and Banda's improvements in order to be correct; choice **H** correctly notes that Banda's legacy could be problematic, but raises an issue (Banda's links to younger politicians) that the passage nowhere discusses. **J** is a trap answer: the author clearly admires Kamuzu Academy overall, but does not argue that the academy's level of publicity has been deficient.

13. Correct Answer: A

The author describes Kamuzu Academy as a Malawian institution "where 'the brightest and the best' children from every village could be educated up to university level at no cost to their families" (lines 32-34). This information supports **A**, while the other answers rely on faulty interpretations of the passage. Though praiseworthy, Kamuzu Academy is nowhere compared to projects in other African countries (**B**). Other answers distort the public reception of Kamuzu Academy: there were criticisms of the Academy, as explained in lines 47-51 (**C**), and there is no information about the fallout of political disputes, aside from a brief description of Banda's political defeat in lines 56-57 (**D**).

14. Correct Answer: F

The passage states that Banda relocated to America and "graduated with a degree in medicine" (lines 13-14). His intention was to return to Malawi: however, "because his own country was a British territory, Banda was required to earn a further medical degree in the United Kingdom before he could do that" (lines 15-18). Thus, *America* and *Britain* were the primary sites of Banda's education. Do not give the wrong significance to *Malawi* and *South Africa*: Banda was born in Malawi, and was a laborer in South Africa *before* pursuing his education.

15. Correct Answer: C

The author describes "village infants chanting rhymes under a Baobab tree" as a Malawian educational practice that is "charming for the tourists, no doubt, but hardly likely to advance a fledgling country" (lines 27-30). Thus, you should expect a strongly negative answer such as **C**. Choice **A** can be eliminated because this description introduces a discussion that moves away from Malawian villagers relates to only a few Malawians, the Kamuzu students. **B** and **D** both overstate the importance of the sight of the "village infants chanting rhymes." This sight may be connected to tourism and Banda's village childhood, but there is no evidence or analysis to show that it is the *primary* reason for tourism or an *important event* that impacted Banda.

16. Correct Answer: J

In describing Banda's education in America and Britain, the author notes that "it was a long haul, but it explains why education became such a priority when Banda rose to the Presidency" (lines 18-19), thus supporting **J**. You may choose other answers if you misconstrue the information contained elsewhere in the first paragraph. Banda's "charm and intelligence" (lines 12-15) helped him to improve himself, but were not necessarily reasons why he wanted to improve Malawian education (**F**). Banda studied extensively, but it is not clear whether this interest in studying was *lifelong* or only formed in South Africa (**G**). In any event, he was helped along in his educational pursuits by a "member of the Methodist church whom he met while he was working in South Africa" (lines 9-10), not by his fellow workers (**H**).

TEST 8 Answer Explanations

17. Correct Answer: C

Banda created the Kamuzu Academy to "tackle the problems created by the widespread illiteracy of the native Malawian population" (lines 20-22), to "build a Malawian civil service for his nation" (lines 29-30), and to assist the "'brightest and the best' children from every village" (line 33). Answers **A**, **B**, and **D** can thus be eliminated. While it is true that Banda had experience of the British education system, Kamuzu Academy was an institution that focused only on native Malawian students. The school was only forced to connect to expatriate schools after Banda left office.

18. Correct Answer: G

The author describes her Malawian students by noting that "I have never had pupils so fiercely determined to seize the chances that they had been given" (lines 65-66). She then goes on to evoke the students' energetic participation in school activities and outstanding academic performance. The students were clearly *eager to succeed*, but were also *cheerful*: whenever the author corrected the students' essays, the students "smiled and laughed and willingly undertook revision after revision" (lines 68-69). Because the students were cheerful, *harshly competitive* (**J**) would be too strongly negative. Because Kamuzu students such as the narrator's came from native Malawian villages, they would most likely be aware of economic hardships of some sort (**H**). And even though the students participated in the "local choir" and "the drama club" (line 70), they were also drawn to other fields of activity that were unrelated to art and literature (**F**).

19. Correct Answer: D

In lines 76-80, the author describes contemporary Malawians in the following manner: "Today, if you travel almost anywhere in the world, it is highly probable that you will meet a Malawian working as a lawyer, a doctor, a scientist, or an engineer, and sending money home every month to help the rest of this optimistic nation." Malawians are thus known for *international travel* and *loyalty to Malawi*, which makes **D** the best answer. The answer is thus strongly positive: **B** (dislike) and **C** (insecurities) employ incorrect negative tones. Trap answer **A** is more difficult to disqualify: Malawians do in fact have strong family connections, but knowledge of history is not emphasized in the final paragraph. Instead, the academic knowledge of Malawian students is the focus of lines 65-71.

20. Correct Answer: G

In lines 57-61, the author describes the situation of Kamuzu Academy after Banda's departure from office: "The new president, Bakili Muluzi, withdrew some of the academy's money in order to provide wider education in the country. Kamuzu had to begin to fend for itself: it had to shed some of its pupils and send them to the expatriate schools." Thus, **G** is the correct choice. The events that impacted Kamuzu were beyond the Academy's control (disqualifying **F**) and were unrelated to issues involving expatriates (a group found only in other schools, disqualifying **H**). **J** is a trap answer: Banda did leave the presidency, but the reason for this was an election defeat (lines 55-57), not his *resignation*.

HUMANITIES

21. Correct Answer: A

Early in this passage on Chinese Taoist doctrine, the author describes the "air of inscrutability that can surround so much Asian philosophy, at least as seen by Americans and Europeans" (lines 18-20). Later, the author explains that essential Taoist beliefs are unsettling "for the Westerner" (75) and conflict with the ideas of "some present-day American politicians" (lines 80-81). Together, these line references justify **A**. Both **B** and **D** can be eliminated as overly negative on the basis of tone, since the author favorably cites Alan Watts and comprehends the "picture of the universe" (line 58) that Taoism sets out. **C** is a trap: the author is favorable to Taoism, but simply contrasts Taoist beliefs with practices in business and politics (first paragraph and final paragraph, respectively). Whether the author wants Taoism adopted in these fields remains an open question.

22. Correct Answer: H

The passage presents contrasts between polarity and conflict in lines 38-41, between Lao-tzu and Rudyard Kipling in lines 28-33, and between Taoist beliefs and current political ideas in lines 78-81. Thus, eliminate **F**, **G**, and **J**. Note that the author repeatedly cites Watts's *Tao: The Watercourse Way* as a book that *explains* Taoism and its central text, the *Tao Te Ching*, so that choice **H** does not involve a contrast at all.

23. Correct Answer: B

In the passage, *yin* and *yang* is described as "a concept that has been popularized shamelessly but seldom fully understood" (lines 25-26). All of the answer choices are negative, but only *irresponsible* accurately captures the shamelessness and poor understanding behind how *yin* and *yang* have been promoted. Because the concept has been popularized, it is in fact accessible (eliminating **A**) and significant (eliminating **C**). There is also no reason to infer that the promotion of *yin* and *yang* has been illegal (**D**): if anything, the popularity of this concept indicates that it has been promoted in a widely accepted way.

24. Correct Answer: G

Early in the passage, the author describes the Taoist idea of non-action and declares that "our hectic modern world, readers across cultures might see this sentence and view it as the height of absurdity" (lines 8-9). Later, the author refers to the typical "Westerner, who likes to believe in the idea of progress from era to era" (lines 75-76). On the basis of this information, **G** is the strongest answer. Throughout the passage, the author describes Lao-tzu's beliefs (but not his life, **H**) and focuses on the ideas behind Taoism (but never mentions any other Asian belief systems, **J**). **F** is a trap answer: despite the author's own openness to Taoist ideas, the passage as a whole indicates that Westerners continue to resist Taoist concepts.

TEST 8 Answer Explanations

25. Correct Answer: C

After providing the excerpt, the author describes its purpose in the passage by writing that, "Thus, we have a picture of the universe in which all opposites are paradoxically intertwined, simultaneously depending upon one another" (lines 58-60). As a "picture of the universe" quoted directly from Lao-tzu, this excerpt provides ideas about the "Taoist order of existence" (C). To eliminate A, keep in mind that no other Chinese writers or philosophers are quoted in the passage. To eliminate B and D, keep in mind that the author is interested primarily in the ideas (the "picture of the universe") that can be found in Lao-tzu's writings. The style of the writing, whether as rhythmic poetry (B) or literary translation (D), is not a declared concern.

26. Correct Answer: F

In the relevant portion of the passage, the author quotes a statement by Taoism expert Alan Watts: " 'Thus the art of life is not seen as holding on to *yang* and banishing *yin*,' writes Watts, 'but as keeping the two in balance, because there cannot be one without the other' " (lines 72-74). *Keeping* is contrasted to a situation that involves *banishing*, or change; thus, keeping means avoiding change or *maintaining* in this context. G (*isolating*) and J (*stockpiling*) both describe activities involving clear changes, while H (*preventing*) is negative in context: to prevent the balance would mean to destroy it.

27. Correct Answer: D

Taoist doctrine is based on principles such as "non-action" (line 3), the rejection of the idea that "it is possible to preserve the good while eliminating the bad entirely" (line 47-48), and the idea that "opposites are paradoxically intertwined" (line 59). This information can be used to eliminate A, B, and C. Because Taoism is premised on the idea of an "intertwined" universe, a Taoist would most likely DISAGREE with the idea of fundamental *isolation* (D).

28. Correct Answer: G

In lines 36-43, a quotation from Watts is used to explain the Taoist idea of *polarity*; then, in lines 72-74, another quotation from Watts is used to describe the Taoist approach to *yin* and *yang*. Thus, G is the best answer, since the quotations from Watts help the author to explain *important principles* from Taoist belief. H can readily be eliminated because of its wrongly negative tone; F and G make assumptions about interest in Taoism and Watts's reputation that are not directly related to the quotes from Watts, which mostly involve analysis and definition of ideas.

29. Correct Answer: D

In the second-to-last paragraph, the author describes yin and yang as "two archetypal poles of cosmic energy" and "the dark and the light" (lines 65-67). Thus eliminate A and B. In addition, the author evokes the Taoist conception of the universe by describing forces that exist "much more like children at play than like two enemy combatants striving for supremacy" (lines 61-63). Since the Taoist universe is premised on yin and yang, you can use this information to eliminate C and choose D (which describes an image that the author openly rejects).

30. Correct Answer: F

In the fourth paragraph, Watts notes that "in the visualizations of other cultures, light is at war with darkness, life with death, good with evil … and thus an idealism to cultivate the former and be rid of the latter flourishes throughout much of the world" (lines 40-43). Taoist polarity is "not to be confused" with such ideas of opposition (line 39). Thus, Watts opposes these ideas and the cultures that support such ideas to Taoists and Taoist principles, so that F is the best answer. Do not assume that Watts is taking a negative tone in the quotation that relates to this question: he is simply developing a contrast between two belief systems. On account of this, negative answers such as G (*criticize*), H (*not … sufficiently*) and J (*neglected*) must be eliminated.

NATURAL SCIENCE

31. Correct Answer: D

In the third paragraph, the author states that captive orcas rarely live "beyond the median age of nine" (line 22). Although this information directly justifies choice D, be careful not to confuse other statistics in the passage for a captive orca's median age. Lifespans of 100 years (A), 60 years (B), and 30 years (C) are all mentioned in the first paragraph; however, these are figures that refer to wild orcas, not captive orcas.

32. Correct Answer: F

The author indicates in the third paragraph that orcas have decreased life expectancy once captured, and uses the fourth paragraph to argue against the idea that "orcas could adapt to captivity, and even flourish under human supervision" (lines 24-25). Later in the passage, the author also designates captive orcas as an "unfortunate group" (line 77). Trap answer G refers to a factor that the passage never addresses: while the author finds the living conditions of captive orcas regrettable, there is no direct evidence that animal rights groups have been successful in releasing orcas from such conditions. H and G both go against the content of the passage: captive orcas are "trainable" (line 31) and an orca "breakdown" (line 43) seems to parallel human emotions.

33. Correct Answer: D

In the quotation, Tranchard begins by stating that "captivity can greatly impact both an orca's lifespan and its behavior" (lines 26-27) and goes on to explain how captivity "redirects and worsens" an orca's natural aggression (line 34). All answer choices are negative, but the false answers refer to topics that Tranchard never discusses: neither she nor the author discusses orca responses to aquarium visitors (A) or orca release attempts (C). Choice B is a trap: the food choices for wild orcas are indeed mentioned in lines 28-30, but these food sources are never compared to the food sources that captive orcas have at their disposal.

TEST 8 Answer Explanations

34. Correct Answer: H

The author defines residential orcas as those that live "within one general area" (lines 62-63), transient orcas as those that are "often on the go" (line 67), and offshore orcas as those "observed in sizable groups" (line 74) near human territory. This information indicates that these orcas distinguished by habitat and travel patterns. The false answers introduce factors discussed elsewhere in the passage: aggression levels are discussed in the fourth, fifth, and sixth paragraphs (**F**), while orca diet is mentioned in the fourth paragraph (**G**). Nowhere is this information related to the different orca distinctions. Trap answer **J** also relies on faulty connections: although transient orcas are known to "communicate vocally" (line 75), their communication habits are not compared to those of other orcas. Thus, communication cannot serve as a way of classifying the orcas.

35. Correct Answer: A

The author develops a sharp contrast between long-lived wild orcas (which can sometimes reach 100 years) and short-lived captive orcas (which have a median age of 9). This is clear or *evident* contrast. Avoid answer **B**; this contrast may anger observers, but is not itself an *angry* contrast. Other answers describe the wrong kinds of things: abrupt (**C**) and expressive (**D**) would both describe actions, not contrasts or ideas.

36. Correct Answer: G

In lines 71-73, the author states that offshore orcas "are often discovered to have large scars and cuts, presumably the results of their encounters with larger mammals or sharks." The passage never mentions ships or motorboats (**F**) or storms at sea (**J**) as the causes of the orcas' scars, though these factors may in fact be present in offshore orca habitats. Also, do not confuse the reference to larger mammals with the idea of competing orca groups in **H**; individual encounters, not entire group-against-group competitions, are the cause of the scars.

37. Correct Answer: A

The author describes the clear standards for classifying orcas in lines 58-83, the infrequency of attacks by orcas (both wild and captive) in lines 35-52, and the differing lifespans of wild and captive orcas in lines 1-22. Thus, you can eliminate **B**, **C**, and **D**. Choice **A** is a statement the author would DISAGREE with because the author states that it is "unlikely" (line 89) that orcas will become endangered in the near future.

38. Correct Answer: G

In the fourth paragraph, the author explains that the presence of "great mental and emotional stress" (lines 40-41) will lead a captive orca to experience a "breakdown," since the whale is deprived of everything that a killer whale instinctively considers natural and important" (lines 44-45). A captive orca will attack humans as the result of such a breakdown, so that **G** is the correct answer. While answer **J** deals with non-captive orcas and is not directly on-topic, **F** and **H** both mention specifics that the paragraph does not provide: deadly orca attacks are mentioned, but specific orca attacks are never named, and an orca breakdown is discussed, but never divided into specifically designated stages.

39. Correct Answer: D

The author explains that there is "a positive side to human interaction with whales" (lines 52-53) and quotes Tranchard's statement that scientists "now understand the complex social life of killer whales—the native conditions that captive orcas are desperate to experience" (lines 54-57). This information supports **D**. Note that the benefits to scientists are matters of understanding and comprehension: the passage does not describe changes in wild orca behavior, only contrasts between wild and captive orcas, so that **A**, **B**, and **C** can all be eliminated.

40. Correct Answer: H

The author notes that captivity "redirects and worsens" orca aggression (line 34), that captive orcas "seldom live long enough to fully nurture their young" (lines 82-83), and that captive orcas rarely live "beyond the medium age of nine" (line 22), a sharp decrease from the average of 30 to 50 years for wild orcas. This information allows **F**, **G**, and **J** to be eliminated. Do not falsely assume that orcas with shorter lifespans will necessarily have sickly appearances; because **H** is never discussed or specified in the passage, it cannot be assumed as a negative effect.

Test 9

READING TEST
35 Minutes—40 Questions

DIRECTIONS: There are four passages in this test. Each passage is followed by several questions. After reading a passage, choose the best answer to each question and fill in the corresponding oval on your answer document. You may refer to the passages as often as necessary.

Passage I

LITERARY NARRATIVE: This passage is adapted from the novella *Eyes on the Ground: A Short Memoir of My Life in Jazz.* The action takes place in the 1950s.

Of course I'd heard of him—we'd all heard of Mick Mercury. As a boy, I used to stay up late to listen to his show, holding my broadband radio tight under the covers, so that Ma wouldn't hear from the kitchen. From out of the tinny
5 speakers came the vibrant notes, rhythms, and melodies that would captivate me for the rest of my life—the songs of Duke Ellington, Dizzy Gillespie, Miles Davis, John Coltrane, and so many more. How I dreamed of being in Harlem, at Minton's, at the Apollo, seeing it all happen! But at the time,
10 I was too young; as much as I begged, Ma wouldn't let me take the subway to see my heroes play live.

"No son of mine is going to waste his time on those *jazz cats*," she declared, throwing all the malice she could into the phrase *jazz cats*. "You focus on school. Understand?"

15 I played by her rules for as long as she could make me, but by high school, I got a job on our local paper—the Brooklyn *Gazette*—and that's when things changed. After convincing the editor that I was serious about, absolutely passionate about jazz, I was soon taking the famous A-Train
20 up to some of the more well-known clubs. At only seventeen years-old, I was a young reporter on the music beat, and I couldn't be happier. But not Ma. As you might expect, staying out all night at jazz clubs doesn't really prepare you for your English and algebra exams—a fact that Ma was
25 quick to remind me of. It wasn't until one night in late January, right in the harsh winter of 1959, that Ma tried something other than losing her temper on me—it was a sneak attack, one that left me reeling at the time and one that I'll never forget.

30 I had come in around 4:00 in the morning, having spent the night covering a performance of the Dave Brubeck Quartet at the Blue Note. As usual, I slid my key into our lock and opened the door as quietly as I could, before slipping into the warmth of our kitchen. But just as I closed the door
35 gently behind me, the lights came on. I froze.

"Late night for you, son?" said a man's voice. It was a deep baritone sound that I knew instantly, and yet I could not convince myself that this voice was emanating here, inside my own kitchen. Slowly I turned, and there he was—the
40 famous radio personality, the host of the iconic Harlem program *Late Night Dyna-Might*, the man himself—Mick Mercury! He was sitting at our very own kitchen table, a steaming mug of coffee set in front of him.

Ma stood leaning against the doorway to her bedroom,
45 still in her work clothes from the day before. I suddenly realized that she'd been up all night, too, waiting for me, and I felt a pang of regret.

"I didn't know what else to do, Winston," she said to me, shaking her head. "Your teacher, Miss Tompkins, called
50 me the other day. You know you're failing English. You might not graduate."

I looked at Mick, who simply sat there, nodding, and sipping his coffee. Then I looked back at Ma.

"Now, I know you stay up listening to Mick's show
55 here, and so I called him. I know you don't listen to a word I say, but I figured that if there's anyone you *will* listen to, it's Mick."

"It's no big thing, ma'am," said Mick, with a smile. "I live around the corner."

60 "You *do*?" I said, unable to hide my puzzlement.

Mick laughed. "Yes I do," he said. "I've lived in this neighborhood all my life. What's nice about being a radio celebrity is everyone knows your voice, but not your face. It helps me keep myself anonymous."

65 He winked once, before taking another sip of his coffee.

"Listen to your mother here," he said, growing stern. "I've read your articles in the *Gazette*, son, and they're good—real good. You could make a career as a writer, I'm sure of it—and who knows, maybe even help me out on the
70 air."

GO ON TO THE NEXT PAGE.

As those last words passed his lips, my heart turned inside-out with joy.

"But your mother's right," he continued. "For now, concentrate on your school work. Jazz doesn't disappear to
75 anywhere. You understand me?" Slowly, I nodded. "Good," he said, finishing his coffee, then getting to his feet and nodding once to Ma.

"Call me when you get that diploma," he said, holding out his hand to me. I shook it, and felt him slip something into
80 my palm. Then he took his leave and was out the door without a sound.

I looked down, and saw that I was holding a business card. *Mick Mercury: Radio Personality*, it said. Underneath, there was a phone number. It was a number I knew that I'd
85 call—just as soon as I'd finished school.

1. The passage establishes that Minton's (line 9) and the Blue Note (line 32) are:

   A. music clubs.
   B. movie theaters.
   C. record labels.
   D. radio stations.

2. As it is used in line 18, the phrase *serious about* most nearly means:

   F. respected for.
   G. devoted to.
   H. talented in.
   J. intimidated by.

3. In the passage, Mick does all of the following things EXCEPT:

   A. finish the coffee that Winston's mother gives him.
   B. give his business card to Winston.
   C. tell Winston that he lives nearby.
   D. discuss a well-known jazz musician.

4. According to Mick Mercury, one of the benefits of being a famous radio personality is the ability to:

   F. avoid unwanted publicity because you are only recognized by your voice.
   G. set your own work schedule and keep late hours because many programs are recorded in advance.
   H. fit into an established community and guide it in a way that inspires respect.
   J. attend performances of important musicians in preparation for radio programs.

5. In line 15, "I played by her rules for as long as she could make me" refers to the fact that the narrator avoided:

   A. staying out late at jazz clubs until he graduated from college.
   B. staying out late at jazz clubs until he graduated from high school.
   C. staying out late at jazz clubs until he started writing for the Brooklyn *Gazette*.
   D. listening to jazz until he learned of Mick Mercury's radio program.

6. Which of the following statements best describes the plot of the passage?

   F. A young man wants to be a jazz writer but finds the business too challenging.
   G. A young man decides to prioritize his education after an intervention by a figure he respects.
   H. A young man is angry with his mother until a radio personality helps them to negotiate calmly.
   J. A young man and his hero explain a challenging goal to the young man's mother.

7. Why does Winston realize that his mother had not gone to sleep while he was out at the Blue Note?

   A. She is up drinking coffee when he arrives home.
   B. She is still wearing her work clothes from the previous day when he arrives home.
   C. She tells him that she was so worried about him that she was unable to sleep.
   D. She is too tired to respond to Mick Mercury's most important questions.

8. The narrator's immediate response to the sight of Mick Mercury in the kitchen is to:

   F. reflect on how poorly he has treated his mother.
   G. react to his visitor with disbelief.
   H. offer Mick Mercury a second cup of coffee.
   J. recall his poor schoolwork.

9. The passage as a whole most strongly suggests that Ma:

   A. accepts Winston but does not like living with him because he frequently keeps her up by coming home late.
   B. is committed to Winston and is concerned that he might sacrifice his future prospects.
   C. dislikes Winston but tolerates him because he is her son.
   D. resents Winston for hiding his real goals and ambitions from her.

GO ON TO THE NEXT PAGE.

10. Near the end of his conversation with Mick, Winston experiences a moment of joy because:

F. Mick Mercury agrees with Winston's mother.

G. Mick Mercury reveals that he lives around the corner from Winston.

H. Mick Mercury suggests that Winston might be able to work on the radio show.

J. Mick Mercury declares that Winston can earn top grades in his English course.

Passage II

SOCIAL SCIENCE: Taken from two essays written by Margery Close, a mystery novelist who lives in the north of France.

Passage A by Margery Close (1993)

To the west of Lower Normandy, the terrain is gentle and open, with low hills and orchards, but to the East, the land becomes more defensive and suspicious of intruders. Steep crags thrust up between ravines that contain fast moving
5 streams that empty into deep, silent lakes. Brooding forests isolate hamlets which are linked only by narrow and winding roads. Even in winter, it is difficult for the eye to pierce the shadows and barriers created by the closely packed trees. There is a sense of ancient mystery, for this is a land of myth and
10 legend and the powers of magic. It is said that the wizard Merlin paced these woods. Certainly, it is believed that this is the land where Lancelot du Lac grew up before he travelled to Camelot where his encounter with Guinevere helped to destroy the Round Table of King Arthur and his knights. You may scoff at the veracity of this legend, but there is magic working here.

15 In the forest of the Andaines, part of the landscape that is described above, the road passes through thickets and trees that line the course of the River Vée. Suddenly, it plunges into a ravine between the two high rocky outcrops that tower on either side. This is Monk's Leap (it's another legend of the
20 area, he made the leap to escape a dragon – of course). It is here that the river flows into a lake around which is set the settlement of Bagnolles de l'Orne.

Bagnolles de l'Orne was once two villages. Their combined population stands now at about 2500, the highest it
25 has ever been. You might expect, then, to see a rather pretty little Normandy village with half-timbered buildings nestling in the forested valley bottom. However, there are no homely cottages, but villas dating from the early twentieth century, elegant, fashionable shops and Art Déco hotels redolent of the
30 1920s. A manicured park, in the center of which lies a lake, marks the center of the town. Here stands the casino with its elegant, terraced restaurant, ballroom, cinema, theatre, slot machines, tables for Roulette and Black Jack and Poker.

Bagnolles de l'Órne is, in the minds of some, a sophisticated
35 Las Vegas situated in the heart of rural Lower Normandy.

Passage B by Margery Close (2005)

I live in France, in the area known as Lower Normandy. This is rural France, full of dairy farms that provide the milk for the making of such cheeses as Camembert and Brie, and orchards of apple and pear. It is a gentle, forested countryside
40 with slow, lazy rivers winding their way to join the greater rivers of the Seine to the North or the Loire to the South. I inhabit a small town in this region: it is called Domfront, and it was once an important center of mediaeval politics, the home of Henry II and Aelinor of Aquitaine, visited regularly by
45 Thomas Beckett, fought over by English and French troops. Today, it has a population of just over two thousand, a number which is gently swollen by tourists in the summer months. Nothing much happens here apart from a tiny market on Friday mornings.

50 So, when, recently, I was invited to New York for a week, it was with some trepidation that I made my way to Charles de Gaulle Airport in Paris and mounted the steps of the Delta airliner that would hurtle me across the Atlantic and dump me in JFK at an hour that was six hours ahead of the time as I knew
55 it in France. Of course, I had been to New York before, but that was in my youth when I was up for any experience. I remembered that, in those days, it had branded itself as "the city that never slept," which had proved to be an accurate piece of messagemaking. Now, as a senior citizen, I was not so
60 certain that I could sustain a week of such constant and electric hustle and perturbation.

The progress from the airport to the hotel did little to dispel my sense of unease. We arrived at a hotel which towered above Sixth Avenue: its forecourt seemed to be a hive of
65 constant motion and a cacophony of shouts, whistles and revving engines. Its lobby, about as large as the Place St Julien, was filled with more guests than there were townsfolk in Domfront. For a moment, I felt panic. Then I took a deep breath, muttered the mantra "You can do this" and strode
70 towards the front desk and asked for my key with what I hoped appeared to be an air of nonchalance and familiarity with the scene. I felt that I was fooling no-one. Had I really grown so old and out of touch?

GO ON TO THE NEXT PAGE.

Questions 11-13 ask about Passage A.

11. In the first paragraph of Passage A, the author establishes what feature of the area "to the East" (line 2)?

    A. its almost complete lack of wildlife.
    B. its welcoming and fertile landscape.
    C. its extensive yet poorly maintained roads.
    D. its association with particular legends.

12. As it is used in line 24, the word *combined* most nearly means:

    F. total.
    G. allied.
    H. confused.
    J. interchangeable.

13. It can be reasonably inferred from Passage A that the village of Bagnolles de l'Orne is:

    A. unexpectedly active and modern.
    B. noted for its old-fashioned architecture.
    C. similar to other Lower Normandy villages.
    D. famous for its beautiful lakes.

Questions 14-17 ask about Passage B.

14. Passage B is delivered from the perspective of an elderly traveler who:

    F. is seeing New York for the first time.
    G. is revisiting New York after a long time away.
    H. lived for several years in New York before leaving.
    J. is returning to New York after a vacation.

15. Which of the following words is used more figuratively than literally in Passage B?

    A. "market" (line 48)
    B. "youth" (line 56)
    C. "hive" (line 64)
    D. "key" (line 70)

16. When in Passage B does the author first begin to experience anxiety or nervousness?

    F. While traveling to Charles de Gaulle Airport
    G. After arriving at JFK Airport
    H. After arriving at the hotel near Sixth Avenue
    J. While approaching the front desk of the hotel

17. As it is used in line 57, the word *branded* most nearly means:

    A. stigmatized.
    B. advertised.
    C. restricted.
    D. embellished.

Questions 18-20 ask about both passages.

18. Which statement provides the most accurate comparison of the narration of each passage?

    F. Passage A is factual and objective, whereas Passage B is both informative and personal.
    G. Passage A is instructive and pompous, whereas Passage B is unrestrained and approachable.
    H. Passage A is fanciful and melancholy, whereas Passage B is realistic and detached.
    J. Passage A is vehement and argumentative, whereas Passage B is both generous and persuasive.

19. According to Passage A and Passage B, "Bagnolles de l'Orne" (line 22) and "Domfront" (line 42) are similar in terms of:

    A. architectural style.
    B. local mythology.
    C. tourist revenue.
    D. population.

20. In contrast to Passage B, Passage A indicates that some areas of rural France are:

    F. reserved and refined.
    G. thriving and energetic.
    H. unknown to tourists.
    J. known for luxury goods.

GO ON TO THE NEXT PAGE.

Passage III

HUMANITIES: This passage is adapted from the article "Film, Crisis, and American Politics."

While all movies serve to entertain, some movies—and probably more movies than you'd expect—also strive to educate. There are historical movies that enlighten the public about a particular time period or event, sometimes under the
5 guise of blockbuster entertainment. There are nature documentaries and films of exploration, often narrated by name actors and designed for sweeping IMAX screens. Entertaining, but undoubtedly educational. In 1983, the television movie *The Day After* appeared; its initial purpose, indeed, was to entertain and educate. But this movie also
10 induced fear and, ultimately, change.

I was a young teen in 1983. Like most teenage boys, I found that the subjects that most occupied my mind were sports (mostly baseball) and trying to be cool for my friends
15 (mostly by setting off firecrackers). If the sports teams that I supported were successful, everything else seemed a little better. In addition, if I made it through the day without doing something embarrassing or being the subject of gossip, I was content. If I worked up the nerve to talk to a girl, well, I was
20 ecstatic. *The Day After* caught me unaware; it is an intensely, disturbingly political film, but its political content does not fully explain its impact.

On the Sunday night of November 20, 1983, I sat in the living room with my siblings and parents. We were gathered
25 around the television to watch a movie that had been prominently advertised in radio and television commercials, in newspapers, and in magazines including *Time*, *Newsweek*, *U.S. News & World Report*, and *TV Guide*. People across the country were all doing the same. In fact, the movie was
30 viewed by more than 100 million people—including half of the adult population of the United States—which was the largest audience for a made-for-TV movie up to that time.

In *The Day After*, a war breaks out between the two Cold War superpowers, the United States and the Soviet
35 Union. This occurs because the Soviet Union is trying to gain control of West Germany, rather than keep to its allotted territory in East Germany. The United States does not back down. One thing leads to another, and the United States issues an ultimatum, which the Soviet Union ignores.
40 Fighting breaks out in Germany and global chaos breaks loose. Unable to find a peaceful solution, the two sides exchange nuclear attacks. One of the Soviet targets is Kansas, and the movie focuses primarily on a few citizens who live in Lawrence, Kansas and Kansas City, Missouri. (The broader
45 nuclear disaster itself is depicted in the middle portions of the movie.) With an array of disturbing images, *The Day After* shows what this stretch of the American Heartland would look like after being devastated by a nuclear holocaust.

The public reaction to the movie was nearly as
50 overwhelming as the advertising build-up. The Joint Chiefs of Staff screened the movie and watched it in silence, clearly moved. President Ronald Reagan himself also viewed the movie; in his diary, he said that *The Day After* was, "very effective & left me greatly depressed."

55 The emotion I felt after watching the movie was fear. My concerns were no longer simply sports and impressing my friends: I now worried about nuclear war. I worried about the arms race, prayed that the Strategic Defense Initiative (dubbed "Star Wars" by the media) would work, and hoped
60 that the summits between President Reagan and the leader of the Soviet Union, Mikhail Gorbachev, would ease the situation.

All of this was part of a bigger plan. ABC, the network that hosted the broadcast of the movie, expected *The Day*
65 *After* to leave viewers anxious. To produce this effect, the network set up toll-free lines and mailed out half a million viewers' guides to help the public cope with the subject matter. Immediately after the movie, ABC ran a live special edition of a news program called Viewpoint. The host of the
70 show, Ted Koppel, posed the following questions: "Is the vision we have just seen the future as it will be or may be? Is there still time?" He even invited the Secretary of State, George Schultz, to discuss the topic.

Throughout the nation at large, the same spirit of
75 questioning and rampant debate arose where the topics of nuclear arms policy and the Cold War were concerned. Virtually all who saw the film agreed that nuclear war should be prevented at all costs. Rallies, forums, and candlelight vigils were held to protest nuclear aggression.

80 And maybe this spirit of unity, too, was part of a bigger plan. The director of the movie, Nicholas Meyer, said that the movie was "the most worthwhile thing I got to do in my life." His reaction was inspired by a note from President Reagan himself. This message arrived just after a summit between
85 the two superpowers in Reykjavik, Iceland, where a nuclear arms deal was reached. The note said, "Don't think your movie didn't have any part of this, because it did."

GO ON TO THE NEXT PAGE.

21. It can be reasonably inferred that *The Day After* was responsible for all of the following EXCEPT:

    A. causing the narrator to think more urgently about international warfare.
    B. inspiring a broad public discussion of the nuclear arms race.
    C. allowing Ronald Reagan to win the loyalty of his former political opponents.
    D. helping along diplomatic efforts between the United States and the Soviet Union.

22. As described by the author, *The Day After* was a notable piece of entertainment because it was:

    F. shocking and transformative.
    G. scholarly and educational.
    H. expensive and astonishing.
    J. accessible and predictable.

23. In *The Day After*, a conflict between the Soviet Union and the United States begins when:

    A. the Soviet Union attempts to gain West Germany.
    B. the United States attempts to gain East Germany.
    C. the United States launches nuclear missiles.
    D. the Soviet Union launches nuclear missiles.

24. The main function of the second paragraph (lines 12-22) is to show:

    F. the origins of the narrator's interest in a single sports team.
    G. a state of immaturity that the author deeply regrets.
    H. a few of the author's interests before he viewed *The Day After*.
    J. a manner of interpreting television programs that the author finds problematic.

25. In order to engage the Americans who viewed *The Day After*, the ABC television network did all of the following EXCEPT:

    A. provide viewers with related written resources.
    B. establish toll-free telephone lines.
    C. host a special interview program.
    D. televise a debate among State Department officials.

26. It can be reasonably inferred that several of the main characters in *The Day After* are:

    F. residents of Lawrence, Kansas and Kansas City, Missouri.
    G. high-ranking military officials in the Soviet Union and the United States.
    H. soldiers and rescue workers who have been newly sent to the American Heartland.
    J. heads of state modeled directly on Ronald Reagan and Mikhail Gorbachev.

27. The fifth and sixth paragraphs of the passage (lines 49-62) establish the idea that:

    A. the broadcast of *The Day After* made Americans more receptive to the Strategic Defense Initiative.
    B. both high-ranking American officials and everyday civilians reacted strongly to *The Day After*.
    C. American officials in the 1980s were kept up to date about trends in popular entertainment.
    D. the makers of *The Day After* were surprised by the intensity of the public response.

28. The author suggests that *The Day After* is similar to a nature documentary in that both of these films:

    F. serve clear educational purposes.
    G. feature actors respected by the public.
    H. are valued today mostly as entertainment.
    J. can be easily adapted to IMAX screens.

29. Based on the last paragraph of the passage, it can be inferred that Nicholas Meyer responded to President Reagan's note with:

    A. confusion.
    B. amusement.
    C. celebration.
    D. satisfaction.

30. The author of the passage indicates that the large viewership for the initial broadcast of *The Day After* can be partially explained by:

    F. President Reagan's positive response to the movie.
    G. televised debates devoted to nuclear warfare.
    H. the popularity of earlier television movies.
    J. an extensive advertising campaign.

GO ON TO THE NEXT PAGE.

Passage IV

NATURAL SCIENCE: This passage is adapted from the essay "Lives of the Mind," a consideration of behavioral or "stimulus-based" psychology.

All of us are different, yet all of us pass through the same stages as we journey from infancy to adulthood. This is the somewhat paradoxical idea that lies behind much of modern cognitive and developmental psychology. In light of
5 this, it is no surprise that children—once seen by researchers as little more than "miniature adults," but now understood to have remarkably flexible and sensitive minds—have become a special subject of psychological study over the past three decades.

10 Of course, it has been argued that many human characteristics and behaviors have innate foundations, and will be automatically evident in all stages of an individual's maturation; thanks to the Human Genome Project of the 1990s, this genetic view of development has even gained
15 some new supporters. However, with the rise of behavioral psychology as a formal field of inquiry, psychologists and sociologists now attest that largely external factors can create personality traits in humans. These factors are especially potent when learned at an early age. Environmental stimuli,
20 also referred to as "learned behaviors," can spur on a multiplicity of changes in the course of a young person's life.

According to the theory of cognitive development first put forward by psychologist Jean Piaget (1896-1980), children go through a few distinct stages as they begin to
25 mentally mature. First, children experience a Sensorimotor Stage between birth and the age of two; this is the condition of learning to walk, talk, and separate out basic perceptions. This stage and the next—the Preoperational Stage, which takes place between the ages of two and six—can sound
30 quite basic. Yet such basics excite researchers. It was Piaget's belief that children, during their earliest growing stages, are like "little scientists," actively trying to understand the reasoning behind the way the world operates as opposed to simply accepting and absorbing information passively—as
35 adults often will. Children question everything and are constantly seeking new experiences; when deprived of such experiences, they are also deprived of the full emotional and psychological capacity needed to mature, develop, and move on to new stimuli. The capacity to interrogate the world is
40 enhanced during the Concrete Operational Stage (ages seven to eleven) but can diminish during the Formal Operational Stage (ages twelve and beyond) as work habits and personality traits really set in.

In truth, what we think of as "good personality" may be
45 mostly a matter of "good upbringing." When children attend school in order to learn the basics of math, reading, writing, and science, they also learn about sharing, compassion, and other social constructs based on cooperation. Some of this knowledge is absorbed without direct thought on the child's
50 part: a classroom with circular tables and an open floor may encourage interaction and spontaneity, while rows of chairs may teach the child to value regularity and uniformity. The child will never think "spontaneity" or "uniformity" as an articulated concept, but the stimulus will leave an impression.
55 These subconscious learning structures may also explain why, although the majority of rote learning takes place in the classroom during early childhood development, many learned behaviors seem to be most profoundly absorbed at home. Those children who are deprived of healthy meals,
60 even in otherwise pleasant environments, will likely react with suspicion and anxiety to images of food and instances of hunger—in contrast to children who are fed properly, or even given too much.

Even the most basic language and communication
65 skills are contracted through such environmental processes. Psychologist B.F. Skinner (1904-1990) suggested during his lifetime that sophisticated language and communication abilities are the results of imitation; often, such skills are reinforced extensions of interactions with adults. For
70 example, when a child is young and the child's parents say, "It's nighty night time," they are inadvertently belittling the child's level of maturity rather than expressing an idea of communicable growth. Instead, the parent or parents would be advised to say, "It's bedtime," or, "It's time to go to sleep."
75 These would be more productive ways of addressing a young child, and would encourage the child to imitate and eventually master relatively advanced means of linguistic expression. These modes of speech would also prevent unforeseen, unfortunate messages. A child that is addressed using such
80 "baby-talk," and then sees its parents use such "baby talk" on the family dog, will be prompted to see itself as somehow alien to the other human beings in its household.

Children's minds are certainly not simplistic, but they certainly are fragile constructs. Beyond the physical needs of
85 food, water, hygiene, and proper shelter or housing, young children need a high degree of emotional care—as any good parent knows. Ultimately, the first five years of a child's life are considered doubly important in regards to growth; the transition from the Sensorimotor to the Preoperational Stage
90 must be navigated, and must be done so in a manner that sets the foundation for a productive life. During this crucial period, infants, toddlers, and young children begin to subconsciously build patterns of behavior, which will eventually determine and shape their future happiness.

GO ON TO THE NEXT PAGE.

31. Which of the following best characterizes the author's overall approach to the field of behavioral psychology?

    A. The author endorses its major principles and indicates deficiencies in earlier approaches.
    B. The author attempts to defend previous developments before reluctantly endorsing Piaget's theories.
    C. The author weighs its strengths against a series of new ideas in genetic biology.
    D. The author uses a single case study to argue for the validity of a behavioral approach.

32. The author of the passage rejects the assumption that:

    F. children will be influenced most strongly by habits observed inside the home.
    G. children consciously look to adults for guidance in forming patterns of behavior.
    H. children's minds can be understood as smaller-scale versions of adult minds.
    J. the theories of Piaget and Skinner were neglected for much of the twentieth century.

33. According to the passage, the stage of development at which children most intensely question the world around them is the:

    A. Sensorimotor Stage.
    B. Preoperational Stage.
    C. Concrete Operational Stage.
    D. Formal Operational Stage.

34. The example of the "classroom" mentioned in line 50 directly supports the idea that:

    F. children will be most clearly impacted by their surroundings in the Formal Operational Stage.
    G. children are incapable of thinking of academic subjects as general categories.
    H. children can acquire a particular behavior without being directly instructed to do so.
    J. children react poorly to ideas of orderliness but do not understand the causes of these reactions.

35. As used in line 84, the phrase "physical needs" refers to requirements that:

    A. must be addressed if children are to develop positive behavior patterns.
    B. have often been belittled by the opponents of behavioral psychology.
    C. children should eventually attend to independently.
    D. are most difficult to fulfill in the Preoperational Stage.

36. The author of the passage indicates that adults should not address children using "baby talk" for all of the following reasons EXCEPT that such talk:

    F. could cause the adults to use less advanced language in other contexts.
    G. may accidentally equate the child with an animal.
    H. can place the child at a troublingly low maturity level.
    J. does not create or reinforce an idea of advanced communication in the child's mind.

37. In the passage, the term "little scientists" is used to refer to a concept that is:

    A. unique to the Peroperational Stage.
    B. disputed by genetic biologists.
    C. attributed to Jean Piaget.
    D. still puzzling to behavioral researchers.

38. In terms of developing the author's argument, the fourth and fifth paragraphs (lines 44-82) primarily serve to:

    F. imply that different types of classroom and home environments communicate different levels of maturity.
    G. explain why language acquisition is a more pressing concern than either academics or nutrition.
    H. apply Skinner's theories to cases that Skinner never envisioned.
    J. present hypothetical instances of how children could be strongly affected by certain stimuli.

39. As described in the fourth paragraph, classrooms can be understood as:

    A. disregarded by most psychological studies.
    B. premised on simplistic concepts of organization.
    C. important to developmental learning.
    D. disadvantageous to highly creative children.

40. According to the passage, which of the following would NOT be of primary interest to behavioral psychologists?

    F. Health and nutritional requirements
    G. Conditions in homes and schools
    H. Processes of language acquisition
    J. Traits determined by an individual's genes

END OF TEST 9
STOP! DO NOT TURN THE PAGE UNTIL TOLD TO DO SO.
DO NOT RETURN TO A PREVIOUS TEST.

Answer Key: TEST 9

Test 9

LITERARY NARRATIVE

1. A
2. G
3. D
4. F
5. C
6. G
7. B
8. G
9. B
10. H

HUMANITIES

21. C
22. F
23. A
24. H
25. D
26. F
27. B
28. F
29. D
30. J

SOCIAL SCIENCE

11. D
12. F
13. A
14. G
15. C
16. F
17. B
18. F
19. D
20. G

NATURAL SCIENCE

31. A
32. H
33. C
34. H
35. A
36. F
37. C
38. J
39. C
40. J

To see your scaled ACT Reading Score (1-36), determine
how many questions you answered correctly and consult the
Scoring Chart on Page 186 of this book.

Post-Test Analysis

This post-test analysis is essential if you want to see an improvement on your next test. Possible reasons for errors, both for the test overall and for each of the four reading passages, are listed here. Place check marks next to the types of errors that pertain to you, or write your own types of errors in the blank spaces provided.

GENERAL

◇ Spent too much time reading the passages
◇ Spent too much time answering the questions
◇ Did not attempt to finish all of the passages
◇ Did not create effective margin answers
◇ Did not use process of elimination
◇ Could not find evidence to answer the questions
◇ Could not comprehend the topics and ideas in the passages
◇ Could not understand what the questions were asking
◇ Interpreted the passages rather than using evidence
Other: _____

LITERARY NARRATIVE

◇ Spent too long reading the passage
◇ Spent too long answering the questions
◇ Could not identify the setting and characters
◇ Could not understand the plot or action
◇ Could not work effectively with tone and clues to tone
Other: _____

> **Use this form** to better analyze your performance. If you don't understand why you made errors, there is no way that you can correct them!

SOCIAL SCIENCE

◇ Spent too long reading the passage
◇ Spent too long answering the questions
◇ Could not understand the author's position or arguments
◇ Used outside knowledge rather than using evidence
Other: _____

HUMANITIES

◇ Spent too long reading the passage
◇ Spent too long answering the questions
◇ Could understand the themes and organization of the passage
◇ Could not understand the author's ideas and uses of evidence
Other: _____

NATURAL SCIENCE

◇ Spent too long reading the passage
◇ Spent too long answering the questions
◇ Found the concepts and ideas in the passage confusing
◇ Found the questions confusing
◇ Could not effectively work with the inference and logic questions
Other: _____

TEST 9 Answer Explanations

1. Correct Answer: A

In the course of a discussion of "vibrant notes, rhythms, and melodies" (line 5) and of his jazz heroes, the narrator mentions Minton's. Later, the narrator states that he spent "the night covering a performance of the Dave Brubeck Quartet at the Blue Note" (lines 31-32). This information indicates that these locations are music clubs. Movie theaters (**B**) are irrelevant to the content of the passage, while record labels (**C**) and radio stations (**D**) are closer to the main topic of jazz but are not accurate descriptions of the narrator's destinations.

2. Correct Answer: G

The narrator notes that he was "serious about, absolutely passionate about jazz" (lines 18-20). Because this statement occurs within a larger discussion of the narrator's commitment to jazz music, *devoted to* is the best answer. The narrator is not respected yet, but is trying to earn respect as a reporter (**F**); he is not talented in playing jazz music itself, but wants to show his knowledge of the topic (**G**). Choice **J** can be eliminated quickly, because *intimidated* falsely gives a negative tone to the narrator's positive feelings about jazz.

3. Correct Answer: D

Mick finishes his coffee in line 76, gives his business card to Winston in lines 79-80, and tells Winston that he lives nearby in lines 61-62. Thus, eliminate **A**, **B**, and **C**. Well-known jazz musicians are discussed in the first paragraph, not during the later stages of the narrative that deal with Mick Mercury's actions.

4. Correct Answer: F

As Mick Mercury states in lines 62-64, "what's nice about being a radio personality is that everyone knows your voice, but not your face. It helps me keep myself anonymous." In other words, he can *avoid unwanted publicity* because only his voice is recognized. Other answers rely on faulty interpretations of the passage. Mick never discusses whether or not his programs are recorded in advance (**G**). He may in fact be a guide to the community (**H**) and may in fact attend performances (**J**), but he never directly points to these as benefits. Because this information is not specified, eliminate these answers.

5. Correct Answer: C

Immediately after the line references, the narrator notes that "by high school, I got a job on our local paper—the Brooklyn Gazette—and that's when things changed" (lines 16-17). He then goes on to describe how he began "staying out all night at jazz clubs" (line 23). This information supports choice **C**. At the time described, the narrator is still in high school; choices **A** and **B** both assume that he is farther along in his education. Choice **D** emphasizes the wrong topic: the narrator temporarily played by his mother's rules regarding live jazz clubs, not listening to jazz on the radio.

6. Correct Answer: G

The early paragraphs of the passage establish the idea that Winston is prioritizing his interest in jazz instead of his education: his mother even notes that he "might not graduate" (line 51). This situation changes when Mick Mercury, a "famous radio personality" (line 40) whom Winston admires, convinces Winston to focus on his studies: by the final sentence of the passage, Winston has decided to put some of his jazz interests on hold until he finishes school. All of this information supports choice **G**, since Mick Mercury intervenes directly in Winston's life. **F** can be eliminated because Winston wants to continue his connection to jazz (as is made clear in the final paragraph), but *after* completing his education. **H** and **J** attribute the wrong roles to the characters. As stated in line 27, Ma (not Winston) reacts by losing her temper. And as the paragraph is arranged, Ma and Mick work together to negotiate with Winston: Winston and Mick never negotiate with Ma.

7. Correct Answer: B

When he comes home at night, Winston observes his mother "still in her work clothes from the day before" and realizes that "she'd been up all night, too, waiting for me" (lines 45-46). This evidence supports **B**. Ma is apparently worried about Winston, but nothing in her dialogue lines up with the information in **C**. Note also that Mick is drinking coffee and that he never questions Ma directly: this information should lead you to eliminate **A** and **D**, respectively.

8. Correct Answer: G

Winston initially reacts to Mick by registering "a deep baritone sound that I knew instantly, and yet I could not convince myself that this voice was emanating here, inside my own kitchen" (lines 36-39). The narrator knows that the voice is Mick's, but is not convinced that the event is real, so that disbelief effectively describes the Winston's response. Reactions of remorse only occur later in the passage (starting with the "pang of regret" in line 47), so that the negative answers **F** and **J** reflect the wrong content. Mick is drinking coffee throughout the passage, but because the narrator never offers him a second cup, **H** must be eliminated.

9. Correct Answer: B

As is made clear in the third paragraph, Winston's Ma persists in trying to get Winston to focus on his studies. She also stays "up all night" (line 46) in an effort to reverse Winston's poor study habits. It is clear from this that Ma is willing to make efforts on Winston's behalf so that he can achieve worthwhile goals, which is why **B** is the best answer. Both **C** and **D** are too negative: do not neglect Ma's interest in Winston's wellbeing, or misinterpret "losing her temper" (line 27) as hatred of her son. Trap answer **A** misstates the content of the passage: Ma actually does not *accept* Winston's jazz activities, and may not be *frequently* kept up by him at all. The late-night meeting in the passage is apparently a one-time occurrence.

10. Correct Answer: H

After Mick declares that Winston could help him out "on the air," Winston feels that his heart has "turned inside-out with joy" (lines 69-72). Actions that resemble both **F** and **G** occur earlier in the

TEST 9 Answer Explanations

conversation; **F** (line 60) confuses Winston, while **G** (line 66) does not receive a direct reaction from Winston. **J** is a trap answer: Mick Mercury in fact praises Winston's abilities as a jazz writer in lines 67-69, but never directly addresses Winston's schoolwork.

SOCIAL SCIENCE

11. Correct Answer: D

Early in Passage A, the author presents a description of the land "to the East" that focuses on two of its major features: its difficult terrain and its "sense of ancient mystery, for this is a land of myth and legend and the powers of magic" (lines 9-10). This information directly supports **D** and can be used to eliminate **B**, which refers more effectively to the "gentle and open" (lines 1-2) land to the west. **A** and **C** both distort actual elements of the passage: the land to the East is described as silent but not as devoid of wildlife (and in fact has prominent woods), and the land has "narrow and winding" (line 6) roads that are, however, never described as poorly maintained.

12. Correct Answer: F

The word *combined* refers to a population of "about 2500" (line 24), a figure that results from *adding* the populations of the two former villages that now constitute Bagnolles de l'Orne. The author is thus considering a single, total figure: thus, **F** is a highly effective answer. **G** wrongly refers to the issue of loyalty (not to simple calculation), **H** is a negative, and **J** in context would indicate that the villages and their populations are identical, an inference that is in no way supported by the text.

13. Correct Answer: A

In describing Bagnolles de l'Orne, the author explains that a "rather pretty little Normandy village" (lines 25-26) might be expected; however, Bagnolles de l'Orne really presents its visitors with an active casino or, "in the minds of some, a sophisticated Las Vegas situated in the heart of rural Lower Normandy (lines 34-35). This information justifies **A** as the best choice. **B** and **C** describe how Bagnolles de l'Orne might be expected to appear, not how it actually is. **D** distorts the passage in a different manner: while Bagnolles de l'Orne does feature a "lake around which is set the settlement" (line 21), there is no indication that the site is famous for its lake. Even the legend that the author cites regarding the lake may be known only to a few people.

14. Correct Answer: G

In lines 55-56, the author explains that "I had been to New York before, but that was in my youth when I was up for any experience." This information can be used to justify **G** and to rapidly eliminate **F**. Both **H** and **J** rely on faulty inferences: it is not clear how long the author spent in New York during her youth (eliminating **H**), but it is clear that the author is not a permanent resident of New York (making a "vacation" from the city a complete misstatement and eliminating **J**).

15. Correct Answer: C

In the final paragraph of Passage B, the author describes a hotel in New York in the following terms: "its forecourt seemed to be a hive of constant motion" (lines 64-65). Since the forecourt is being compared to a hive, the author is using the word "hive" figuratively; thus, **C** is an effective choice. **A** refers to a literal market that can be visited in Normandy, **B** refers to the actual years of the author's youth, and **D** refers to a physical key that the author obtains at the hotel. Although some of these terms can be used figuratively in OTHER contexts (as in "key to success"), they are all used in direct, literal references in the passage itself.

16. Correct Answer: F

After beginning with an opening description of the region where the author lives, the passage describes the author's journey to New York in chronological order: the author notes that "it was with some trepidation [nervousness] that I made my way to Charles de Gaulle Airport in Paris" (lines 51-52). Choices **G**, **H**, and **J** all describe later stages of the passage: while the author may feel INCREASED anxiety at these points, the question asks when the author FIRST experienced anxiety, not when the author's anxiety was greatest.

17. Correct Answer: B

The word *branded* refers to an activity performed by New York, which branded itself as "the city that never slept" in "an accurate piece of messagemaking" (lines 57-59). In the context of "messagemaking," to *brand* would mean to *advertise*, thus making **B** an excellent answer. Both **A** and **C** are inappropriate negatives for a city that is trying to promote itself, while *embellished* (**D**) means *decorated* or *beautified* and is thus out of context: this word does not directly fit the theme of presenting or of sending a message.

18. Correct Answer: F

Unlike Passage A, which is an impartial and entirely third-person account of specific areas in Normandy, Passage B considers some of the same issues from the author's explicit perspective ("I inhabit a small town in this region", lines 41-42) before going on to explain what happened when the author "was invited to New York for a week" (line 50). While both passages emphasize factual information about Normandy, only Passage B takes an approach that involves a personal narrative: **F** is thus the best answer. **G** introduces negatives that may be felt by students who are bored by the passage, but that are not substantiated by any context clues. **H** wrongly assumes that Passage B (which has a strongly personal tone) is "detached", while **J** wrongly assumes that both passages present central arguments instead of simply providing overviews of facts.

TEST 9 Answer Explanations

19. Correct Answer: D

While the population of Bagnolles de l'Orne "stands now at about 2500" (line 24), Domfront "has a population of just over two thousand" (line 46). This information makes **D** the correct answer. While the architecture of Domfront is never directly analyzed (eliminating **A**), only Bagnolles de l'Orne has a local mythology (eliminating **B**, since all of the figures who played a role in Domfront are famous historical leaders, not creations of myth and legend). **C** relies on a faulty inference: while both sites do welcome tourists, the author does not directly discuss revenue figures in a way that would justify this choice. If anything, Bagnolles de l'Orne seems to be a much more popular tourist destination.

20. Correct Answer: G

In Passage B, the author focuses on a region of rural France where "Nothing much happens" (line 48) and contrasts her life in this region with her experiences in New York. However, Passage A explains that one town in rural France, Bagnolles de l'Orne, is the site of a lively "casino with its elegant, terraced restaurant, ballroom, cinema, theatre, slot machines" (lines 31-33) and other forms of entertainment. This information makes **G** the correct answer. Both passages indicate that some areas of rural France are reserved and quiet (eliminating **F**), both mention tourism (line 47 of Passage B, eliminating **H**), and neither discusses luxury goods at any length (eliminating **J**, although Passage B does mention the cheeses and fruits produced in Lower Normandy).

HUMANITIES

21. Correct Answer: C

The author notes that, after seeing *The Day After*, he "worried about nuclear war. I worried about the arms race" (lines 57-58). Thus, eliminate **A**. The author also notes that a "spirit of questioning and rampant debate arose where the topics of nuclear arms policy and the Cold War were concerned" (lines 74-76) and that "a nuclear arms deal was reached" and was partially attributed to Nicholas Meyer, director of *The Day After* (lines 82-87). Thus, eliminate **B** and **D**. However, the passage does not indicate that Ronald Reagan won the loyalty of his former opponents (who are in fact never mentioned): the author simply states that Reagan reacted strongly to the film (lines 52-54) and that Reagan's negotiations with Russia had a positive outcome (lines 84-86).

22. Correct Answer: F

Unlike other movies, which only "entertain and educate," *The Day After* was important because it "induced fear and, ultimately, change" (lines 10-11). Thus, the movie would be shocking (fear) and transformative (change), making **F** the best answer. It is unlikely that a film that produced change would be predictable, so eliminate answer **J**. The other answers rely on misreading of the passage's content. *The Day After* inspired debate, but did so because it was shocking and popular (not scholarly or academic, **G**). And the film was widely and perhaps expensively publicized, but is never described as itself expensive to make (**H**).

23. Correct Answer: A

In *The Day After*, "a war breaks out" because "the Soviet Union is trying to gain control of West Germany, rather than keep to its allotted territory in East Germany" (lines 33-37). Thus, **A** is the correct answer. Do attribute the aggression to the wrong country (**B**) or assume that the "nuclear attacks" mentioned in line 42 are the initial cause of the conflict (**C** and **D**).

24. Correct Answer: H

The author states that he was "a young teen in 1983" (line 12) and goes on to describe "the subjects that most occupied my mind" (line 13) in the rest of this paragraph. As is explained at the end of the paragraph, *The Day After* caught the author "unaware" (line 20) or changed the state of mind described earlier. Thus, **H** gives the best description of the function of this paragraph. Despite his responses to sports and television, the author mentions neither a specific sports team (**F**) nor multiple television programs (**J**). Although the author may in fact have been immature at the time and appears to be good-naturedly poking fun at his youthful self, the tone of this paragraph is not one of strong *regret*, so that negative answer **G** can be eliminated.

25. Correct Answer: D

After broadcasting *The Day After*, ABC "set up toll-free lines and mailed out half a million viewers' guides" (lines 66-67); the network also "ran a live special edition of a news program called *Viewpoint*" and invited Secretary of State George Schultz to participate (lines 68-73). This information enables you to eliminate **A**, **B**, and **C**. Schultz is never mentioned in the context of other State Department officials, so it would be wrong to assume that a debate among such officials (**D**) was part of ABC's programming.

26. Correct Answer: F

In his description of *The Day After*, the author explains that "the movie focuses primarily on a few citizens who live in Lawrence, Kansas and Kansas City, Missouri" (lines 43-44). This information supports answer **F**. Although United States officials (**G**) and Reagan and Gorbachev (**J**) are mentioned elsewhere in the passage, the description of the movie disqualifies this answer. And although the setting is the American Heartland, the characters are citizens of this area, not people who have been newly sent there (**H**).

27. Correct Answer: B

It is explained in lines 49-54 that the Joint Chiefs of Staff were "clearly moved" by *The Day After*, and that President Reagan was "greatly depressed" by the movie. Then, it is explained in lines 55-62 that the author, who was a teenage boy at the time *The Day After* appeared, felt "fear" and "worried" about new issues. Thus, the movie caused strong reactions in the two groups of Americans designated in choice **B**. Choices **A** and **C** are two narrow: we only know that the author was more receptive to the Strategic Defense Initiative, and we only know that that American officials viewed *The Day After*. (Other Americans and other trends are not mentioned in these contexts.) The makers of *The Day After* are not mentioned at all at this point, so **D** must be eliminated.

TEST 9 Answer Explanations

28. Correct Answer: F

In the first paragraph, the author describes "nature documentaries" as "undoubtedly educational" (lines 5-8). The author then goes on to state that the initial purpose of *The Day After* "was to entertain and educate" (line 10). This information lines up to support **F**. Respected actors (**G**) and IMAX screens (**J**) are only mentioned in line 7, in the context of nature documentaries alone. Choice **H** is beyond the scope of the passage: the author is concerned throughout with the impact of *The Day After* when it first appeared, not with its status *today*.

29. Correct Answer: D

According to the passage, Meyer referred to *The Day After* as "the most worthwhile thing I got to do in my life," a reaction "inspired by a note from President Reagan himself" (lines 82-84). Thus, expect a strongly positive answer and eliminate **A** and **B**. Of the remaining choices, **D** is the best answer: we do not know if Meyer outwardly *celebrated* the note (**C**) but we do know that he found his accomplishment and subsequent recognition worthwhile, or *satisfying*.

30. Correct Answer: J

In describing the massive audience for *The Day After*, the author notes that the movie had been "prominently advertised in radio and television commercials, in newspapers, and in magazines" (lines 26-27). Thus, an advertising campaign would be a likely cause for the movie's large viewership. Reagan's response (**F**) and televised debates (**G**) were results of the movie, not reasons why it was widely viewed. Note also that the author never discusses or even names other television movies, so that **H** must be eliminated.

NATURAL SCIENCE

31. Correct Answer: A

The author refers to the rise of "behavioral psychology," which places emphasis on how "largely external factors can create personality traits in humans," in lines 15-18. In the remainder of the passage, the author argues that there are strong links between external factors, such as classroom settings and modes of dialogue, and how children think. Note also that the author mentions and contradicts psychological ideas that place little emphasis on learned behaviors and adaptations (children as "miniature adults" in line 6, the "genetic view of development" in line 14). Together, all this evidence supports **A**. Choice **B** distorts the author's tone: the author never questions Piaget's theories, and instead questions opposing schools of thought. Choices **C** and **D** misstate the emphasis of the passage: the author only considers genetic biology broadly and briefly (not as a series of ideas sustained through the passage) and uses multiple case studies to argue for a behavioral approach (not a single case study).

32. Correct Answer: H

In lines 5-7, the author describes children as "once seen by researchers as little more than 'miniature adults,' but now understood to have remarkably flexible and sensitive minds." The author then references Piaget's theories (lines 22-43) to show how children and adults differ, so that the author would reject the equivalence between children and adults in choice **H**. The author would in fact endorse choices **F** and **G**, as is made clear by textual evidence: many learned behaviors "seem to be most profoundly absorbed at home" (lines 58-59) and many childhood skills are "reinforced extensions of interactions with adults" (line 69). Choice **J** is never addressed: the passage is concerned with explaining the ideas of Piaget and Skinner, not with the historical reception of these ideas.

33. Correct Answer: C

In the Preoperational Stage, children try "to understand the reasoning behind the way the world operates" (lines 32-33). However, this "capacity to interrogate the world is enhanced during the Concrete Operational Stage" (lines 39-40), so that **C**, NOT **B**, is your answer. Remember that the Sensorimotor Stage involves "basic perceptions" (line 27), not intense questioning, and that the Formal Operational Stage involves diminished questioning and steady "work habits" (line 42). Thus, eliminate **A** and **D**.

34. Correct Answer: H

The example of the classroom illustrates the idea that "knowledge is absorbed without direct thought on the child's part" in certain scenarios (line 49). In other words, the children are not being directly instructed in certain behaviors, yet the children's surroundings will "leave an impression" (line 54). Choices **F** and **J** rely on faulty inferences: it is never explicitly mentioned that the children in the classroom are in the Formal Operational Stage, or that they have negative reactions to the orderly classroom mentioned. Choice **G** is a trap: though the children do not think of general categories in the classroom situation (as explained in lines 52-54), this one case does not indicate that children are absolutely incapable of thinking of general categories. Also, the categories here refer to ideas of arrangement, not to *academic subjects*.

35. Correct Answer: A

The author states that "beyond the physical needs of food, water, hygiene, and proper shelter or housing, young children need a high degree of emotional care" (lines 84-86). Later, the author describes early childhood as a crucial period when children begin to "build patterns of behavior" (line 93). It can be logically concluded that physical needs are essential elements of positive childhood development. Use false words to eliminate the other answers: the opponents of behavioral psychology (**B**) are mentioned earlier in the passage, and a comparison of the Preoperational Stage to other stages (**D**) is never undertaken. (The author does mention the transition from the Sensorimotor to the Preoperational Stage, but does not say which stage entails more pressing needs.) Although children may independently attend to some of these needs in adulthood, the author does not explicitly set this idea forward as a recommendation (**C**).

TEST 9 Answer Explanations

36. Correct Answer: F

The "baby talk" mentioned in the passage could align a child with a "family dog" (line 81), belittle the "child's level of maturity" (line 72), and would not express "an idea of communicable growth" (lines 72-73). This information can be used to eliminate choices **G**, **H**, and **J**, respectively. **F** misstates the danger of baby talk: the author argues that baby talk places a child (not an adult) in danger of acting on a low maturity level.

37. Correct Answer: C

In lines 30-32, the author writes that "it was Piaget's belief that children, during their earliest growing stages, are like 'little scientists,'" a piece of evidence that directly supports answer **C**. Choice **B** deals with a topic (genetic biology) that occurs only in the second paragraph, while choice **D** misstates the attitude of researchers, who are not puzzled (negative) but excited (positive, line 30) by ideas such as Piaget's. Trap answer **A** relies on a faulty analysis. The idea of "little scientists" involves intense questioning on the part of children, and the third paragraph indicates that children are inquisitive both in the Preoperational *and* in the Concrete Operational Stages, not in the Preoperational stage alone.

38. Correct Answer: J

In the fourth paragraph, the author describes the effects of different classrooms (lines 50-52) and of different diets (lines 59-63); in the fifth paragraph, the author describes the effect of "baby talk" on a child (lines 69-82). These are set forward as realistic scenarios, yet specific children and locations are not named. Thus, the author provides hypothetical instances of the role of certain stimuli in the lives of children. Skinner is only mentioned in the fifth paragraph (**H**), while language acquisition is only mentioned in the fifth and is never construed as superior to academics or nutrition, which may be equally pressing concerns (**G**). Trap answer **F** misdirects the passage's argument: different modes of dialogue (as discussed in the fifth paragraph) communicate different maturity levels. This argument is never applied to the classroom environments mentioned in the fourth paragraph.

39. Correct Answer: C

The author states in lines 50-52 that "a classroom with circular tables and an open floor may encourage interaction and spontaneity, while rows of chairs may teach the child to value regularity and uniformity." In other words, classroom arrangements form behavior, or are important to developmental learning. The author never directly mentions psychological studies of classrooms (**A**) and may even be mentioning classrooms because they are valuable to current studies. Both **B** ("simplistic") and **D** ("disadvantageous") go against the passage by applying negative tones to the classrooms.

40. Correct Answer: J

In the second paragraph, the author points to the importance of "environmental stimuli" or "learned behaviors" in developmental psychology (lines 19-20). Some examples which the author goes on to provide include nutritional requirements (lines 59-63), school conditions (lines 50-52), and language learning (lines 64-82). Thus, eliminate choices **F**, **G**, and **H**. In the second paragraph, the author also notes that there is a "genetic view of development" which contrasts with the approach taken by behavioral psychology, so that **J** is the correct answer.

Test 10

READING TEST
35 Minutes—40 Questions

DIRECTIONS: There are four passages in this test. Each passage is followed by several questions. After reading a passage, choose the best answer to each question and fill in the corresponding oval on your answer document. You may refer to the passages as often as necessary.

Passage I

LITERARY NARRATIVE: This passage is adapted from the short story "Estuary." The action takes place in Florida during the 1990s, and concerns members of the Seminole Tribe of Native Americans.

It was a balmy day, and even the blue of the sky appeared somehow warm. Jessie steered her red Mercedes-Benz deftly through the midday traffic on I-95, circumventing the elderly motorists who drove far too slowly in all the
5 wrong lanes.

"I sure haven't missed this!" Jessie yelled, with a smile, over the roar of the wind. The convertible's top was down, and the Jessie's long black hair flew all about in the warm air. Around her neck hung the traditional tortoise-shell necklace
10 that Lucy had given her as a present at the Green Corn Dance—the ceremony in which Jessie and Lucy, at the age of sixteen, had been recognized as women by the tribe. Lucy smiled, and, for a moment, felt as though she and her friend were again just teenagers, making the drive down from Ft.
15 Lauderdale to Miami to do nothing other than hang out on the beach all day, without worry or care. But she knew that those days were over, and that this meeting was not carefree. Jessie had told Lucy that "they needed to talk," which hadn't surprised Lucy in the least. She knew all about this particular
20 trouble.

They drove on. Lucy ran her fingers across the smooth brown leather of the seat; the silver Mercedes logo glinted upon the steering wheel of her friend's car. Lucy had grown used to it all a long time ago. Jessie, as the only daughter of
25 Joe Okobee—tribal chief of the Florida Seminoles for over thirty years—had always lived a very different life than she had.

Jessie put on the signal, taking the exit for A1A, towards South Beach. As the car ascended the causeway,
30 Lucy looked out, and felt a familiar thrill: for as far as her eyes could see, the clear water of Biscayne Bay glittered like a jewel. Minutes later, they were pulling up under the porte-cochère of the Fontainebleau, and Jessie was handing her keys to a well-dressed valet. Soon, the two women were
35 seated at a beachfront table overlooking the ocean, under the

cool shade of a wide umbrella.

"So," said Jessie, getting straight to the point, as usual. "Do you know why I've asked you here?"

Slowly, Lucy nodded.

40   "Then you understand that my father needs you to stop printing your editorials," said Jessie, matter-of-factly.

Lucy was quiet, and took a sip of her water. Of course Jessie's father didn't like the editorials. In them, Lucy railed against Joe Okobee's number-one policy as chief of the
45 Seminole tribe: the use of casino gambling as a source of tribal revenue.

"You know how I feel," said Lucy, looking up at her friend. "I'm concerned about our heritage. That so few Seminoles can even speak our language anymore. It's become
50 purely about profits and—"

"I understand your concern," interrupted Jessie. "And my father has plans to allocate money towards cultural preservation, including hiring linguists to create instructional language DVDs. But in order to do that, we need our funding.
55 It doesn't make sense to cut off our largest and biggest lifeline. But your editorials are stirring up a lot of anti-casino sentiment, which isn't helpful either for my father's reelection *or* for your cause."

Lucy didn't respond—a familiar tactic that aggravated
60 Jessie. Lucy had always been an impractical dreamer, unable to understand the realities of the world. What Lucy couldn't see was that Jessie really *did* sympathize with Lucy's point of view—she knew that there was nothing particularly "noble" in running a casino, that casinos didn't have anything to do
65 with traditional Native American values—but the fact remained that in the past thirty years since her father had become chief, profits from the casino had lifted the Seminoles out of poverty. It was these very profits that were made available to young tribe members such as themselves, and
70 which had paid for their college educations. Arguably, it was *because* of Jessie's father's policies that Lucy even had her

GO ON TO THE NEXT PAGE.

journalism degree from New York University—an irony that seemed to be lost on Lucy. Thinking about it, Jessie felt herself growing angry. Still, she held her tongue.

75   "Come on," Jessie said, after a time. "At the end of the day, we're old friends. Isn't there some way we can work out a compromise here?"

Lucy placed her napkin down on the table, before looking her friend right in the eye.

80   "Jessie," she said. "Do you know what the word 'Seminole' means?"

Jessie tried not to roll her eyes; she hadn't come here to be lectured.

"It means 'No surrender,' " said Lucy. She placed her
85 napkin down on the table, and got to her feet. "I'm sorry," was all she said, before she turned to go.

"Me too," said Jessie, but it was no use. Her friend was already gone.

1. Jessie and Lucy would most likely agree with which of the following statements about the casinos run by Jessie's father?

   A. The casinos were only set up as a last resort effort to keep the tribe from disappearing.
   B. Jessie's father is not aware of the harmful effects of the casinos.
   C. The controversy surrounding the casinos has received more publicity than it deserves.
   D. There is no fundamental link between the casinos and respected Seminole customs.

2. Lucy can most accurately be characterized as:

   F. determined and histrionic.
   G. principled and uncompromising.
   H. optimistic yet misguided.
   J. pragmatic and flexible.

3. One of the functions of the third paragraph (lines 21-27) is to:

   A. provide background information about the two primary characters in the passage.
   B. explain why Joe Okobee became popular as a tribal chief.
   C. describe the setting where the dialogue that follows takes place.
   D. shift the reader's sympathy from Lucy to Jessie.

4. As it is described in the passage, the Green Corn Ceremony is important because it represents:

   F. a tradition that Jessie has gradually forgotten.
   G. a new stage of maturity for Seminole women.
   H. a turning point in the career of Jessie's father.
   J. a time when Jessie and Lucy's friendship was tested.

5. Which of the following policies does Jessie's father support as a means of preserving Seminole heritage?

   A. Setting up college funds for gifted Seminole students
   B. Using casino revenue to build a local museum
   C. Encouraging tourists to attend Seminole ceremonies
   D. Hiring language experts to create educational DVDs

6. Lucy's attitude toward the Biscayne Bay can best be described as:

   F. delighted
   G. perplexed.
   H. sullen.
   J. agitated.

7. It can be reasonably inferred that the "irony" mentioned in line 72 is the idea that:

   A. Lucy's university education has put her in contact with people who do not value her degree.
   B. Lucy's own life has been improved by the policies she opposes.
   C. Jessie's growing anger causes her to address her friend more politely.
   D. Jessie's father respects his political opponents.

8. As it is used in line 79, the word *right* means:

   F. abruptly.
   G. correctly.
   H. directly.
   J. ethically.

9. In her discussion with Lucy, Jessie uses all of the following arguments against Lucy's editorials EXCEPT:

   A. the editorials could hurt the reelection efforts of Jessie's father.
   B. the casino funding could actually enable Seminole culture to be preserved.
   C. the casinos have provided poorer Seminoles with new employment opportunities.
   D. speaking out against the casinos could backfire and harm Lucy.

GO ON TO THE NEXT PAGE.

10. The final four paragraphs of the passage (lines 80-88) are important because they indicate Lucy's

    F. desire to popularize Seminole culture outside the tribe.
    G. conflicted attitude toward Seminole history.
    H. unwillingness to negotiate with Jessie over deeply held principles.
    J. inability to understand Jessie's perspective.

Passage II

SOCIAL SCIENCE: These passages are from two different recent essays on British politics.

Passage A, "No Satisfaction: The Profumo Affair"

If you want to know how the decade beginning in 1960 had such an impact on British life and overturned the traditional attitudes of society, then you need to begin with a dramatic trial in the High Court of London that took place in 1963. Performing
5 in what turned out to be both a tragedy and a farce was a free-ranging cast of characters quite surprising for a plot-line that would seem on the surface to be tacky even by the standards of a Hollywood melodrama. The "Profumo Affair," as the case was called, had its origins on the outskirts of London at the
10 Cliveden Estate, which belonged to Lord Astor, a backstage political tsar. John Profumo, the British Minister of War, was a frequent guest at Cliveden and had the bad luck to fall for one Miss Keeler, a woman with exactly the wrong connections for the Cold War era.

15 Sadly, even back in the sixties private lives had a way of becoming public property. Miss Keeler, the short-lived sweetheart of Mr. Profumo, had an almighty—and rather public—bust-up with an ex-boyfriend who had been angered by a more serious fling she had engaged in with a suspected
20 Soviet spy. The press questioned publicly why the Minister of War should have connections to a Communist enemy. Foolishly, Profumo stated to the Parliament that he had never met the man, and "no impropriety had occurred." The press can follow a scent, emitting more noise and embodying more
25 intensity than a pack of foxhounds: they discovered that both Miss Keeler and Miss Davies had been paid to catch the attention of the Soviet ambassador. This international intrigue climaxed in two spectacular events: John Profumo admitted that he had perjured himself and was then immediately expelled
30 from office and Parliament.

For the first time, the corruption of the ruling class of England was being exposed. As a result of Profumo's indiscretions (and of subsequent investigations of the shady morals that, apparently, were running rampant at Cliveden),
35 the career of an able but naïve politician was ended, a Prime Minister resigned "on the grounds of ill health," the ruling political party lost the next election, the freedom of the press was encouraged to a level never before seen in Britain, and, most importantly, the existing class system was upended.
40 England would never be the same again, no longer fettered by what "the great and the good" of the nobility decided. From 1963 onward, at any rate, the youth of Britain felt free to bring on the liberating, almost revolutionary idea of "Swinging London."

Passage B, "Events, Dear Boy, Events"

45 In the United Kingdom since the end of the Second World War, there have really only been two political parties providing a choice for the voter: Conservative and Labour. Each party has what it calls its core voters: those who, irrespective of what was actually happening in politics, voted for the same party
50 every time. This has led to a complacency in British politics and certainly in the way that the parties in Westminster have regarded the electorate, perhaps because the number of people actually using their votes has been falling gradually over the last forty years. Politicians have assumed that this is a result of
55 general satisfaction in the way Britain is governed. The electorate, if asked, might have a quite different response.

No one doubts that power is often accompanied by scandal and corruption. In that respect, the British Parliament has never been different from any other government. However, since the
60 beginning of the 21st century, perhaps because of the growth in the speed and powers of writers and photographers on the Internet, revelations about the life style of the "rich and famous and powerful" have become much more immediately available. This has had an effect on the response of the general public
65 towards the lifestyles of those who govern. What offends and alienates most is the patronage of voters as an inferior, uncomprehending, gullible class, who should leave government to those who are educated enough to understand these things. A spate of revelations in the first few years of this century that
70 MPs (Members of Parliament) were using their status to financially improve the life of their own families, the suggestions that they were manipulating public opinion have widened the gap between the those who govern and those who are governed. In addition, the economic chaos caused by the
75 arrogance of banks and the rise of unemployment, especially among the young, have widened this lack of trust between the electorate and traditional government. All together, M.Ps are seen to be members of an exclusive upper class club, the members of which are only allowed to those who
80 could afford to go to private schools and Oxbridge. In the words of Benjamin Disraeli, "The Privileged and the People have formed two nations, between who there is no intercourse and no sympathy."

GO ON TO THE NEXT PAGE.

Questions 11-14 ask about Passage A.

11. According to Passage A, which of the following events occurred last?

    A. Profumo was expelled from his position as Minister of War.
    B. Profumo made the acquaintance of Lord Astor.
    C. Profumo admitted that he had perjured himself.
    D. Profumo denied wrongdoing in his connection with Mrs. Keeler.

12. The main purpose of the first two paragraphs of Passage A (lines 1-30) is to:

    F. mock individuals such as Profumo and Astor for their lack of political knowledge.
    G. establish the historical context for a major change in British society.
    H. contrast Profumo's haplessness and dishonesty with Miss Keeler's apparent cunning.
    J. present a theory of political gain that was refuted by the events of 1963.

13. As it is used in line 26, the word *catch* most nearly means:

    A. attract.
    B. understand.
    C. overpower.
    D. foil.

14. The author uses quotation marks with the phrase "the great and the good" (line 41) most likely because this phrase:

    F. was always unpopular among the public.
    G. was widely used by the British media.
    H. was not truly accurate as applied to the nobility.
    J. was developed by the nobility to selfishly promote its own interests.

Questions 15-18 ask about Passage B.

15. According to the author of Passage B, the British are most offended by what tendency of the "rich and famous and powerful" (lines 62-63)?

    A. This group's sponsorship of unpopular legislation.
    B. This group's condescending stance towards voters.
    C. This group's disregard for valued national traditions.
    D. This group's links to elite educational institutions.

16. A "core voter" (line 48) can be defined as a voter who:

    F. agrees with all the positions of the party he or she supports.
    G. is uninterested in politics but sees voting as a patriotic activity.
    H. is extremely loyal to a single party and votes in a predictable pattern.
    J. is either extremely liberal or extremely conservative and votes accordingly.

17. The author of Passage B quotes Benjamin Disraeli most likely because Disraeli's words:

    A. are known to a large number of the passage's readers.
    B. were written during a time period mentioned in the first paragraph.
    C. sum up the author's bias against the British elite.
    D. encapsulate an important point from the passage.

18. Passage B was published in 2015. On the basis of this information, voter participation in Britain, according to the passage, began falling in what year?

    F. 1945 (end of World War II)
    G. 1965
    H. 1975
    J. 2005

Questions 19-20 ask about both passages.

19. A similarity of the two passages is that they both:

    A. single out one or two especially inept British politicians for criticism.
    B. describe the role of the media in exposing cases of corruption.
    C. argue that corruption is growing in British politics despite reform efforts.
    D. praise British voters for their intolerance of poor government.

20. How would the author of Passage B most likely respond to the ideas about the "existing class system" that conclude Passage A?

    F. The overbearing influence of the privileged classes in British society continues to this day.
    G. Profumo's actions are excusable compared to current abuses of power.
    H. Journalists have failed to address corruption in the 21st century.
    J. The corruption of the British political system is now mostly confined to Parliament.

GO ON TO THE NEXT PAGE.

Passage III

HUMANITIES: This passage is adapted from the article "The Modern Dance Revolution."

Created in 1958 as the first dance company composed primarily of African Americans, the Alvin Ailey American Dance Theater is no longer just a group of innovative dancers. Today, it would be better described as an institution. An
5 Alvin Ailey performance can be a visceral spectacle, a back-and-forth play of color, motion, order and seeming disorder—yet this should not obscure the agenda that has always been behind the company's performances. There was, of course, the vision of the actual Alvin Ailey, a man raised in the rural
10 South and determined to find a sophisticated audience for African-American culture and history. He crafted modern ballets such as *Revelations* (1960)—always a crowd-pleaser and an Alvin Ailey company favorite—but also did everything possible to nurture new generations of promising African-
15 American dancers. Between 1969 and 1974, he ushered into being two closely linked dance schools: the Ailey American Dance Center and the Ailey Repertory Ensemble, both of which are active to this day.

Yet perhaps Ailey's greatest success was creating a
20 vision of dance that would survive, ever evolving yet never compromised, well beyond his death in 1989. Whether by luck or by design (probably a bit of both), the company directors who appeared after Ailey remained true to his mission, but brought their own strong personalities to Alvin
25 Ailey choreography and performances. For instance, Judith Jamison was brought on as an Ailey dancer in 1965, was named Artistic Director in the last year of Ailey's life, and lifted the entire troupe to new heights of recognition. Under her leadership, the Ailey dancers embarked on a 50-city
30 global tour to celebrate the company's 50th anniversary. Jamison, in turn, selected Ailey choreographer and artist in residence Robert Battle to take her place; he became Artistic Director in 2011, thus adding another honor to a resume that already included an award from the Kennedy Center for the
35 Performing Arts and a speaking stint at the United Nations Leaders Program.

So the Ailey Dance Theater, indeed, is an institution, and one of the best dance institutions that Americans of all ethnicities have at their disposal. But it is necessary to
40 distinguish a great institution from a perfect one; even Ailey's company has had to endure criticisms—including a few that are very hard to overlook in a century as troubled and backward-looking as our own.

Perhaps the single greatest problem with the early Ailey
45 dances (as the critics say) is that these works look straight past the historical afflictions that African Americans have faced. *Revelations* is a cheery, dynamic, even funny work—and that is what is wrong with it, or so its critics contend. Try to find slavery, poverty, or segregation in *Revelations*, and

50 you will instead find churchgoing folk in their Sunday best and bobbing masses of bodies. In fact, the only sequence in *Revelations* that signifies suffering is a detour to the underworld: here, the movements of the dancers are frenzied and kinetic and the colors—lurid greens and reds—are
55 unusually blistering even for Ailey. But the whole sequence comes off as a sort of cartoon nightmare, not as a response to historical tragedy.

Ailey's contemporary critics are in the habit of posing dances such as *Revelations* against the creations of other
60 black artists, including those who have little direct involvement in dance. Certainly there is less agony in Ailey's piece than in the *Blue Rider* paintings of Chris Ofili, with their images of violence against African Americans, or in the stencil scenes of Kara Walker, which treat slavery as a
65 grotesque tragicomedy. Where is Ailey's social consciousness? And what of the consciousness of his successors, many of whom have created dance sequences that are more cryptic than anything in *Revelations*?

But those who find fault with classic Alvin Ailey content
70 don't realize how radical Ailey and his followers were, and in many cases still are. Remember where America was in 1960, when *Revelations* premiered: the desegregation of American schools only became the law of the land in 1954, and the Civil Rights Act was still four years away. In this climate, for
75 an all-black troupe of dancers to take the stage and deliver something so alien to traditional European ballet was a self-assertive gesture of the highest order.

It was a hopeful gesture, too. Instead of looking back to what was most tragic in African American life, Ailey looked
80 to what was most vital—religion, music, community gatherings, individual romances. *Revelations* celebrates these social foundations, and can be reinterpreted in ways that only reinforce its underlying optimism. In the past few years, the Ailey troupe has more aggressively courted dancers of Asian,
85 Latino, and Caucasian descent. And when these dancers perform *Revelations* as part of Ailey's predominantly African American company, Ailey's dance simultaneously becomes a symbol of ethnic pride and of ethnic unity.

GO ON TO THE NEXT PAGE.

21. One of the main arguments of the passage is that:

   A. Alvin Ailey was a transformative artist, even though the dances he created have been subject to debate.

   B. Alvin Ailey promoted new forms of dance, but was never a renowned dancer himself.

   C. dances such as *Revelations* are pleasing because they avoid political and religious content.

   D. recent Alvin Ailey artistic directors have been reluctant to stage Ailey's *Revelations*.

22. As they are characterized in the passage, Alvin Ailey's critics are notable for their:

   F. belief that the work of the Ailey company will eventually become more pragmatic.

   G. extensive knowledge of fields other than modern dance.

   H. failure to grasp how groundbreaking Ailey's work really was.

   J. unwillingness to analyze art that challenges common assumptions.

23. The author repeatedly refers to the Alvin Ailey American Dance Theater as an "institution" in order to emphasize the idea that Ailey's work has been:

   A. influential and widely imitated.

   B. broad-reaching and enduring.

   C. popular yet predictable.

   D. radical and award-winning.

24. In terms of developing the author's argument, the sixth paragraph (lines 69-77) serves to:

   F. show why Ailey was not impressed by European ballet.

   G. discuss themes that Chris Ofili and Kara Walker have consciously avoided.

   H. provide historical context for one of Ailey's signature dances.

   J. determine why it took so long to improve social conditions for African Americans.

25. It can be reasonably inferred from the passage that the Alvin Ailey Dance Company was originally designed to:

   A. entertain audiences with dreamlike dances.

   B. depict African-American traditions.

   C. provide funding to reform movements.

   D. improve African-American schooling.

26. The author describes *Revelations* as a "hopeful gesture" (line 78) most likely because this dance:

   F. highlighted positive and inspiring aspects of African-American culture.

   G. was instrumental in bringing political change to African-American communities.

   H. is now performed by dance companies very different from the Alvin Ailey Dance Theater.

   J. motivated new innovations in the visual arts.

27. Between what years was Alvin Ailey most active in forming new institutions for dance education?

   A. 1958 and 1960

   B. 1960 and 1969

   C. 1969 and 1974

   D. 1974 and 1989

28. According to the passage, which of the following was NOT an honor given to Robert Battle?

   F. A central role in the Alvin Ailey company's 50th anniversary tour.

   G. The position of Alvin Ailey Artistic Director

   H. Recognition from the Kennedy Center for the Performing Arts

   J. The opportunity to address the United Nations Leaders Program

29. In discussing Alvin Ailey dances, the fourth and fifth paragraphs (lines 44-68) do all of the following EXCEPT:

   A. identify specific critics of Ailey and his art.

   B. make extended reference to a single Ailey work.

   C. provide a visual description of a dance sequence.

   D. mention a few prominent individuals who can be contrasted with Ailey.

30. As it is used in line 85, the word *descent* means:

   F. ministry.

   G. heritage.

   H. misfortune.

   J. dynamism.

GO ON TO THE NEXT PAGE.

Passage IV

NATURAL SCIENCE: This passage is adapted from "Uncommon Reactions: New Perspectives on Old Problems in Chemistry."

It's one of the most visually exciting reactions in all of basic chemistry: drop sodium metal into liquid water, and watch the explosion. Students love this classic demonstration, which is undertaken not only to impress young minds, but
5 also to illustrate a pair of fundamental chemical principals: oxidation and reduction. When sodium metal comes into contact with liquid water, the sodium is *oxidized* (that is, it loses an electron), and the water is *reduced* (that is, water gains an electron). Ultimately, this reaction produces
10 positively charged sodium ions, a basic solution, hydrogen gas, and—most importantly—a tremendous amount of heat. As the famed neurologist Oliver Sacks described one instance of this reaction, the sodium "took fire instantly and sped around and around on the surface [of the water] like a
15 demented meteor, with a huge sheet of yellow flame above it." It is thanks to this spectacular, fiery evidence that chemists have presumed for centuries that the explosion must be the result of the ignition of the hydrogen gas formed in the reaction. However, chemist Pavel Jungwirth of the Czech
20 Academy of Sciences in Prague has recently put forth an entirely new explanation for the spectacle, and his theory soundly disproves the former assumptions surrounding one of chemistry's most fundamental phenomena.

According to Jungwirth, the violent reaction of sodium
25 and water could not be an explosion in any traditional sense. This is because in a traditional explosion, the reactants need to mix easily and to be in continuous contact, at least in order for the explosion to last. (Think of a burning candle: if the wick of the candle is not continuously exposed to the air, the
30 flame will go out.) When considering the case of sodium and water, Jungwirth reasoned that it is not possible for the two reactants to be in continuous contact. This is explained by the fact that as sodium metal produces hydrogen gas at its surface, the formation of the gas will push additional water
35 molecules *away* from the sodium. This process should thereby slow down and inhibit the reaction. The overall result will be that there should be no lasting explosion at all, only a quick burst of fire that fizzles out in just a few seconds. Yet as chemists have known for years, the reaction of sodium and
40 water is anything but a fizzle. This signaled to Jungwirth that something else must be going on.

In order to more deeply explore the mechanism behind the sodium-water reaction, Jungwirth used an ultra-high-speed camera to record droplets of a sodium-potassium alloy
45 colliding with water in an atmosphere of argon gas. (The argon atmosphere ensured that the sodium-potassium alloy would not react with the oxygen in the air before hitting the water.) The camera captured the reaction at a rate of 10,000 frames per second, which allowed Jungwirth to document the
50 reaction from its initial stages. What he discovered was something far different from anything ever mentioned in any

conventional explanation of the reaction. Within the first 0.5 milliseconds of hitting the water, the sodium-potassium alloy shot out a series of "spikes," and a deep blue color was
55 observed.

"The deep blue color is indicative of solvated electrons," notes Jonathan Ayer, an inorganic chemist from the University of Dortmund. By "solvated," Ayer means to refer to electrons that have left the sodium metal and entered the water. But as
60 sodium metal ejects its electrons, which carry a negative charge, the sodium metal is left with a net positive charge. The result is that, as sodium loses its electrons, it becomes a dense ball of *positive* charge that then explodes outwards, due to electrostatic repulsion. This explosion of the sodium
65 through the water is so powerful that, as Ayer himself noted, "The spikes accelerate outward at an initial rate of thirty thousand meters per second squared. If this acceleration were to be maintained for just one second, the spikes would soon be traveling at the speed of sound."

70 As such, Jungwirth and his colleagues are now referring to the sodium explosion as a "Coulomb explosion" in order to distinguish it from more traditional explosions. The word "Coulomb" is also found in the name of the "Coulomb Force" in physics; this force is understood as the electrostatic
75 attraction of positive and negative charges, as well as the electrostatic repulsion of like charges from one another.

After reading the results of Jungwirth's research, published recently in *Nature Chemistry*, inorganic chemist James Dye of Michigan State University remarked, "The
80 paper gives a complete and interesting account of the early stages of the reaction." Indeed, Jungwirth's work is a reminder that, in the scientific world, we cannot take anything for granted—not even the facts we preach in Freshman Chemistry.

31. The function of the quotation from Oliver Sacks in lines 13-16 is to:

A. question whether the reaction was in fact a traditional explosion.
B. emphasize the popularity of the chemical reaction between sodium metal and water.
C. underscore the intensity of the chemical reaction between sodium metal and water.
D. illustrate what most oxidation-reduction reactions look like.

GO ON TO THE NEXT PAGE.

32. Jungwirth used an argon atmosphere in his experiment in order to:

   F. allow the sodium-potassium alloy to react with the argon
   G. prevent the sodium-potassium alloy from reacting with water.
   H. allow the sodium-potassium alloy to react with oxygen in the air.
   J. prevent the sodium-potassium alloy from reacting with oxygen in the air.

33. According to the passage, the deep blue color observed in Jungwirth's experiment is the result of the presence of:

   A. solvated electrons.
   B. sodium metal.
   C. sodium-potassium alloy.
   D. argon gas.

34. Jungwirth and his colleagues have classified the sodium explosion as a Coulomb explosion because it was propelled by the:

   F. electrostatic repulsion of negative charges.
   G. electrostatic repulsion of positive charges.
   H. electrostatic neutralization of negative and positive charges.
   J. electrostatic attraction of negative and positive charges.

35. According to Jungwirth, why is the chemical reaction between sodium metal and water NOT a traditional explosion?

   A. A traditional explosion produces flame, which was not observed in the reaction between sodium metal and water.
   B. A traditional explosion involves oxidation and reduction, which was not observed in the reaction between sodium metal and water.
   C. A traditional explosion requires the reactants to be in constant contact with air, which was not possible in the reaction between sodium metal and water.
   D. A traditional explosion requires the reactants to be in constant contact with each other, which was not possible in the reaction between sodium metal and water.

36. The author explains that Jungwirth used a high-speed camera in order to:

   F. determine whether an argon atmosphere would affect the mechanism of the reaction.
   G. record only the first 0.5 milliseconds of the reaction.
   H. study a chemical reaction with great precision across very small increments of time.
   J. record the speed, acceleration, and color of the spikes formed by the argon atmosphere.

37. The "facts we preach" (line 83) include the idea that:

   A. the reaction between the sodium-potassium alloy and water is an oxidation-reduction reaction.
   B. the explosive nature of the reaction between the sodium-potassium alloy and water is due to the ignition of hydrogen gas.
   C. the reaction between sodium metal and water is an oxidation-reduction reaction.
   D. the explosive nature of the reaction between sodium metal and water is due to the ignition of hydrogen gas.

38. Regarding Jungwirth's experiment, it can be most reasonably inferred from the passage that:

   F. the deep blue spikes traveled at the speed of sound during the experiment.
   G. the deep blue spikes did not reach the speed of sound during the experiment.
   H. the speed of the deep blue spikes exceeded the speed of sound during the experiment.
   J. Jungwirth and his colleagues could not hear the explosion.

39. As it is used in line 48, the word *captured* can be understood to mean:

   A. prevented.
   B. recorded.
   C. acquired.
   D. comprehended.

40. The tone of the quotation from James Dye in lines 79-81 is:

   F. supportive.
   G. awestruck.
   H. outspoken.
   J. lighthearted.

END OF TEST 10
STOP! DO NOT TURN THE PAGE UNTIL TOLD TO DO SO.
DO NOT RETURN TO A PREVIOUS TEST.

Answer Key: TEST 10

Test 10

LITERARY NARRATIVE

1. D
2. G
3. A
4. G
5. D
6. F
7. B
8. H
9. C
10. H

HUMANITIES

21. A
22. H
23. B
24. H
25. B
26. F
27. C
28. F
29. A
30. G

SOCIAL SCIENCE

11. A
12. G
13. A
14. H
15. B
16. H
17. D
18. H
19. B
20. F

NATURAL SCIENCE

31. C
32. J
33. A
34. G
35. D
36. H
37. D
38. G
39. B
40. F

To see your scaled ACT Reading Score (1-36), determine
how many questions you answered correctly and consult
the Scoring Chart on Page 186 of this book.

Post-Test Analysis

This post-test analysis is essential if you want to see an improvement on your next test. Possible reasons for errors, both for the test overall and for each of the four reading passages, are listed here. Place check marks next to the types of errors that pertain to you, or write your own types of errors in the blank spaces provided.

GENERAL

◇ Spent too much time reading the passages
◇ Spent too much time answering the questions
◇ Did not attempt to finish all of the passages
◇ Did not create effective margin answers
◇ Did not use process of elimination
◇ Could not find evidence to answer the questions
◇ Could not comprehend the topics and ideas in the passages
◇ Could not understand what the questions were asking
◇ Interpreted the passages rather than using evidence

Other: _____

LITERARY NARRATIVE

◇ Spent too long reading the passage
◇ Spent too long answering the questions
◇ Could not identify the setting and characters
◇ Could not understand the plot or action
◇ Could not work effectively with tone and clues to tone

Other: _____

> **Use this form** to better analyze your performance. If you don't understand why you made errors, there is no way that you can correct them!

SOCIAL SCIENCE

◇ Spent too long reading the passage
◇ Spent too long answering the questions
◇ Could not understand the author's position or arguments
◇ Used outside knowledge rather than using evidence

Other: _____

HUMANITIES

◇ Spent too long reading the passage
◇ Spent too long answering the questions
◇ Could understand the themes and organization of the passage
◇ Could not understand the author's ideas and uses of evidence

Other: _____

NATURAL SCIENCE

◇ Spent too long reading the passage
◇ Spent too long answering the questions
◇ Found the concepts and ideas in the passage confusing
◇ Found the questions confusing
◇ Could not effectively work with the inference and logic questions

Other: _____

TEST 10 Answer Explanations

1. Correct Answer: D

Support for this is found between lines 47 and 65. The author quotes Lucy, who says, "I'm concerned about our heritage." Jessie responds by saying, "I understand your concern." The narrator then explains that "What Lucy couldn't see was that Jessie really *did* sympathize with Lucy's point of view—she knew that there was nothing particularly "noble" in running a casino, that casinos didn't have anything to do with traditional Native American values." Choice **A** is incorrect because nothing in the passage supports the idea that the Seminole tribe was in danger of disappearing without the casinos. (Since Lucy is an activist acting against the casinos, it is unlikely that she would agree with this point.) Choice **B** is incorrect because there is no indication that either girl believes that Jessie's father is *unaware* of the harmful effects of the casinos. It can even be inferred from the efforts toward cultural preservation mentioned in lines 51-54 that Jessie's father is aware of possible negative press. Finally, choice **C** is incorrect because the central disagreement in the passage is over Lucy's efforts to create public awareness about the harmful effects of the casinos. Lucy would even disagree strongly with the ideas in **C**.

2. Correct Answer: G

In lines 43-46, the author writes that "Lucy railed against Joe Okobee's number-one policy as chief of the Seminole tribe: the use of casino gambling as a source of tribal revenue." Later Lucy expresses her concern that "so few Seminoles can even speak our language anymore. It's become purely about profits" (lines 48-50). In these excerpts, Lucy is depicted as *principled*. Then, at the end of the passage, Lucy endorses the idea of "no surrender" (line 84) and turns away from her friend Jessie. Here Lucy is shown as *uncompromising*. Of the false answers, **F** is incorrect because while Lucy might be described as *determined*, she isn't *histrionic* (too negative for a character who stays calm throughout the passage). **H** is incorrect because there's no evidence that Lucy is *optimistic* (too positive) about her conflicts with Jessie and the tribe. Choice **J** actually goes against the evidence in the passage, which indicates that Lucy is neither *pragmatic* (lines 60-61 directly contradict such a characterization) nor *flexible* (lines 80-84 suggest the opposite).

3. Correct Answer: A

In this line reference, we learn who Jessie is and discover differences between Jessie and Lucy. Thus, we learn "background information about the two" of these characters. Choice **B** is incorrect because the third paragraph suggests nothing about the political popularity of Jessie's father (who is not described at any length here), while **C** is incorrect because the setting of the dialogue is described in the next paragraph (lines 34-36). **D** must be eliminated because, even the narrator is arguably sympathetic to Lucy here (when the paragraph implies that she's not as wealthy as Jessie), it isn't clear that this paragraph or those that follow immediately are intended to evoke sympathy with Jessie. This latter point would be necessary for **D** to be correct.

4. Correct Answer: G

The support for this answer can be found in lines 11-12. The author tells us the significance of the *Green Corn Ceremony* by describing it as, "the ceremony in which Jessie and Lucy, at the age of sixteen, had been recognized as women by the tribe." **F** is incorrect because nothing in the passage suggests that Jessie has forgotten the Green Corn Ceremony. (In fact, because she still has a memento of this ceremony, she may remember it well.) **H** is incorrect because the passage gives no indication that the ceremony has any connection with the political career of Jessie's father, who is not mentioned until line 25. **J** is incorrect because the passage suggests that the opposite of this choice is true. Lines 10-16 indicate that the ceremony took place at a time when the Jessie and Lucy were still close friends.

5. Correct Answer: D

The support for this answer can be found in lines 52-54, in which the author quotes Jessie's statement that "my father has plans to allocate money towards cultural preservation, including hiring linguists to create instructional language DVDs." **A** is incorrect because while lines 68-70 indicate that casino profits have been used to provide college educations, no connection is made between these efforts and the preservation of Seminole heritage. Despite the educational nature of the efforts, both **B** and **C** completely misrepresent the details of these efforts: no museum is mentioned and there is no discussion of the relationship between tourists and the preservation of Seminole heritage.

6. Correct Answer: F

The author, in lines 30-32, writes that Lucy "felt a familiar thrill," upon seeing the *Bay*. Lucy then describes *Biscayne Bay* by saying that it "glittered like a jewel." We thus know she regards the *Bay* positively. The only positive answer is **F**, *delighted*, which is a synonym for *thrilled*. **G** is incorrect because nothing suggests that Lucy was *perplexed* or confused upon seeing the bay, while **H** is incorrect because *sullen* (strong negative) is the direct opposite of Lucy's feelings. **J** can be eliminated because there is no indication that Lucy is *agitated* (subtle negative) or disturbed by the sight of the bay.

7. Correct Answer: B

We know that Lucy *opposes* the policy of "the use of gambling as a source of tribal revenue." But, as we learn in lines 70-72, it was arguably "because of Jessie's father's policies that Lucy even had her journalism degree from New York University." This can also be described as *irony*, a state of affairs that seems contrary to what one expects. **A** falsely introduces a new topic: the passage mentions nothing about whether her degree is valued by any particular people with whom Lucy has been in contact. **C** misrepresents Lucy's reactions: while Lucy remains polite despite her growing anger (line 74), her politeness is not *caused by* her anger. **D** is incorrect because the passage makes no explicit mention of Jessie's father's respect for his political opponents; the only opponent of any sort who is named is Lucy, and it is not clear how Jessie's father feels about her. Lucy and Jessie, not Jessie's father, are the author's main concerns in the relevant lines.

TEST 10 Answer Explanations

8. Correct Answer: H

In context, the best synonym for *right* is *directly*. In the following sentences (lines 80-84), we learn that "Jessie tried not to roll her eyes," which suggests a break from the direct eye contact previously established by Lucy. **F** can be eliminated because *abruptly* is not the best synonym in context. The passage notes that Lucy is deliberate and direct in her actions, rather than abrupt, which means "sudden and unexpected." **G** can also be eliminated because *correctly* makes no sense in context. Since Lucy has been Jessie's friend since childhood, it's unlikely that there is a "correct" way for Lucy to look her friend in the eye. **J** is also incorrect because *ethically* makes no sense in context. Ethically means, "of or relating to moral principles," which doesn't describe the act of looking a friend in the eye. Rely on the structure of the sentence, and do not falsely assume that the author's emphasis on correct or ethical behavior as a theme justifies **G** or **J**.

9. Correct Answer: C

The support for this answer comes from lines 51-58. Jessie initially states that her "father has plans to allocate money towards cultural preservation, including hiring linguists to create instructional language DVDs. But in order to do that, we need our funding." This eliminates choice **B**. In reference to Lucy, Jessie then goes on to say that "your editorials are stirring up a lot of anti-casino sentiment, which isn't helpful either for my father's reelection *or* for your cause," eliminating choices **A** and **D**. The correct answer is therefore **C**. Jessie doesn't mention anything about either *poorer Seminoles* or the *employment opportunities* provided directly by the casinos themselves; by funding college educations, these casinos have allowed Native Americans to find employment in other contexts.

10. Correct Answer: H

This line reference entails a response to Jessie's question: "Isn't there some way we can work out a compromise here?" In the line reference itself, the author quotes Lucy: "Do you know what the word 'Seminole' means... It means 'No surrender.'" Remember, to *compromise* is to *negotiate*. Of the false answers, **F** is incorrect because nothing in the final four paragraphs suggests that Lucy has any desire to popularize Seminole culture (which she simply wants to preserve and defend). **G** is incorrect because the passage mentions nothing about Seminole history (beyond the building of the casinos). Furthermore Lucy's attachment to her heritage and strong sense of purpose suggest the very opposite of *conflicted* feelings. **J** is incorrect because it contains an overstatement. While Lucy is certainly unwilling to compromise with Jessie, nothing indicates that Lucy is *unable to understand* Jessie's perspective, which Lucy could in fact understand and still reject.

SOCIAL SCIENCE

11. Correct Answer: A

The passage describes, in chronological order, the major events in a scandal that ended the career of John Profumo, a British Minister of War. In order, Profumo "was a frequent guest at Cl23veden" (line 12) or Lord Astor's estate (**B**), stated that "no impropriety had occurred" (line 23) in his connection with Miss Keeler (**D**), "admitted that he had perjured himself" (lines 28-29, **C**), and "was then immediately expelled from office and Parliament" (lines 29-30, **A**). Thus, **A** is the correct answer.

12. Correct Answer: G

The author begins Passage A by indicating that "the decade beginning in 1960 had such an impact on British life and overturned the traditional attitudes of society" (lines 1-3), then links these changes in British life to the "Profumo Affair" (line 8), which is explained in the remainder of the first two paragraphs. This evidence supports **G** as the most effective answer choice. **F** wrongly focuses on Astor (only mentioned in the first paragraph) and wrongly states that the passage is mocking instead of informative. **H** places too much emphasis on Miss Keeler (whose personality and motives are minor considerations at best), while **J** wrongly states that the author is presenting and disproving a theory, not recording an episode from history.

13. Correct Answer: A

The word *catch* refers to the "attention of the Soviet ambassador" (line 27), which two young woman would *draw forth* or *attract* through interaction. Thus, **A** is an effective answer, while **B** refers to a different issue (extent of comprehension, rather than extent of influence) and **C** and **D** are both negatives that do not relate to this specific context. Profumo might have been generally overpowered or foiled in the passage, but the sentence is describing how two women managed to catch or attract one man's attention.

TEST 10 Answer Explanations

14. Correct Answer: H

In context, the author is describing how "the corruption of the ruling class" (line 31) was brought to light by the Profumo Affair: describing members of the nobility as "the great and the good" should thus be seen as an ironic or sarcastic reference in light of the author's focus. **H** is an effective choice, while **F**, **G**, and **J** all wrongly assume clear sources for the phrase "the great and the good". The author never describes a source such as the public, the media, or the nobility (and could in fact be making up the phrase for the passage), so that all of these answers must be eliminated.

15. Correct Answer: B

In lines 65-67, the author of Passage B explains what is most objectionable about the behavior of Britain's powerful groups: "What offends and alienates most is the patronage of voters as an inferior, uncomprehending, gullible class". Thus, **B** is an effective answer. **A** must be eliminated because the author never discusses legislation directly, while **C** misstates the true approach of Britain's powerful classes (which uphold elite national traditions in a problematic way) and **D** states a reason why these groups are disliked, but not the reason that "offends and alienate most".

16. Correct Answer: H

In lines 48-50, the author of Passage B defines "core voters" as voters who, "irrespective of what was actually happening in politics, voted for the same party every time" (line 50). This predictable pattern of support justifies **H** as the best answer. **G** introduces an issue that is not directly relevant ("patriotism"), and may actually contradict the author's tone, since the author refers to the "complacency" (line 50) of core voters instead of labeling them as patriotic. **F** and **J** are both tempting answers, but both distort the logic of the passage: the author only indicates how core voters VOTE, not what they BELIEVE. Oddly enough, a voter who is either completely uninformed or politically moderate could still be a core voter, so long as he or she always votes for the same party.

17. Correct Answer: D

Earlier in the passage, the author states that negative economic factors have "widened the lack of trust between the electorate and traditional government" (lines 76-77): the second of these groups, as defined by the author, consists of elite members of society. Disraeli's quotation is itself about a split between the Privileged and the People, and thus returns to one of the author's major criticisms of Britain's governing system. Thus, **D** is a correct choice. **A** and **B** both assume specific context about the passage's audience and about Disraeli, yet the author never situates the passage in a way that would justify these answers. (Disraeli, for instance, is only mentioned in lines 80-81 and his position is never explained.) **C** is correct about the author's stance, but incorrect about the function of the quote: this answer neglects the role of the "People" in Disraeli's point.

18. Correct Answer: H

The author of Passage B notes that "the number of people actually using their votes has been falling gradually over the last forty years" (lines 52-54). Since the passage was written in 2015, this trend began in 1975; thus, **H** is the best answer. **F** could result from a faulty use of the "Second World War" references in lines 45-46, **G** could result from a calculation error, and **J** could result from the faulty assumption that voter indifference (which has continued into recent times) BEGAN in recent times.

19. Correct Answer: B

In describing the Profumo Affair, the author of Passage A notes that "The press can follow a scent, emitting more noise and embodying more intensity than a pack of foxhounds" (lines 23-25). The author of Passage B notes that "perhaps because of the growth in the speed and powers of writers and photographers on the Internet, revelations about the life style of the "rich and famous and powerful" have become much more immediately available" (lines 60-63). Together, this information indicates that both passages discuss the role of the media in cases of corruption, justifying **B** as the best answer. **A** only refers to Passage A (since Passage B does not directly name any flawed politicians, and instead criticizes politicians as a large group), **C** is undermined by the positive conclusion of Passage A, and **D** is undermined by the discussion of voter "complacency" (line 50) in Passage B (since current British voters in fact seem to both dislike and ACCEPT the state of their government).

20. Correct Answer: F

While the author of Passage A states that Britain's hierarchical class system was "upended" (line 39) by the Profumo Affair, the author of Passage B argues that Britain has a powerful and elite governing class that treats voters as "an inferior, uncomprehending, gullible class" (lines 66-67). This information supports **F**, since the "upending" in Passage A is not construed as a lasting change in Passage B. **G** is out of scope because the author of Passage B never addresses Profumo or pardons any other politician for corruption. **H** is contradicted by Passage B, which in fact argues that "writers and photographers" (line 61) can reveal corruption, while **J** is out of scope. Parliament (line 70) may be the author's focus, but there is no basis for this answer because OTHER forms of British government are never explicitly compared to Parliament.

TEST 10 Answer Explanations

21. Correct Answer: A

As the author writes in the beginning of the second paragraph, "Ailey's greatest success was creating a vision of dance that would survive, ever evolving yet never compromised, well beyond his death in 1989" (lines 19-21) According to this line reference, Ailey created a *vision of dance* that has *survived* till this day, while still *evolving*, supporting the word *transformative*. But then the author writes in the following paragraph, "But it is necessary to distinguish a great institution from a perfect one; even Ailey's company has had to endure criticisms," (lines 39-41), which means that Ailey's work has "been subjected to debate." **B** is incorrect because, although the passage suggests that Alvin Ailey, was celebrated as an artistic director and choreographer, the author mentions nothing about Ailey's competence as a dancer. Thus, there is not enough information to draw this conclusion. **C** is incorrect because the passage never draws a correlation between a lack of political or religious content and the aesthetic pleasure felt by those who attend performances. **D** is incorrect because the passage makes no mention of artistic directors who have been reluctant to stage *Revelations*. In fact, lines 84-88 suggest that *Revelations* continues to be performed.

22. Correct Answer: H

The support for this answer can be found in lines 69-71, in which the author writes, "But those who find fault with classic Alvin Ailey content don't realize how radical Ailey and his followers were, and in many cases still are." Remember, *radical* is another word for *groundbreaking*. Thus, **H** is the best answer. **F** is incorrect because the passage provides no evidence to suggest that Ailey's critics believe that the company will become more *pragmatic*, which means "dealing with things in a practical rather than idealistic or theoretical manner." **G** is incorrect because, even though Ailey has in fact been compared to artists "who have little direct involvement in dance" (lines 58-68), the passage mentions nothing about the critics' *expertise* in these other fields. **J** is incorrect because the passage makes no mention of the critics' unwillingness to analyze any particular form of art. Such critics may in fact analyze many forms of art, and simply argue against Ailey.

23. Correct Answer: B

In lines 19-21, the author asserts that "Ailey's greatest success was creating a vision of dance that would survive, ever evolving yet never compromised, well beyond his death in 1989." Since Ailey's vision of dance has "survived well beyond his death," we can say that it is *enduring*. In addition, in the first sentence of the passage,

the author tells us that Ailey's dance theater "is no longer just a group of innovative dancers," but rather an organization that is well-established, or (by definition) an *institution*. Of the false answers, **A** is incorrect because, although the passage indicates that Ailey's work has been *influential* (lines 19-21), nothing explicitly suggests that the work of the company has been widely imitated. Such a conclusion requires speculation beyond what is written in the passage, and direct comparison to other dance companies. **C** is incorrect because while the passage suggests that Ailey's work is popular, nothing indicates that the work is *predictable*. **D** is incorrect because the only awards mentioned can be found in lines 33-36, which apply to the current artistic director, and not the company itself. Further, it is inappropriate to automatically characterize the institution as *radical*, given the discussion of critics who have argued that the company's work hasn't been radical enough.

24. Correct Answer: H

In this line reference, the author tells us, "Remember where America was in 1960, when *Revelations* premiered: the desegregation of American schools only became the law of the land in 1954, and the Civil Rights Act was still four years away." Such information tells us "where America was" in terms of "historical context," thus making **H** the best answer. **F** is incorrect because while the passage does state that the performances were "alien to traditional European ballet" (line 76), it never claims that Ailey was not impressed by European Ballet. **G** must be eliminated because the argument in the sixth paragraph neither compares Ailey's dances with the works of Ofili and Walker (who are only mentioned in lines 62-64) nor suggests that these other artists consciously avoided any particular themes. **J** must be eliminated because such a general statement about the history of African American social conditions goes beyond the scope of the passage, which is confined mostly to a discussion of Alvin Ailey's legacy.

25. Correct Answer: B

The author writes in the first paragraph, "There was, of course, the vision of the actual Alvin Ailey, a man raised in the rural South and determined to find a sophisticated audience for African-American culture and history." Another word for *culture and history* is *traditions*. **A** is incorrect because the only reference to dreamlike dances ("cartoon nightmare," line 56) is not in reference to Ailey's original intentions for forming the dance company. **C** is incorrect because the passage does not discuss whether the company ever sought to raise money for social reforms. **D** is incorrect because there is no mention of a relationship between the Dance Company and African-American education in general.

26. Correct Answer: F

In the sentence following the line reference, the author explains that "Instead of looking back to what was most tragic in African American life, Ailey looked to what was most vital—religion, music, community gatherings, individual romances." These are vital, or *positive and inspiring aspects* of *African American culture*. **G** is incorrect because the passage never draws a direct relationship between performances of *Revelations* and political change. **H** is incorrect because the passage doesn't state whether or not any company other than Alvin Ailey Dance Theater ever performs *Revelations*. **J** is incorrect because the author never mentions any works of visual art that may have been influenced by *Revelations*. At most, the author notes a *contrast* between Ailey and visual artists such as Kara Walker and Chris Ofili.

27. Correct Answer: C

This answer can be found in lines 15-16, in which the author writes, "Between 1969 and 1974, he [Ailey] ushered into being two closely linked dance schools." Answer choices **A**, **B**, and **D** are all incorrect because these time-spans are not mentioned in connection with the topic in question. For the other years mentioned, Ailey created his entire dance company in 1958 (line 1), devised *Revelations* in 1960 (line 12) and died in 1989 (line 22).

28. Correct Answer: F

For this question, the essential information can be found in lines 32-36, in which the author writes, "he [Robert Battle] became Artistic Director in 2011, thus adding another honor to a resume that already included an award from the Kennedy Center for the Performing Arts and a speaking stint at the United Nations Leaders Program." Thus, eliminate choices **G**, **H**, and **J. F** is the correct answer because Robert Battle is NOT mentioned in connection with the company's 50th anniversary tour, which was directed by Judith Jamison (lines 28-30).

29. Correct Answer: A

The author states in lines 47-48 that "*Revelations* is a cheery, dynamic, even funny work— and that is what is wrong with it, or so its critics contend." Thus, eliminate choice **B**. Then in lines 51-55, the author states that "in fact, the only sequence in *Revelations* that signifies suffering is a detour to the underworld: here, the movements of the dancers are frenzied and kinetic and the colors—lurid greens and reds—are unusually blistering even for Ailey." Thus, eliminate choice **C**. Finally, in lines 61-65, the author writes, "Certainly there is less agony in Ailey's piece than in the *Blue Rider* paintings of Chris Ofili, with their images of violence against African Americans, or in the stencil scenes of Kara Walker, which treat slavery as a grotesque tragicomedy." Eliminate choice **D**, and choose **A** as the best option. Keep in mind that the passage only refers to Ailey's critics in general terms, and never mentions any particular critics by name.

30. Correct Answer: G

The author uses the word *descent* after referring to the various ethnicities of current members of the company ("Asian, Latino, and Caucasian"). The final sentence refers to these ethnicities as sources of "ethnic pride and of ethnic unity" (line 88), supporting the conclusion that, in context, *heritage* is the best synonym for *descent*. **F** is incorrect because, although positive, *ministry* suggests that the dancers look on their work as a form of outreach or religion. (Ailey was involved in outreach, but whether his dancers are similarly involved is never specified.) **H** is incorrect because *misfortune* is much too negative for this positive concluding paragraph, while **J** makes little sense in context. It is clear that *descent* refers to the dancers' ethnicity or cultural heritage, rather than to their *dynamism*, even though Ailey dancers may themselves be dynamic.

NATURAL SCIENCE

31. Correct Answer: C

The author writes in the first paragraph, before he introduces the quote, that "Ultimately, this reaction produces … a tremendous amount of heat" (lines 9-11) Another way of saying *tremendous amount* can be *intensity*. The author then goes on to call the process that is being described *spectacular, fiery evidence*, further supporting choice **C**. **A** is incorrect because the author doesn't quote Sacks in order to *question* the nature of the explosion. (Sacks simply describes the explosion; *questioning* only occurs later in the passage.) **B** is incorrect because, while the quotation *emphasizes* the appearance of the reaction, it doesn't emphasize the reaction's popularity as a classic chemistry demonstration. (Popularity is addressed mostly in lines 1-4). **D** is incorrect because nothing suggests that the reaction involves characteristics that are present in *most* oxidation-reduction reactions. Indeed, it is reasonable to infer that the reaction is popular with chemistry teachers because it offers a uniquely dramatic example.

32. Correct Answer: J

The support for this answer can be found in the parenthetical statement in lines 45-48, in which the author writes that "the argon atmosphere ensured that the sodium-potassium alloy would not react with the oxygen in the air before hitting the water." **F** is incorrect because, while the passage indicates that the argon atmosphere inhibits reactions between the alloy and atmospheric oxygen, it doesn't say that the alloy would react with argon instead. (In fact, if the argon and the alloy reacted, the alloy would change form before reaching the water.) **G** is incorrect because the passage notes that the argon ensured that the alloy would not react with atmospheric oxygen "*before* hitting the water." (Remember, the point of the argon is to make the alloy and water react without major impurities.) Nothing is mentioned about preventing the alloy-water reaction itself. Be sure to read **H** carefully; this choice states the opposite of what is claimed in lines 45-48 of the passage.

33. Correct Answer: A

According to Jonathan Ayer, "the deep blue color is indicative of solvated electrons" (line 56). This justifies choice **A**. Choices **B**, **C**, and **D** must all be eliminated because, while each is mentioned in passage, none is mentioned as a cause of the blue color Jungwirth observed. Keep in mind that the other answers are discussed in lines 1-55, *before* Jungwirth presents his conclusion.

34. Correct Answer: G

According to the passage, during a sodium explosion, "as sodium metal ejects its electrons, which carry a negative charge, the sodium metal is left with a net positive charge. The result is that, as sodium loses its electrons, it becomes a dense ball of positive charge that then explodes outwards, due to electrostatic repulsion" (lines 59-64). Compare this to the force involved in a *Coulomb explosion*: "this force is understood as the electrostatic attraction of positive and negative charges, as well as the electrostatic repulsion of like charges from one another" (lines 74-76).

TEST 10 Answer Explanations

Since the sodium described in the passage only has a *positive* charge, the answer is **G**. **F** is incorrect because the passage states that the explosion was driven by the repulsion of positive rather than negative charges. **H** and **J** must both be eliminated because the Coulomb explosion in the passage involves positive charges only; in addition, **H** is incorrect because the passage notes that a "dense ball of *positive* charge accumulates that then explodes outwards" (lines 62-63). To *explode* would be the opposite of to *neutralize*.

35. Correct Answer: D

Evidence for the correct choice can be found in the second paragraph, since the author writes that "in a traditional explosion, the reactants need to mix easily and to be in continuous contact" (lines 26-27). But in the sodium reaction, "it is not possible for the two reactants to be in continuous contact" (lines 31-32). Thus, **D** is the best answer. **A** is contradicted by the passage: in line 15, Oliver Sacks describes the sodium and water reaction as presenting "a huge sheet of yellow flame." **B** is incorrect because, while it is true that a "traditional explosion" involves oxidation and reduction, the second part of the answer choice is incorrect. Lines 6-11 even describe how the sodium and water reaction is a classic demonstration of the principles of oxidation and reduction. **C** is incorrect because the passage only states that the reactants need to be in continuous contact with each other, and not necessarily with air. In Jungwirth's experiments, the explosion still occurred when atmospheric air was replaced by argon gas.

36. Correct Answer: H

Your support can be found in the third paragraph, in which the author outlines Jungwirth's method: "In order to more deeply explore the mechanism behind the sodium-water reaction, Jungwirth used an ultra-high-speed camera to record droplets of a sodium-potassium alloy colliding with water in an atmosphere of argon gas … The camera captured the reaction at a rate of 10,000 frames per second, which allowed Jungwirth to document the reaction from its most initial stages" (lines 42-50). Thus, **H** is correct, while other answers mis-arrange ideas from the passage. **F** must be eliminated because the effect of the argon atmosphere (as described in the third paragraph) is already known. **G** must be eliminated because, even though the passage describes a phenomenon that was observed "within the first 0.5 milliseconds" of the reaction (lines 52-53), the author never states that the camera *only* filmed these first 0.5 milliseconds. **J** is incorrect because the spikes described are formed by the potassium, not by the neutral *argon atmosphere*.

37. Correct Answer: D

In context, we can infer that the "facts we preach in Freshman chemistry" refer to the ones "that chemists have presumed for centuries" (lines 16-17), as described in the first paragraph. The passage suggests that the sodium metal and water reaction is commonly taught; in addition, lines 17-19 state "that the explosion must be the result of the ignition of the hydrogen gas formed in the reaction," though the passage ultimately rejects this conclusion. Thus, the "facts we preach" are sometimes faulty, and **D** is the best answer choice. **A** is incorrect: the pure sodium metal mentioned in the first paragraph is not identical to the sodium-potassium alloy mentioned in the third paragraph. There is no reason to assume that the sodium-potassium alloy reaction (particular to Jungwirth's experiment) is commonly taught in "Freshman chemistry." Similarly, **B** is incorrect because Freshman chemistry students are typically exposed to the reaction between sodium metal and water, and NOT that of the sodium-potassium alloy and water. Trap answer **C** is factually true, but is not a "fact we preach" as the author understands the term in context:" such "facts" cannot be taken "for granted" (line 83) and are ultimately negative, unlike the information given in **C**.

38. Correct Answer: G

As the author writes in lines 67-69, "If this acceleration were to be maintained for just one second, the spikes would soon be traveling at the speed of sound," which means that in reality the speed was not *maintained* and that the spikes did not reach the *speed of sound*. This logical conclusion justifies **G**. We know this because the author starts out the statement with the word *if*, indicating a condition that was not actually met. Answer choices **F** and **H** are incorrect because they state that the spikes either reached or exceeded the speed of sound, which is contradicted by the conditional statement in lines 67-69. **J** is incorrect because the passage gives no indication that the sound of the explosion was a consideration of Jungwirth and his colleagues. Here, the *speed of sound* is used only as a measure of velocity.

39. Correct Answer: B

Your clue in this sentence is the word *camera*. Cameras *record* information. **A** is incorrect because the negative *prevented* makes no sense in context; the camera, instead, would naturally be used in a positive way as a component of the experiment. **C** is not the best synonym in context. While data were likely *acquired* from the camera's images, it is more correct to say that the camera *recorded* the initial stages of the reaction. (To acquire means to take ownership, a very different concept.) **D** must be eliminated because is unreasonable to conclude that the camera, an inanimate object, *comprehended* anything.

40. Correct Answer: F

In the sentence following the quote, the author starts out with the word *Indeed*, which indicates that the comments that follow are in agreement with Dye's statement. Of the answer choices, *supportive* makes the most sense because it is logical to conclude that the author uses Dye's quote to *support* the conclusion about "the early stages of the reaction" (lines 80-81) made in the final paragraph. Answer choices **G** and **J** are incorrect because the quoted statement is a succinct appraisal of Jungwirth's research, which is described only as a "complete and interesting account" (line 80). Nothing in the final paragraph suggests that Dye was either *awestruck* (highly impressed) with Jungwirth's findings or was speaking in a lighthearted (cheerful and carefree) manner: these positives are too strong. **H** is not a good characterization of the quotation's tone. While Dye does state a frank opinion of Jungwirth's research, it is a stretch to assume that the opinion is either straightforwardly critical or highly assertive in any way, as an *outspoken* opinion would need to be.

ACT **Scaled Score Conversion**

To obtain your Scaled Score on the 1-36 system used by the ACT,
simply total the number of questions you answered
correctly on a single Reading section.
The conversion is provided below.

QUESTIONS CORRECT	SCALED SCORE RANGE	QUESTIONS CORRECT	SCALED SCORE RANGE
40	36	20	20-18
39	36-35	19	19-17
38	36-34	18	18-16
37	35-32	17	17-15
36	34-31	16	17-15
35	33-30	15	16-14
34	32-29	14	15-14
33	30-28	13	14-13
32	29-27	12	13-12
31	28-26	11	13-12
30	27-25	10	12-11
29	26-24	9	12-11
28	25-23	8	11-10
27	24-23	7	10-9
26	23-22	6	9-8
25	23-21	5	8-7
24	22-20	4	7-6
23	21-20	3	5-4
22	21-19	2	4-3
21	20-18	1	2
		0	1

TRY ALL OF OUR ADVANCED
PRACTICE SERIES BOOKS

If you like this easy-to-use workbook, check out our other great volumes. The *ACT Reading Practice Book* is part of the *IES Advanced Practice Series*, which currently includes a *Reading Comprehension Workbook*, a *Math Workbook*, a *Grammar Workbook*, and the soon to be released *New 2016 SAT Workbook*. Please visit www.ILEXpublications.com to order these resources, or find our complete line of SAT workbooks on Amazon.com.

Made in United States
North Haven, CT
13 June 2022